Better Than Fiction 2

Better than Fiction 2

Published by Lonely Planet Publications

90 Maribyrnong St, Footscray, Victoria, 3011, Australia
150 Linden St, Oakland CA 94607, USA
240 Blackfriars, London, SE1 8NW United Kingdom

Published 2015

Printed in China

Edited by Don George and Samantha Forge
Project managed by Robin Barton
Proofread by Karyn Noble

Cover Design by Tom Jay
Design & Layout by Daniel di Paolo and Amanda Scope

1st Editon

978 174360 749 7 (pbk.)

National Library of Australia Cataloguing-in-Publication entry

Better than Fiction 2: true adventures from 30 great fiction writers / edited by Don George

Contents

Introduction

DON GEORGE

For most of the year, Lonely Planet's varied creations focus on the how and the where of travel; from guidebooks to apps, they're designed to help travelers decide where and when to go, and how to get the most out of their journeys once they get there. But once a year Lonely Planet also publishes a special literary anthology that focuses on the why: the rigors and the rewards that travel confers.

Three years ago, we decided to devote that anthology to true travel tales written by acclaimed fiction writers. We called the collection *Better Than Fiction*, and it was a resounding success. We were so pleased with that delightful and inspiring spectrum of stories that we decided to reprise the theme for this year's anthology.

At the beginning of the year I contacted a globe-girdling

list of notable fiction writers, a marvelous mix of esteemed
literary stars and emerging prize-winners, and asked if they
would like to write a true tale of an especially memorable travel
experience – one that had profoundly moved, delighted, taught,
and/or transformed them. I said we were open to virtually any
kind of experience, in any setting around the world. Despite
their demanding schedules, 30 of these writers responded with
passionate descriptions of tales they'd love to tell.

While I was waiting for these stories to arrive, I began to
worry that they might not meet the heady standards set by the
first collection. But then the pieces began to trickle in, and I was
transported. As I read each one, my picture-puzzle panorama of
travel's infinite possibilities wondrously expanded, piece by piece –
as yours will too, when you read them.

The tales assembled herein embody a moving microcosm
of our modern world. The settings roam from Azerbaijan to
Vietnam, with stops in Iceland, India, Italy, and Idaho, Samoa,
Saudi Arabia, and Scotland, and some 20 more places around the
globe. The themes vary widely as well, from youthful coming-of-
age adventures, to middle-age misadventures and meditations on
journeys past and to come, to wistful older-age homages to the
most lasting of life's road-lessons. And the subjects encountered
along the way encompass sex, romance, the end of romance,
surfing, fear, potential kidnappings, a hotel that isn't a hotel,
hitchhiking, a mysterious sadhu, a Kazakh flash mob, wrong
turns, right turns, an almost-arrest on an English train, dengue
fever, laughter clubs, fire jumping, healing along the Boudin
Trail, and canyon gazing. As I wrote: a moving microcosm of our
modern world.

While these pieces vary invigoratingly in setting, style, and
subject, they all manifest two unifying lessons. The first is that

great fiction writers are also artful travel-tale-spinners: Just as they do when creating an imagined story, in recreating a lived experience, writers evoke a vivid sense of place with just a few finely chosen details, use dialogue to propel a plot and reveal the character of a person and a locale, and shape the arc of an adventure toward a meaningful end.

The second lesson is that whenever we venture into the world as travelers, our capacity for wonder, engagement, and growth is directly related to the capacity of our hearts. Wherever we may be in the world and in the pilgrimage of our lives, if we can wholeheartedly embrace the adventures we encounter, travel offers life-changing opportunities for discovery, renewal, connection and transformation.

Grounded in these truths, *Better Than Fiction 2* celebrates the power of storytelling and risk-taking, and the peril and promise that travel presents. The ultimate message these artful, heartful tales all convey is that stepping into the world alchemizes adventures even the most imaginative novelist could never foresee – and leads to resolutions that transmute our lives more rarely and richly than any of us could dream, even better than fiction too.

KAREN JOY FOWLER has written literary, historical, and science fiction books. She's published three collections of short stories, most recently *What I Didn't See*. Her novels include *Sarah Canary* and *The Jane Austen Book Club*. Her most recent novel, *We Are Completely Beside Ourselves*, won the 2013 PEN/Faulkner Award and the California Book Award, and was shortlisted for the Man Booker Prize. She lives in Santa Cruz, California.

An Italian Education

KAREN JOY FOWLER

In 1966, when I was sixteen years old, I went on a trip to Italy. This was my first trip to much of anywhere without my parents. It was billed as educational. We would be enrolled at the University for Foreigners in the lovely hilltop city of Perugia to learn whatever Italian we could pick up in four weeks. Students from several high schools were participating; my English teacher was coming, along with three other girls from my English class – Carolyn, Janice, and Ellen, all friends of mine.

We students were lodged in a number of places, but on the cheap. My particular cohort of four landed in a convent. We shared a room on the second floor, spartan but bright, which looked down on the street below. There were bars on our bedroom windows, which we wondered about.

The nuns did not speak English and we, despite the dozen or so hours we'd eventually put in, did not speak Italian. We called

the Mother Superior the Hitchcock nun, because she resembled
the creepy sort of painting whose eyes follow you around an
empty room. Her expression soured visibly whenever she looked
at us. The other nuns were friendlier and we had friendlier
names for them.

Imagine a trip to Italy, only with terrible food. Perhaps we
ate what the nuns always ate: dry rolls, fatty meats, tasteless
cheese, bitter tea. One of the teachers complained every morning
that they must be making a pretty penny off us. She eventually
bought her own jam, taking it out of her purse ostentatiously,
this jam that they should have provided, but didn't. We found
the ugly-Americanism of this embarrassing, though in fairness
to her, the food was truly terrible. I lived those four weeks on
bread and water and a daily trip to the gelato stand.

So there we were, tucked up in the nunnery, and yet most of
my memories of the trip have something to do with sex. Not real
sex, but the rumor of sex, the specter, the shadow. I was sixteen
years old. Sex came in all manner of guises.

This same teacher, the teacher with the jam, was often in a bad
mood about something or other. Our guide, a young man from
England, told me one day she was probably going through the
change of life. He had a girlfriend back home and occasionally
asked one or another of the prettier students to model some bit
of clothing he was thinking of buying for her. He sang Frank
Sinatra songs when we were on the bus, but even this did not
diminish his appeal, because it was 1966 and all it took to be sexy
was to be British.

The change of life was a phrase and a phase of which I was
ignorant. Once explained, it was unwelcome knowledge –

someday I would be in a continual bad mood and young men would find that amusing. Yet I was flattered to be confided in. Taken in all, the conversation had provided about equal amounts of pain and pleasure.

At orientation, this British guide had warned us about the Italian boys. They were very handsome, he said (as it turned out, some of them were and some of them weren't), but very aggressive. They mustn't be encouraged. We must, at all times, be demure in our dress and deportment. No pants, no short skirts, no bare arms. No make-up. Sensible shoes. We were told to be actively unfriendly.

We four walked to school every morning and went out again on our own after siesta, exploring Perugia's steep, narrow streets and hidden staircases. We made a game of looking for 12 steps, 39 steps. We saw few girls of our age, but many boys to whom we were not friendly. They didn't appear to notice. Despite the warnings, it was startling to be pinched and prodded. Carolyn was not the oldest of us (that would be me) but she looked the oldest. Blond and curvy, even in her demure clothes, she was tormented beyond her endurance. One day in a small public square, she turned and slapped a boy across his face. He instantly slapped her back. She began to cry.

An old woman appeared, hugged her. '*Brava!*' she said. '*Brava!*' She turned to shout at the boy. He shouted back. Red-faced, he gestured furiously at Carolyn. Slowly a crowd gathered, men shouting at women, women shouting at men. A gender war had broken out. Since we could understand none of it, we slipped away while it was still escalating. I have no idea how or when it ended. For all I know, they are shouting there still.

Another day, an older man, a man about the age of our fathers, came and chased the boys off for us. He spoke good

English and was courtly and kind. After that, we often saw him and often talked to him. We felt that we had made an Italian friend. One sunny afternoon, on our way home to dinner, we passed him seated at an outdoor cafe. He waved us over, got us chairs. It was soon clear that he was very drunk. He moved close to Carolyn. He put his arm around her. He put his other hand in her lap. Something happened under the table. When she jumped up, he spilled his drink down her dress and over my legs and that was the way we had to go back and face the Hitchcock nun, wet and reeking of alcohol.

Janice was our resident expert in all matters sexual, the one who explained the change of life to me. She was the only one of us with a boyfriend back home. She wrote him letters and talked about him endlessly. He was sort of a boyfriend and sort of her piano teacher. He was much older, and had an actual girlfriend, so their affair had to be conducted in secret. All this seemed adult and sophisticated to me, not a bit sad or unseemly. The fact that it was also illegal interested us not at all, since it carried the suggestion that we were not capable of making the smart choices we were so obviously making.

Toward the end of our trip, the university hosted a dance. I could see only two possible outcomes to this. The first was that I wouldn't be asked to dance. The second was that I would. And I didn't see how I could manage it, dancing while being actively unfriendly. Both possibilities made me so anxious that I told my friends I wasn't feeling well and stayed behind at the convent, playing checkers with the nuns. We had a rousing game and I went to bed early.

My friends returned around midnight and woke me. A group

of boys had followed them back from the dance. They were in the street now, calling up to the open windows. 'I can kiss you! I can kiss you!' Several of them made it, hand over hand on the columns and cornices, to the second floor. They hung there, looking in. Their hands came through the bars. They howled at us.

The nuns sprang into action. Checking first to make sure we were all in our bedroom where we belonged, they armed themselves. Not Catholic myself, I had imagined the nuns would command a certain respect. They did not. We watched from our windows as they attacked the boys with mops and broom-handles, trying to knock the ones on the edifice to the ground, to chase the ones on the ground away.

In the end, they triumphed, as nuns will do. They came back inside, heads high. 'How was the dance?' I asked my friends and they said it was good. Really fun! I should have come!

A few days later, there was a drama involving one of the girls from a different high school. She'd gotten engaged to an Italian boy, our British guide told us. Her parents arrived as quickly as you can fly from California to Italy, possibly quicker, to whisk her home. They had some words with the guide to the effect that he was not supervising us properly. He pointed out that none of the rest of us had gotten engaged, only *their* daughter. It was a stand-off.

After four weeks, we left Perugia, down one student, no more fluent than when we'd arrived. There followed a week of travel on the bus. The food improved immeasurably, which was a great relief, as I'd spent all my remaining gelato money on a local artist's rendition of Don Quixote.

We saw the iconic works of art – the Sistine Chapel, the *Pietà*.

I remember *David* the best, but mostly because Janice bought
a small replica and shipped it off to her boyfriend with a ribald
note. The note was very funny, she told me, but she wouldn't read
it to me, because she said I wouldn't approve. There is nothing
more annoying than being told there is a funny joke that you
can't hear. How did she know what I would approve of? I was the
one who made her whole affair possible, driving her to meet him
in out of the way places, lying to everyone about where we were,
providing the cover of my own spotless reputation. I felt hard
done by.

In Florence, we aroused little of the attention we'd gotten in
Perugia; in Rome, none at all. Our remaining adventures were
less sexual than life-threatening.

We were booked home through Shannon Airport on Saturn
Airways in a modest four-propeller plane. Janice had the window
seat. About twenty minutes out, she turned to me. 'One of the
propellers has stopped,' she said. Across the aisle, Carolyn and
Ellen were sleeping. 'Should we tell them?' she asked and we
decided we would not.

Moments later, the pilot spoke over the intercom. 'We're
returning to Ireland. We've had a little engine trouble, but not to
worry. We could get back on a single propeller if we had to.'

Those on the right side of the plane didn't know a propeller
was out on the left. Those of us on the left didn't know that both
propellers were out on the right.

Plus the wing was on fire.

The pilot continued to talk to us. He was calm and
cheerful. The crew behaved less professionally. Perhaps I'm
misremembering that we could hear one of the flight attendants

throwing up in the bathroom. I'm certain one of them quit on the spot, loudly and publicly.

We had a beautifully smooth landing. When we debarked, the runway was lined with sobbing Irish. They seized and hugged us. 'You had the best pilot in the world!' they said. They shook their hands heavenward. 'The best pilot in the world!' The best pilot in the world had completely persuaded me that we were in no danger; this was my first understanding otherwise. I turned to watch him come down the stairs. His hands were shaking; his face was drained of color. Someone handed him a bottle of whisky. He stood and drank it right there on the tarmac while people cheered him and cried.

Again, there were compensations. A cute boy from another high school who'd never said a word to me before asked if I was all right. Saturn Airways was forced to buy us all a lovely supper and put us up for the night. I remember this as one of the most amazing meals of my life. Roast chicken. Rhubarb pie. We had hotel rooms with feather beds. And also this – a whole new plane sent from Germany.

We finally arrived in New York in the middle of the great airline strike of 1966. We spent a night at the airport, which was crammed with people sleeping on the chairs and floors. If our parents ever wanted to see us again, they were going to have to pony up for first class. This remains the only time in my life I have ever flown first class and I slept through the whole thing. Janice told me they served frogs' legs.

But these final adventures, dramatic as they were, are not what I think of first when I remember my trip to Italy. Instead, I remember how it rained every day during siesta, but stopped politely when we wished to go out. I remember the pantomimed amazement of the nuns that we could sleep in the large curlers we wore to bed. I remember our British guide singing 'Strangers in the Night' and our English teacher telling me I should write it all down, because I would be a writer someday. (I did write it all down. I lost that diary decades ago.)

And all this is still not what I think of first. The very first thing I remember, and with enormous pleasure, is the great battle at the convent. The boys on the walls, the nuns with their brooms. The four of us watching from above, just sixteen years old and already that epic struggle below, waged for us and only us.

REBECCA DINERSTEIN was born and
raised in New York City. She studied
English at Yale, and upon graduating
received the Frederick Mortimer
Clapp Fellowship, a year-long poetry
grant. Dinerstein spent the year in the
Norwegian Arctic, writing and learning
Norwegian. In 2012 her first collection
of poems, *Lofoten*, was published
by Aschehoug in a bilingual English-
Norwegian edition. Her debut novel, *The
Sunlit Night*, was published in 2015 to
praise from *Publishers Weekly*, *Kirkus*,
Booklist, *Library Journal*, the *Huffington
Post*, *The Forward*, *Bustle*, *ELLE*, and
others. Rebecca holds an MFA in Creative
Writing from NYU and lives in Brooklyn.

Into the Fjord
REBECCA DINERSTEIN

I showed up in Oslo with a suitcase and the name of one man. Arnulf Egeland, I'd been told, directed research at the National Library of Norway and could possibly award me a writing station of some kind, where I could work on my novel in one of the library's corners. The trouble was, Arnulf wasn't at the library, and he wouldn't be for a few months. He was in a cabin, on a rock, in the middle of a fjord, as all Norwegians are during the summer.

Arnulf's cabin had been built two generations before on an island off Norway's southeastern coast. It was a genuine example of Norwegian carpentry and Arnulf suggested I join him there, to discuss my work. If I rode the Sørlandsekspressen bus for four hours, I would reach a town named Tvedestrand, where he'd be waiting with his boat. The bus stop, he said, was steps away from the dock. He'd be wearing a green hat.

The bus traced Norway's shoreline as we drove west from
Oslo and then south, past Tønsberg and Sandefjord and
Porsgrunn, past Bamble and Kragerø and Gjerstad, towns
with red and yellow station houses. I sat on the east side of the
bus, where I could look out the window and see the water that
separated Norway from Denmark, a strait with a dragon's name:
Skagerrak. In the Tvedestrand harbor, I found Arnulf wearing
a lime green beanie, waving to me from his speedboat. 'Let's get
some bread', he said with a smile, as I boarded.

We shot out into the fjord. Arnulf's zigzag steering seemed
like pure enthusiasm, but he soon explained that we were
dodging underwater rocks – the bed of the fjord was a maze of
threatening, invisible boulders the locations of which he knew by
heart. The water was full of visible rocks too – small islands like
gray cupcakes with the strangest toppings: one entirely covered
with white goats, one sporting a gasoline pump, one bare except
for a one-room house that served as a general store.

The store was out of bread. The fjordwater had been choppy
overnight and the late shipment hadn't come. We zoomed on
to the next rock, where another little house sold household
essentials. Arnulf bought a loaf of dark, unsliced bread and
a tube of mayonnaise. We hit the water again, only briefly
this time, before Arnulf slowed the boat and we pulled into a
narrow cove. A long-legged, red-headed child stood at the top
of the nearest cliff, completely still and expressionless, a spaniel
alert beside her.

Arnulf hopped out onto one of the lower boulders, helped me
out of the boat, and then pulled the boat into a wooden shack.
I'd be sleeping in the boat shack, he explained. The girl on the
cliff came to meet us and the dog licked Arnulf desperately.
We climbed from the shack to the main cabin, over a jagged

rock formation that offered no clear path – the girl's feet had memorized its contours and she didn't need to look down as she floated over it, fleet as the dog. My feet had never felt rocks this hard and spiky – I'd grown up in Manhattan – and my ankles gave out over and over again. The girl waited for me at the cabin door, patient and confused by my needless stumbling. Eventually she climbed back onto the rocks and gave me her hand. She said her name was Vilde, the Norwegian word for 'wild.'

Vilde led me to the family cabin and it was beautiful – white wood, red trim, large windows reflecting blue – but before we had taken a seat, Arnulf suggested we go for a swim. He'd already put on his goggles, somehow, and Vilde removed her sweater to reveal a bathing suit. I hurried to change and we marched out, back over the rocks, to the water. The water, he announced, was full of jellyfish. The poisonous kind? *Ja.* Arnulf's eyes blinked enormous behind his goggle lenses. He dove, without hesitation, into the mess of tentacles.

The creatures dispersed momentarily, and Vilde jumped into the clearing. I followed her in, as the orange vines began to reassemble around us. Arnulf led us in a loop: we circumnavigated the jelly family as they hovered, wiggling in place, swam out to a small white buoy, and soon returned to the rock where we'd started. This mandatory splashing lasted less than a minute. But now that we'd done our lap, we dried off and sliced our loaf of bread. All questions about where I would go, or how I would get there, subsided for a few hours, under the weight of being right where I was. I'd come to Norway to be nourished by its clear Nordic light, to let one of the earth's farthest corners energize my writing. Here was the far place I'd craved. After a quiet dinner of open-faced sandwiches, I ventured back across the rocky hill – even more path-less in the dark – and went to sleep in the boat shack.

The next day, Arnulf's wife, Hilde, and eldest daughter, Marthe, arrived. Arnulf, Vilde, and I rode back to the Tvedestrand harbor and watched the bus pull up. The passengers exited. Arnulf's wife, from my sea-level perspective, appeared over 6 feet tall and, in terms of species, somewhere between horse, wolf, and woman. Arnulf's dog jumped out to greet her and she began bounding up and down the dock in great big strides that impressed and intimidated me, crouched as I was in the speedboat. The dog loved the exercise and soon left Hilde to lick Marthe's face – an older, stronger, more befreckled version of Vilde's. In the context of this family, I was a measly, miniature thing. It took the entire ride back to explain to Hilde and Marthe, in stumbling English, why and from where I had come.

Still, I *had* come, and I stayed a week. After a few nightless days, Marthe and Vilde became my sisters, the dog became my dog. We swam with the jellyfish every day. Every night, after dinner, we'd wash the dishes outdoors, and let them air-dry like laundry. The island was in bloom and multicolored flowers grew everywhere. If photographed, the scenery would have resembled the set of Munchkin Land. The sun set at midnight and rose again at two. During those two darker hours, the fjord retained a milky glow. Arnulf was a talented guitarist and loved to play jazz standards, the same songs I'd been raised on in New York. Before bed, we'd sing 'Don't Worry 'Bout Me.'

I felt I no longer needed a destination. The world had crystallized into one island, and its landscape and inhabitants served as an endlessly vivid setting and characters – a book spun into action. Still, eight days after my arrival, I returned to the Tvedestrand bus stop and retraced the shoreline route. Arnulf had found me a writing station after all: a desk in the Arctic, on the Lofoten Islands, in a community building where his uncle developed photographs. His wife and daughters would soon leave the cabin and return to their non-summer lives. Arnulf would return to the National Library, but I'd do my writing in a far wilder place. In Oslo, I boarded a train that would take me straight up the length of the country to the edge of land, and at that edge I would cross one final fjord. I pictured Vilde standing on the distant cliffs, beckoning the ferry. But only the islands waited for me in their freezing water, under their monarch sun.

JANE SMILEY'S novel *A Thousand Acres* won the Pulitzer Prize and the National Book Critics Circle Award in 1992; her novel *The All-True Travels and Adventures of Lidie Newton* won the 1999 Spur Award for Best Novel of the West. She has been a member of the American Academy of Arts and Letters since 2001. Her novel *Horse Heaven* was shortlisted for the Orange Prize in 2002, and her novel *Private Life* was chosen as one of the best books of 2010 by the *Atlantic*, the *New Yorker*, and the *Washington Post*. She has written several works of nonfiction, including *Thirteen Ways of Looking at the Novel* and *The Man Who Invented the Computer*. She has also published five volumes of a horse series for young adults, *The Horses of Oak Valley Ranch*. Most recently, she has written the fictional trilogy *The Last Hundred Years*, comprising *Some Luck, Early Warning*, and *Golden Age*.

Alone in Iceland

JANE SMILEY

The thing you want to remember most about going to Iceland is all the hiking you did – up the hills and across the dales, wind, rain, and sunshine pouring over you and through you. You were always facing down the elements, maybe with the aid of a little hat and a poncho. You will have knitted your own socks from oily (but natural) Icelandic wool, and your own gloves, too. Your backpack will have contained dried reindeer meat for sustenance, a few containers of *skyr* (like yogurt), and, because you were so adventurous, some *hákarl*, which is shark meat allegedly buried in the sand, and then preserved by fishermen who urinate on it as they go by every day for a few months, until it is truly inedible to everyone but Icelanders. You will not have had even a sliver of *rjomaterta* (cream cake) in your backpack because you were too sturdy for that, and your only reading matter will have been by medieval saga writers (Halldór Laxness being way too modern for you).

But I am unlike you – my main memory from my eight months in Iceland is sleeping. My favorite dream was of myself swimming in the waters of the north Atlantic (unrealistically warm and bright), and being approached by a pod of dolphins, who lifted me out of the water as they leapt into the blue sky, then let me down gently to float again in the waves. Almost all of my dreams there were more vivid than any I had ever had, and from them I understood some of the incidents in the Icelandic Sagas – for example, the monster who sits astride the roof of a house in *Grettis Saga*, and rides it until the roof beams crack.

As the nights grew longer and the days shorter (down to two hours in December), I remained on American East Coast time – I would go to sleep around 4am and get up at dawn (which was 1pm in the afternoon), go swimming at the local pool (hail and ice on the concrete between the locker room and the hot tub – the hotter one, not the hottest one, where the old men were boiling themselves and talking), then walk home in the dusk, stopping at the American consulate to take out a book from the library, something that I had never read (*The Grapes of Wrath*) or never heard of (*The Man Who Loved Children* by Christina Stead) or that was long enough to require many dark hours of concentration (*Anna Karenina*).

Iceland made me.

I was always a traveler. I do not remember my earliest journey – my mother and father driving from LA to Michigan when I was a year old – but I think I remember all of them after that, from St. Louis to Chicago on the train with my grandmother to visit cousins when I was three; to Grand Rapids around the same time to visit the other grandparents; down to the Current River in southern Missouri when I was nine and ten;

camp in northern Wisconsin and Vermont when I was eleven, twelve, and thirteen. I was always staring out the window of the plane or the train or the back seat of the car, fascinated by the landscape, listening to people around me talk. When I was a senior in high school my parents let me go to England for two weeks during spring vacation, and that's where Iceland was planted, right there in those cathedrals and those dialects that my very saintly hosts exposed me to, day after day.

After college there were no jobs, so my first husband, John, and I scraped together three thousand dollars and went to Europe for a year, first working on an archeological dig in Winchester, England, then hitchhiking through France, Italy, Greece, Crete, Yugoslavia, Austria, Switzerland, France again, Denmark, and back to England. He was six-foot-ten, my mentor and protector. We met other travelers who had been scammed and robbed and frightened. The closest we came to being taken advantage of was in an Italian train station, where we fell asleep on some benches, and my husband woke up just as a man was attempting to steal his shoes from under his head. Much more typical was our experience at an outdoor bazaar, where we ponied up the asking price for some item, and the seller took pity on us. He taught us how to bargain, then gave us the item half off. In grad school, after my husband and I had parted ways, my new boyfriend and I thought nothing of heading out from Iowa to California, Oregon, Idaho, New York, and Martha's Vineyard, by car or motorcycle.

But until I went to Iceland, I had never traveled alone.

There were seven or eight of us – my fellow Fulbright recipient, Elizabeth, and other students from England, Denmark, Norway, and even the Soviet Union (he said his father was in the KGB, which was why he was allowed to leave; he also knew how to knit, thanks to his grandmother, so he fit right in). Elizabeth had gone to Radcliffe and graduated *summa cum laude*. She had grown up on the Upper East Side of Manhattan and read *War and Peace* when she was ten. We got along well. While I was catching up on classics, she was plowing through Barbara Cartland. The Danish boy (four years younger than I was) was Knud. He was handsome and personable, with blond hair and a square, open face. He was a whiz at Icelandic – not all the Danes were. There was one woman in my class who knitted in the lobby before class and who was rumored to be stuck between the liquid pronunciation of Danish and the harsher, multi-consonantal pronunciation of Icelandic, unable to go either back or forward. She knitted like a whiz, though – the whole front of a baby's sweater in twenty minutes.

Elizabeth and I lived in a dorm on the campus of Háskóli Íslands, the country's largest university. From the front door you could see the mountains beyond Reykjavik rearing into the sky, crusty and barren. Once I was sitting at my desk and three swans flew by outside the window, close enough to touch, it seemed. An American professor was in Iceland on a teaching Fulbright. His name was Oscar, and he hosted informal parties every Sunday, where we ate the food he liked to cook, chatted, and played hearts or whist. What was eerie and alluring was the walk to his house, along the dark beach at night (it was always night), listening to the water lap the sand, to the wind slithering here and there.

It was an easy walk to downtown Reykjavík, and I loved to observe the Icelanders, who spoke loudly and stood closer to one another than New Yorkers. My favorite episode was at the local grocery store. I was walking past the meat counter. A woman customer and the woman butcher were looking at a plate sitting on top of the butcher case that contained two stalks of celery. The butcher said, very clearly, 'SELL-ER-EE'. Then the two women shook their heads slightly and shrugged. No idea what that green thing was for. The greatest difficulty when I went to the grocery store was bringing home eggs – there were no cartons, just plastic bags. I could never get more than three or four home intact. But the *skyr* was great, the granola was great, the precious oranges from somewhere far, far away were great, and there were other vegetables, too, grown in Iceland, in thermally heated greenhouses. My fellow students were more gustatorily adventurous than I was, and even ate whale meat (which was cheap).

Occasionally, we went to the movies, if only to test our Icelandic, and many Fridays we went to the philharmonic hall, which was within walking distance, where we listened to the Icelandic Symphony Orchestra. At Christmas I went to New York, where I stayed with a friend on the Upper West Side. The first morning I sat up in bed, wide awake, thinking it was noon. The sun was pouring through the windows and it was eight in the morning. After Christmas in New York, I went back to Iowa for a few days, where my boyfriend broke up with me (not unexpected).

Now I didn't even have a reason to write letters. When I got back to Reykjavík the days were getting longer, but I didn't notice. All I did was read and read and walk. In late January I got so depressed that the only book that could help me was a collection of humorous essays by S.J. Perelman that made me laugh in the bathtub while I was hiding out from the darkness and my shirked responsibilities toward my language class and my dissertation. At some point, one of those points that are so sunk in the endless passing of time, I started writing a novel, always from about 11 at night until about 4, when I fell onto my couch/bed and continued to dream of what I was writing. It was set in Idaho, and concerned my grandparents and my grandfather's brother trying to start a ranch with a little money my great-grandmother had given them, and their winnings from as many poker games as they could get into. The best episode was very Icelandic – they were caught in a blizzard and had to dig a hole in the snow. They saved themselves by lying in each other's arms until the blizzard covered them over and then subsided. My Idaho had no trees.

I wrote and read, read and wrote, went once a week to the best hotel in Reykjavik where I did eat *rjomaterta*, a six-inch-tall wedge of layer cake, all the layers made of cream flavored with different liqueurs. The other meal I remember was a traditional Icelandic end-of-winter feast, *Þorrablót*, consisting of everything that traditional Icelanders would have found in their frozen storerooms at about the time when the grass greened up and the sheep were allowed out into the pastures. The most startling thing on the plate, to me, was the singed sheep's head *(Svið)* – eyes restfully closed. I took one look and opted for one of the alternatives, maybe a roast chicken. Elizabeth ate everything on her traditional plate with relish, including the liver sausage and the *Súrsaðir hrútspungar*, which were lambs' testicles cured in lactic acid.

The days got longer. The Fulbright Committee packed Elizabeth and me onto a plane and sent us to Berlin for a meeting with all of the European grantees. The hosts showed us around and invited us to appreciate the difference between West Berlin and East Berlin, then still behind the Wall. I did appreciate the difference, but not as they wanted me to – what I saw in East Berlin was some kind of patience, letting the ruins from the war

sit there until someone came up with a better idea than replacing
everything with chrome and neon lights. We were taken to
Dahlem, where we visited the Botanic Gardens and a few of
the museums. The best piece of art I saw was a Japanese scroll
painting that ran along the entire wall of one of the galleries, the
story of a single journey up mountains and through forests that
unfolded as you walked past it, peering carefully at the trees and
the rocks and the tiny figures. The principal difficulty of solitary
travel, I decided, was not being able to turn to your companion,
to say, 'Look at that! I love that!' Whatever revelations were
pouring into you and out of you, they were yours alone.

I felt this the following week, too, when I hiked in the
southwest of England, a region John and I had missed in our
months spent in Winchester, York, and the Lake District.
Exeter, Dartmoor (which reminded me of *The Hound of the
Baskervilles*), Newton Abbot, Dawlish – the place names, the
wide landscape, the grass and blossoming trees and the wealth
of flowers seemed to sink into me and disappear, escaping all of
my attempts to capture the view, the fragrance, the warm feel of
the air in letters or diary entries. When I read the old letters now,
I am embarrassed at how desperately they grasp at the things I
was seeing and try to push them into the minds of my recipients.
When we returned to Iceland we had five weeks left, the sun was
everywhere, and I went back to work, this time relating the tale
of my grandfather winning a diamond ring in a poker game,
giving it to my grandmother, who had no wedding ring, and
then my grandmother losing it down the drain of the kitchen
sink when she was washing the dishes.

I began preparing to go back to Iowa City. I would move into
my ex-boyfriend's apartment, I would work on my dissertation,
applying modern theories of literary criticism to the Icelandic

Sagas; I would continue my solitary existence and come to enjoy it as well as rely upon it. Then Duncan asked me to go driving with him.

Duncan was an oboe player from Edinburgh who had by that time been in the Icelandic Symphony for two or three years, though he was a year younger than I was. He was maybe the only person I knew then who was gainfully employed. He was also handy (he did, after all, have to make his own reeds, and they had to be good). He was outdoorsy, he was adventurous, and he had a car. In the last three weeks (now April and May, sun up at 4, down at 9 or 10), we drove to Dritvik, Laugarfell, Hlíðarendi (the setting of *Njáls Saga*), and Eyjafjallajökull. We saw Skógafoss, and stayed in a youth hostel near Bergþórshvoll. The grass in every valley was brilliantly green. On our second morning in the hostel, another Brit arrived – a sailor taking a break, as I remember. The two men talked all day about sailing and life on the ocean, and never once acknowledged my presence, which was an illuminating experience, the first time in my life as a six-foot-two American woman that I was entirely overlooked. Which is not to say that Duncan was unkind. Every time we met during those three weeks, he had a plan or an idea about something that might be fun to do. He also had a lot to say about Scotland, the oboe, the orchestral life, music, nature, haggis, his former plan to sail from Scotland to Iceland to Greenland to America by himself. He wore glasses, his hair was red, he was as easygoing as any man I had ever known.

We knew that our relationship was neatly circumscribed by my imminent departure. He didn't ask me to stay and I didn't ask him if I could. What Iceland had to offer me was strangeness, the theme of seven and a half months on my own now gently expanded by his knowledge and mobility. My vocation, I knew, was to return to America and keep writing, but to have Iceland deeply engraved into my own sensibility, not only by the land and the people I met, but by the ghostly presence of the Saga writers and the living Icelandic writers whose work I read, most notably Halldór Laxness, who was still alive and writing not far from Reykjavik, and whose books, especially *Independent People*, entered into me as if they had existed forever.

On the way home my plane flew over Greenland. The sky was clear, and I stared down at the glaciers and the icy coast, and felt more deeply into my fascination with that far-flung offshoot of Nordic restlessness. After I arrived in New York, the first movie I saw was *Annie Hall*, perhaps the least Icelandic film ever, and the first food I ate was a bagel with lox and cream cheese from Zabar's, Icelandic in a much-translated but still evocative way.

I went back to Iowa City. My old boyfriend was gone for the summer. I moved my suitcase and my typewriter into his apartment. Now, when I wrote, I was looking out the window at green grass and the white siding of the Foursquare house next door. I kept on with the grandparents in Idaho, my mother as an adventurous two-year-old wandering among the cattle while my grandmother cared for the new baby in the house. But I knew that the work to come, whatever it would be, had taken on a deep Nordic tinge, let's say a combination of wind and sky and snow and grass, of making the best of isolation and hard work, tragedy, luck, and magic.

AVI DUCKOR-JONES is a New Zealand-born writer. Trained as a lawyer, he graduated from Victoria University's International Institute of Modern Letters with a Masters in Creative Writing in 2013. His short stories, essays, and travel articles have been published in various literary journals, magazines, newspapers, and websites. He teaches creative writing for National Geographic Expeditions and currently lives in Western Ghana directing the reading and writing program at Trinity Yard School.

Discovering Fear in Baja

AVI DUCKOR-JONES

The journey ended with a knife. It wasn't in me, but it was directed at me, by a swaying drunk in Loreto. I don't recall anything about his face, but instead the shiny sweat of his torso combining with the Sea of Cortez behind him, until it became one thing.

The plan was to hitchhike, camp, and surf my way around the Baja Peninsula in Mexico. My reasons for choosing this particular trip are now somewhat hazy, but I suspect that I simply liked the geography of it: an enormous finger of land, from top to bottom, from Norte to Sur, a point to reach and say I had made it. I had also spent the previous year living and surfing in Hawaii and after grueling wipeouts, being held down and used as a pin cushion by an ocean floor comprised mostly of spiky black sea urchins, I had graduated to the next level of surfing and as any fresh graduate, I wanted more.

The border crossing from San Diego to Tijuana was filled with the same trepidation as any trip into the unknown, but with added fear from the horror stories of Tijuana that various fearmongers had instilled in me prior to departure. The bus passed row upon row of white crosses, marking the deaths of those who had attempted to cross the border illegally, and I saw these as some ominous warning.

I had already promised the aforementioned fearmongers that I wouldn't stop in Tijuana, so I continued south to the not-much-safer beach of Rosarito. I camped on the beach that night while a family had a fiesta around me, booming mariachi and sizzling various meats to be cupped in soft tortillas later. I was happy for their company. Earlier in the day, a drunken fellow had stumbled across the dunes to where I was setting up camp. He had held a glass coke bottle as a black and yellow snake weaved out of it. He kept thrusting the snake towards me and laughed when I flinched. I was twenty-three and it was my first trip to a foreign country alone. That night I slept with my surfboard next to me, like two soldiers before an ambush.

The next few days were spent oscillating between my ambitions to get decent mileage under my belt and my agonies over every potential surf break I passed. I decided to take it slow and ease my way into the trip, stopping for nice gentle surfs in Calafia, La Fonda, and Salsipuedes. Things were going well, and by the end of the first week, I had reached Ensenada. I wandered the streets and visited the fish markets where I saw a man selling enormous lobsters, a tattoo of a woman making love to a swordfish on his arm. That evening I surfed the famous point break of San Miguel. It was a magnificent session and I stayed out after sunset. As the wind dropped, the waves seemed to break in slow motion and my fellow surfers turned to silhouette, moving seamlessly around me like seals in the thick, oily water.

Then, when I left Ensenada, something changed. The tourists disappeared. So did the traffic, buildings, and any sense of comfort. Things were drier and the landscape opened up. There was no longer anything to hold onto and I felt untethered, like a balloon let go. I leapt out of the tray of a truck in San Vicente. It was a small dusty town after San Isidro just before the turn-off to Erendira, where I planned to spend the following couple of nights. Women with creased faces sat on stools outside closed-up shops and everything was covered in a thin veil of red dirt.

I turned and started to walk down the road towards the coast. Endless plains dotted with scrub rolled on like an ocean of rust. I began to sing aloud, elated at being in the middle of nowhere, heading towards the unknown with nothing but my bag on my back and my board under my arm. As I kept walking, though, small seeds of doubt planted themselves in my mind more frequently, and before long I was drenched in sweat. I was also almost out of water. No car had passed. The brittle scrub on the side of the road shuddered as a hot breeze passed through. Then fear started to leak into the place where doubt had been.

I walked for over two hours before I heard the thin buzz of a motor. I turned and squinted in the direction it was coming from, and the relief I felt when I saw a small rusty red thing moving in the distance was overwhelming. As it neared, I took off my battered straw hat and waved it down. The car came to a stop and the guy wound down the window. Crucifixes and beads swayed from the rearview mirror and tinny mariachi music rattled from the speakers. He was speaking in rapid Spanish and moving things around in the back, which I took as an invitation to get in. I somehow managed to squeeze myself and my board into the car and we raced off. I felt the warm wind battering my face, closed my eyes, and dissolved in relief.

There was a beautiful rustic old backpackers that stood out at the point of Erendira and I pitched my tent under a palm tree nearby. Later I would regard this chapter as the safest, and possibly happiest, part of my trip. I suppose it is the way the entire trip should have gone. I met fellow travelers; we had bonfires. There were beers and striking sunsets. We dove for mussels. On my final night, I surfed with a pod of slick dolphins as the sky became streaked with red. It was an adventure, but part of me wanted it to be harder. I had already begun to romanticize the walk out here and knew that my time at the backpackers was simply too safe to achieve what I wanted from this trip. So, somewhat reluctantly, I packed in the pre-dawn haze and left the comfort of Erendira to head back out into the unknown.

The following weeks instilled the fear and wonder and triumph that I was after. I hiked down long roads, lay out under the stars, sat with small local fishing families as they rolled up small tortillas on a grill. I rode in the back of seaweed trucks over impossibly bumpy dirt roads. I climbed dormant volcanos and watched the sun set, turning the small islands into spilled coffee beans. My map of Baja was now cross-hatched, scarred, and dotted with markings and asterisks of where I had traveled, surfed, and slept.

I was getting too confident, too far ahead of myself, already imagining the retelling of my glorious adventures, when I crashed the car. I had been so fanatic about hitting every surf spot on my map, and making it out along every spidery dirt road that straggled off towards the coast, that I was now running out of money and time. I needed to get further down Baja towards Todos Santos and the coast that stretched down to Cabo San

Lucas, where I would celebrate the completion of my adventure. Then, hopefully bearded, stronger, and wiser, I would turn around and head back up to California in one straight shot.

The man said he was driving all the way down to La Paz and could drop me wherever I liked. As we drove on, though, I could see that my driver was nodding off. Looking back, I shouldn't have offered to drive. We should have pulled over and napped. But what good is retrospect? I took over while the man slept. I clunked along, wrestling with the gearstick that jutted from the floor of the pickup. I had to swerve to avoid potholes that pockmarked the road. It was my first time driving on the other side of the road too, and in my disorientation I was veering dangerously close to the curb. It was when a herd of cattle started wandering onto the road and three trucks appeared racing down the center line from the opposite direction that it happened. I swerved to avoid the cattle, then swerved to avoid a collision with the trucks, and I lost control. It all happened in a blur of brown and red. When the car settled, the front window was smashed. Dust and smoke hung around us. It could have been worse; we suffered only minor injuries and managed to get the thing going again. I wasn't murdered for my recklessness. We drove on silently, in our separate fury and guilt. When we reached the small town of Guerro Negro, the driver stopped by an ATM, pointed at it, and leaned over to open my door.

After emptying most of my bank account to the man whose car I had crashed, I was determined to finish what I had started, so I kept going. I spent the next three days sleeping in a freight truck carrying 3000 cartons of pineapple juice. The driver and I were stranded together in the small fishing village of Santa Rosalita due to flash floods that had torn out an entire chunk of the road that led out of town. On the third day, after assisting in the clearing of a new makeshift road, we drove on through La Paz and I was dropped in Todos Santos, which would serve as the next chapter of my journey.

I lived frugally, surviving on only soft flour tortillas and tomatoes, and the trip started to find its foothold and sense of purpose again. There were some big swells, full moon surfing, and bonfires with scattered travelers who had found each other there. Baja didn't let me get too comfortable, though. After a horrendous hurricane that tore my tent to shreds with me in it, and a heavy swell that snapped my board in half, after being chased down by a pack of dogs, witnessing an intense fist fight, and getting stung fairly seriously by jellyfish, I decided to draw this chapter of the trip to a close and get to Cabo so that I could get home.

The morning after I snapped my board, a mid-fortyish surfer whom I had seen around gave me a lift into town. He introduced himself as Kristoff from Canada, and mentioned that he had seen my snapped board on the beach that morning. Kristoff was typical of the *gringos* I met down here. He had made some 'wise investments' before coming down to build his dream surf house. Unmarried and without children, he was hesitant to talk about himself but eager to surf. He said he was going to Punta Conejo on the East Cape to catch a big swell that was approaching and asked if I wanted to jump on board. He had a whole stack of boards I could choose from. Exhausted and penniless, without a tent or a board, I heard myself say yes.

We packed up the campervan and drove straight through Cabo San Lucas, where I was meant to have celebrated my crossing of the finish line and the conclusion of my trip. But I didn't feel like I had reached anywhere. I was in the clutches of something bigger now, and it was seeming less and less like a peninsula rather than a labyrinth of dirt roads and deserts, dogs, snakes, cacti, and dust. California no longer seemed like a place I could ever reach again. As we sped down the dirt road to the coast, wild horses galloped in front of us, appearing then disappearing in the dust they left behind.

Punta Conejo was wild. We camped for three days on a sand dune down the beach from the small collection of oyster farmers' shacks. I don't remember any specific waves that I dropped into. I remember it was quiet and grey and cold for brief moments before sound returned and I roared across the face of giants.

When we returned to Todos Santos and Kristoff's house, I got food poisoning. In various lucid intervals, as sweat poured from my body and drenched the sheets, I watched the fan turning slowly above me and realized that the trip had ended. When I was well enough to leave, Kristoff drove me to a highway and wished me luck. I hitched with a great urgency to reach the border and California, where my uncle and my credit card waited for me. I had no more money. None. People often say they are broke when traveling on a shoestring budget of sorts, but I really had spent everything I had and had nothing left but my thumb to get me home.

I hadn't eaten for two days when I woke to the knife in my face. I had managed to get to Loreto, where my friend from the hostel in Erendira had given me the number to his trailer. I hadn't counted on the endless neighborhoods of trailers, huddled together like cattle, and after searching for what seemed like forever, I lost hope and laid out my board bag to sleep on the beach. The next thing I knew, there was a knife in my face and the sweaty torso of a man blending into the light bouncing off the Sea of Cortez behind him. I gave him three t-shirts. He spat on me and left.

There isn't much else to say. Desperate but extremely doubtful, I inserted my card into the ATM machine to see if some sort of miracle had occurred overnight. My mum told me later that she had received my final check from Hawaii and thought I might need it on my big Mexico adventure, so had taken the liberty of depositing it into my account. I had moved through everything, all the car crashes and hurricanes and knives and sickness, all the isolation and loneliness with a numbness that I suppose was some sort of survival tactic. In that moment, I cried. I cried for everything that had happened, knowing that it was over, that I could go home, and that I would live.

The strangest part is that now, after many journeys, I actually long for that fear. Not the fear of a certain neighborhood dog on your paper round as a twelve-year-old, or the fear of being caught as you snuck back into your house drunk as a teenager, or the fear of failing exams, but the true fear that you may not survive something. I'm relatively older and wiser now, so there is always enough money, a rental car, a hotel, and friends to mitigate the likelihood of finding myself in situations where true fear could exist, and it's begun to feel as though I've lost the capacity for it. I have been close, during huge swells, or extreme hikes, but it hasn't reached the glorious despair of my journey down the Baja Peninsula when I was twenty-three. Still, I continue to search for it, as far as my mind and body will let me, because it is what lets me know, in the strongest voice and in the clearest way, that I am alive.

CATHERINE LACEY is the author of
Nobody Is Ever Missing, a finalist for
the New York Public Library Young
Lions Fiction Award. It was released in
the UK by Granta Books and is being
translated into French, Italian, and
Spanish. Her short fiction and essays
have been published in *The New York
Times, Guernia, Granta, McSweeney's
Quarterly, The Believer*, and other
magazines. She was named a Granta
New Voice in 2014 and awarded an
Artist's Fellowship from NYFA in 2012.
Her second novel and first short
story collection are forthcoming from
Farrar, Straus & Giroux.

Awkward Situations

CATHERINE LACEY

I once sublet an apartment in New York that had a tiny, triangular closet and because the closet had a small window and because I tend to put myself in awkward situations, I crammed a tiny desk and chair inside and began wondering if I should spend that winter in New Zealand. I knew no Kiwis, knew nothing of their history or culture, felt ambivalent about *The Lord of the Rings*, and was a compliant though not always enthusiastic outdoorswoman, but I felt there was something in New Zealand for me, some reason I had to go – and soon – to the other side of the world, alone and ignorant.

Some superficial reasons were created, not quite lies but close. I told friends and family I wanted to someday write about agriculture laws and politics and I thought that volunteering for Willing Workers on Organic Farms would be a thorough introduction to farming, and cheap; I'd be given housing and food in exchange for a half-day's labor at one of the small farms in their network. The unfortunate acronym of the organization is WWOOF, which means one goes WWOOFing, which makes one a WWOOFer, which does not help in the feeling, at times, that you are a slightly more useful stray dog for whom a farmer leaves out food.

I told a few others I was going to New Zealand to write a book about the ocean, a book I suppose I am still theoretically writing though no actual words have made it to the page. I doubt anyone believed this 'reason'.

I still had half the money from donating my eggs and the belief that I should do something more substantial with it than set it ablaze on the New York rental pyre, but I told only a few friends that I was planning to make the egg cash last by hitchhiking. I had once met a sparkling young Dutch woman at a dance party who had hitchhiked on every continent, even, somehow, by plane; I thought I might become sparkly or somewhat Dutch if I could trust strangers in cars the way she did. The Kiwis seemed like a good demographic to try this theory on. Any time I mentioned this plan I was encouraged to buy bus tickets. I said I would consider this. I did not.

Maybe the real reason that I went on that three-month solitude bender with no cell phone, no companion, and no clear plan was the appeal of all the awkward situations I could get myself into. I likely didn't see this at the time, and it certainly wouldn't have made a good explanation for my impulsive, isolating trip, but I've come to understand that I'm one of those people who often travels the inconvenient route or wedges herself into precarious arrangements. Even as I write, I am scrunched into a Butoh-like tangle at the edge of a couch. I cannot explain, even to myself, why.

In general, hitchhiking is series of awkward moments. The hitchhiker stands on the side of the road as people drive past thinking, *That's sad*, or *That's stupid*, or *What a fucking weirdo*. The hitchhiker knows this, is made awkward by this, and yet must look on to the next car, the next driver, retain some hope. Then there are the awkward times when a car pulls over *near*, but not *for*, the hitchhiker; those drivers caution the hitchhiker away as if she is the neighbor's unpredictable dog. Stay.

Then there's the awkwardness of actually getting into someone's car, seeing what they have in it, what they carry around, the struggle of small talk, the sinking reality that you have just put your life into a stranger's hands. The risks that both driver and hitcher have taken hotboxes the car – *Will you kill me? Something worse? Do you think I could kill you? What if we just annoy each other?* There is no gratitude like the gratitude of a hitchhiker who has safely arrived and the driver who has safely done their good deed.

I lied to the first driver who picked me up. I said I'd done this before, that I wasn't afraid, that I knew what I was doing. Gabriella, an easy talker with a maternal sense, made it easy for me to fake experience. I played the sort of make-believe that children do, mimicking a life they hope will soon happen. I stared out the window as a muted, grey afternoon fell on the shrubby landscape, and pretended. When I got out of her car a few hours later, she told me to be careful, to stay away from men; I shrugged like a teenager, as if it was something she told me every day.

When the next driver picked me up, it was harder to impersonate confidence. He was shirtless and sinewy and wore sunglasses despite the dull sky. Midway through the trip, he cracked open a beer, offered me one, and asked if his driving made me uncomfortable. I said it did. He laughed. I could hardly understand him through his accent and whatever else might be numbing his mouth, but I got that his name was Leong, that his father was Chinese, that his mother was something else, that he preferred his music to make his ears bleed, at least a little. He invited me swimming. I declined. He asked me again. I said, not convincingly or truthfully, that someone – no, not someone, a man – a man was waiting on me in Takaka. He didn't seem to care.

The moment I got out of his car, I felt a wave of relief that nearly took me out at the knees. This wasn't the only time I feared the hitchhiking skeptics might be proven right, that something terrible could happen, but it was the most memorable. After this I began to scrutinize all my strange choices – why this car, why this person, why this town? And what, exactly, did I think I was doing? But I never had an answer. I faked assurance with a thumb.

After Gabriella and Leong, I WWOOFed for a week in one of the more isolated parts of the South Island. This old man had a garden and a shed-like situation that he had long ago rigged up from construction scraps. He was senile and often stoned and had a habit of wandering around his yard all morning naked from the waist down, like he had some kind of pact with noon. I pretended to be unfazed by this, but I was very much fazed. This was a different sort of awkward, one that didn't have much to teach me, much of a skill to gain.

On other farms I faked my way into actual knowledge. I weeded fields and vegetable gardens and pumpkin patches and hillsides. I picked plums, grapes, kiwi fruit. I landscaped. I endured a couple weeks of the pain required to produce a single glass of Sauvignon Blanc. I did learn some of what I wanted to learn about agriculture, though I never applied that knowledge to anything other than an acceptance of the high price of organic produce. Considering how hard it is to produce quality organic crops en masse, I sometimes marvel at how anything is grown at all.

What I wasn't prepared for was how difficult the solitude would be. I'd always thought of myself as a solitary person; when friends asked me if I'd be lonely on this trip, I assured them I'd be fine. It had never occurred to me that so much time alone could curdle something in a person. Of course I found short-term friends – a stoic winemaker, that artist and mother in Napier, a boy in the backseat of someone else's car – but I spent most of those months walking in silence.

I thought of myself as a writer at the time, though my writing routine was more an emotional buoy than a productive process; I had still finished very little. That routine mostly stopped in New Zealand. All I could do was record dismal accounts of my day – *Weeded pumpkin patch all morning. Walked for a few hours in one direction. Walked back. Had supper. Slept.*

In the end it wasn't the hitchhiking or the semi-indentured servitude, but my own loneliness and lack of context that were the most paralyzingly awkward. I was embarrassed by this at the time, the inevitable realization that I still needed more than just myself to survive. And not just the occasional stranger to drive me or house me somewhere; I needed people who knew me as more than a stranger.

Perhaps gravitating toward awkwardness isn't about the discomfort of that moment, but what comes later, sometimes after months or years. After New Zealand I re-settled in Brooklyn, no longer in the triangular office-closet, but tossed into a cooperative living situation with seven strangers, the opposite of solitude. As we all became un-strange to each other, my writing began to take on new life, and fiction like I'd never written before, all set in New Zealand, emerged in huge chunks. I treated it exactly as I had treated those first hitchhiked rides – I pretended I knew what I was doing, faked a competence. Surprisingly, this worked and after a couple of years' work I had completed and sold a novel set in New Zealand about a woman even more confused and lost and awkward than I had been.

Perhaps this was all I was doing on those pointless walks through fields and towns of nothing. I acted like I knew where I was going until, years later, I did know. This may be all a young writer needs to know about their work: all you can do is pretend to know what you're doing until you do know what you're doing and when you forget again, pretend again, and the sense will return. It might also be all there is to travel, all there is to life.

PORORCHISTA KHAKPOUR is a novelist, essayist, journalist, and professor. She is the author of the forthcoming memoir *Sick*, and of the novels *Sons and Other Flammable Objects*, which was chosen as the 2007 California Book Award winner in First Fiction, one of the Chicago Tribune's Fall's Best, and a New York Times Editor's Choice, and *The Last Illusion*, named a 2014 Best Book of the Year by NPR, *Kirkus*, *Buzzfeed*, *Popmatters*, and *Electric Literature*, among others. She has had fellowships from the NEA, Yaddo, Ucross, the Sewanee Writers' Conference, Northwestern University, the University of Leipzig, and many others. Her writing has appeared in *Harper's*, *Bookforum*, *The New York Times*, *The Los Angeles Times*, *The Wall Street Journal*, *Al Jazeera America*, *Slate*, *Salon*, *Spin*, *The Daily Beast*, *Elle*, and many other publications around the world. She is currently Contributing Editor at the *Offing*, a channel of the *Los Angeles Review of Books*, and Writer in Residence at Bard College. Born in Tehran and raised in Los Angeles, she lives in New York City.

My Mississippi
POROCHISTA KHAKPOUR

In the spring of 2000, I had lost myself again. Mere months from college graduation, I could no longer hold it together to be the student I had been for nearly four years. Drugs, drinking, smoking, unstable flings, and weird friends (at one point a stripper was living with me, sleeping in my twin bed) had made it so I could no longer concentrate. All my classes – the usual fiction workshop, lit class, and philosophy class, all I ever took at Sarah Lawrence, where you could take anything you wanted with no grades and no exams and still be encouraged to complain – seemed a burden. I had one independent study with my American Studies professor that was meant to be journalistic somehow. I was supposed to be giving it some direction and I had none.

Professor Sizer and I would stare at each other in those tense office hours, every second feeling like an hour.

'Your skin is gray,' she once said to me.

I had nothing to say, because I no longer looked in mirrors, but I trusted her.

'Are you depressed?' she asked.

I didn't know then, but I was.

'When was the last time you were excited? What excited you?'

I was sick of my friends, going out, substances, so my mind went to books. 'I used to read a lot,' I finally said.

'Go on.'

'I loved it.'

Professor Sizer smiled at me for the first time all semester. 'Now you sound more like yourself. Keep going.'

She had never known what *myself* was like, so I didn't believe her, but I went on because there was nothing else to do.

In all my years at college, this was the first time I had spoken of him: William Faulkner, my first literary love. I had just come back from a year abroad at Oxford because that was where I had thought I could study the Western canon without too much ridicule. Identity politics were at a fever pitch then, and I was tired of living in so many margins: I was brown, bisexual, from a Muslim background, of the dreaded Middle East, of the even more reviled Iran, always poor from parents who were originally not poor and then had become very poor – I was always outside a norm, at every layer. I was sick of the fringes. Oxford had seemed like my only hope to have the most conventional Western education possible: reading the classics like Dante, Shakespeare, the Old and New Testaments. But even there, any interest I had in American literature didn't hit the surface with my professors; Faulkner didn't come up once.

'What was it about him?' Professor Sizer asked.

How do you explain to anyone why you, as a 15-year-old suburban Pasadena, California, teenager, latched onto Faulkner?

How do you explain that when your best friend had picked up the Vintage paperback of *The Sound and the Fury*, the one with the pink and blue sunset, and recommended it to you, you had just rolled your eyes? But that then you had told your English teacher you wanted to do it for your author report for honors English, and he disapproved, knowing you'd have to read more than just one book, and that in spite of you being a great student, you'd need a whole year just to do that.

There was no explaining how: I just did it. The text moved me. Though it was hard to understand, I developed a strategy: *You just keep going, you plow through it,* I told my best friend, who would look over my shoulder after school perplexed by the gift she had handed down. (*You just keep going, you plow through it,* I would tell my Columbia MFA students in a seminar 20 years later.) Benjy was always a problem, but *The Sound and the Fury* was a great excuse to get to Quentin Compson, who was destined to become a huge love of mine – so much so that soon I was deep into *Absalom, Absalom*, and, eventually, I couldn't stop reading Faulkner. One by one, I read on and on until I had indeed read all his books.

'But what was it about him?' Professor Sizer asked again.

I didn't know. I thought maybe it was the language – the maximal stream of consciousness somehow mirroring my own psyche, the lush style and winding rhythms of Southern writing somehow reflecting the lattice and arabesques of my own first language, Farsi. (A decade later my comp lit-studying brother would tell me that Middle Easterners always have a special affinity for Faulkner.) Perhaps there was something of the story of the South, too, its rise and fall, the Reconstruction era and beyond, the blood in the soil, the civilization on a pedestal and then questioned and then lost…

But I wasn't thinking about all that – I was thinking about escape. I told her all I did know, and then I said, 'I don't know why he spoke to me, but maybe I could find out,' and right then and there, I had an idea.

I could go there, couldn't I?

I imagined Professor Sizer looking at me mockingly, so when I got the courage to meet her eyes, I was surprised. She looked earnest, her head was nodding. 'I think that's the best idea you've had for me ever,' she said.

And so for my spring break of senior year, just months before I would begin my life as a college graduate in New York City, I set off to the Deep South to find something, anything, of a self I didn't quite know I'd lost.

It was my first airplane ride that didn't follow a route determined by my parents, no longer LAX to JFK. I was flying to Memphis, Tennessee, which I had discovered was the only way to get to Oxford, Mississippi – a flight there and then a Greyhound Bus to Oxford. I hadn't learned this from the Internet – it wasn't really a source you could trust then – but from phone calls to the Faulkner estate and museum where a curator named Bill Griffith had offered to meet me and put me in touch with some Southern Studies students at the University of Mississippi in Oxford.

I had no idea what I was doing, but I also told myself I had no other choice. Youth told me – falsely, of course – that I'd never have an adventure like this again, and that I had to see more of the South, and that perhaps a day or two in Memphis was the right thing. I booked two nights at a chain motel near Graceland. Elvis was an icon I had largely ignored, but I thought lodging nearby would be a good idea: nice area, full of tourists, no big deal for a young woman like me who had seen it all in New York.

Upon arrival, I realized Graceland was not in the best part of town – I didn't know what the best was, but it couldn't have been that. I walked to a gas station to get some water bottles and realized there was no actual sidewalk on the main road. I walked carefully alongside the road, the lone pedestrian, as cars honked and young guys hooted at me from their windows. At first I imagined I was in my native California, where walking in the streets was rare, but there was something different in the air. I wasn't sure if it was my cut-off jean shorts that were somehow inappropriate or that somehow they could tell I was *different*. By the time I got to the hotel room, my heart was racing. What had I done? Where was I? Who was I?

That dark dusty motel offered little consolation. I remember sitting for hours on the creaking twin bed, trying to cancel out the smell of all sorts of conflicting body odors – not mine! – by eating soy jerky I'd brought from New York. I was a vegetarian and had no idea what was in store for me food-wise. I sat and ate, my mind mostly blank except paralyzed with fear. What was I doing?

By morning, I submitted to my setting and took the Graceland tour and then even took a tour of downtown Memphis. All I remember of Graceland is that it was cramped, kitsch, a place of stale Elvis jokes, sad and camp. It seemed disappointing to everyone in that long line with me. And all I remember of Memphis is the Peabody Hotel, a big gilded grand hotel, where their claim to fame was a daily duck processional through the lobby. This was less disappointing, but still it meant nothing to me.

All around Memphis, a bleak sprawl reminded me of Los Angeles; all around, there was a quiet tension that I recognized from the days following the LA riots. A place certainly of divisions, a place maybe of intentional misunderstanding. I did not belong in this discussion. Had I come all this way to not belong all over again? To compare this to what I knew and to come short, as all who do not belong always do? Why was I here again?

I remember walking again along that sidewalk-less highway, this time to buy cigarettes – so much cheaper than in New York, I realized for the first time in my life – and ordering my first biscuits and molasses at a lonely diner. Was this the real world? Was I about to get to a realer world? Before I could even attempt to answer those questions, the next morning – drizzly and gray – I was on a Greyhound bus, arriving in no time at all in Oxford, Mississippi.

Bill Griffith, a tall man with curly brown hair and kind brown eyes – the sort of guy who had the look of universal trustworthiness – picked me up at the bus station and before I knew it we were pulling into Faulkner's home, the literary landmark: Rowan Oak.

It was a house both tall and slight, awkward and grand, a rigid white columned mansion in the woods, the smallest example of what I didn't know then was called Greek Revival architecture. A row of cedar trees lined the driveway. It was an 1840s structure bought by Faulkner in the 1930s and renovated extensively. Faulkner gave it the name Rowan Oak– after a tree of Scottish legend that is supposed to signify security – and this was the location where his mythical Yoknapatawpha County came to life, the bulk of his books having been written here, the kitchen being where he got the call for his Nobel Prize. He lived here until 1962 and it was the Faulkner home until 1972 when his daughter Jill – who was born in the house – sold it to the university.

We stood in the main lobby, me nibbling at granola bars I'd

packed from New York. Bill was an affable guy, not as Southern as I'd imagined, excited to talk about New York. He'd arranged one night in the alumni house for me and the rest I was to stay with Robin Morris, a Southern Studies student I'd managed to reach over email.

I had spoken to Bill once over the phone and he'd mentioned getting in touch with 'Jimmy,' apparently Faulkner's oldest living relative, a 77-year-old nephew, who was known to be identical to Faulkner.

'He likes to go on about it all,' Bill said with a mischievous grin, just moments before dialing Jimmy.

After just a few words on the phone, it turned out he'd be coming to see us.

'Oh, wow,' I cried both in excitement and in anguish, digging into my purse for spare batteries and a tape for my tape recorder, always nervous I'd not get my story.

'It's not that unusual,' Bill assured me, more consolation than slight.

He filled me in about Jimmy, who was one of the two sons of William's brother, John. (The other, 'Chooky,' was around but not as *social*, Bill euphemistically put it.) Jimmy was a WWII Marine fighter pilot and had also fought in the Korean War. He had an engineering degree and had owned a construction company; he'd been retired for over 15 years. Apparently 'Brother Will' (the only way he referred to William Faulkner) had called him 'the only person who likes me for who I am.' For all these reasons, he had become the primary Faulkner family spokesman and informal historian.

Soon enough he made it there, a slight, white-haired old man, with eyebrows and a mustache that refused to blanche quite that far, an aristocratic nose and piercing blue eyes: indeed a carbon copy of any Faulkner image I'd ever seen.

He asked my name and asked it again.

'Pia?' he said. 'I can't hear well. Pia, is that it?'

Bill tried to correct but I jumped in. 'Pia is great.'

No one had called me Pia before, but for whatever reason I thought it might be the best way to go. I was nervous and the politics of my Iranian name was the last thing I needed to throw into the mix, where foreign regions and distant eras especially were involved. I was still tiptoeing, still a few days from realizing that in this region there was black and white only, and this was going to be the first place in my life that I would pass as one hundred percent white.

Bill walked us through the house, but I was mesmerized by Jimmy the whole time – *I was in contact with a living, breathing Faulkner.*

By the time we finished, he turned to me and wondered what time I wanted to get up tomorrow.

I had no idea what he meant and must have looked confused.

'Well, don't you want to see some things?' he said.

'You don't want to miss this,' Bill whispered in my ear, perhaps worried I was hesitating.

But I was already there. 'I'm in,' I remember saying, a sentence I would say again and again in my life to subjects whenever there was a fork in the road. 'I'm in for whatever.'

I remember that night feeling a little less lost, thinking I had a piece of myself I had never found in college: *I was a person who could be in for things.* I could do this, and probably could do it again and again.

The Center for the Study of Southern Culture at the University of Mississippi – 'Ole Miss,' as I was getting slowly though uneasily used to saying – was over two decades old, a place 'to investigate, document, interpret, and teach about the American South through academic inquiry and publications, documentary studies of film, photography, and oral history, and public outreach programs.' And it was a program in a public co-ed research university, Mississippi's largest university with well over twenty thousand students. I, meanwhile, was coming without a major – all Sarah Lawrence students graduated with a generic 'Liberal Arts' diploma – from a small private liberal arts/arts conservatory with a population of 1200 then. Even academically, I was from a different planet.

Robin, the Southern Studies student I'd connected with, decided I could stay at her apartment as long as I wanted. She was an always-smiling, always-helpful, bottle-blonde nerd – all novel to me. I experienced many firsts with her: She was the first stranger I ever sent an email to (since 1994 I'd been 'online' in chat rooms, but I'd never actually emailed a stranger). The first Southern woman I'd befriended. The first graduate student I had ever met. And she had the first fold-out couch I'd ever slept on.

Robin introduced me to some of her friends and that meant going to bars and restaurants around the main square. It was with her I had my first grits and my first hushpuppies, foods that would come to be my favorites in life. Even the air was something I was to notice – they told me to take it in, that mix of magnolia blooms and bourbon, could I smell it? I closed my eyes and concentrated and let that particular delicate sweetness rush over me and realized I could. They laughed knowingly and I came to understand it was a game for them at first – *let's see what the New York girl can take* – but even I was surprised at how at home I felt with it all.

It was also the first time I was *a New York girl*. In New York I was an LA girl. In LA, an Iranian girl. But here there was no other interpretation. 'You are so New York,' one of Robin's friends said, though I couldn't bring myself to get her to elaborate. I took it as a compliment.

One place they seemed determined to take me was Graceland Too. At first I thought this was because I told them I'd been to Graceland – perhaps they thought I was an Elvis fanatic – but then it became clear to me: it was a major destination. Thirty miles north of Oxford, in Holly Springs, there was apparently a private home that was its own informal Elvis museum, a sort of shrine to the man by an eccentric guy named Paul McLeod who stayed up 24 hours a day they said to give these 'tours.'

It was apparently also something students in town did after drinking. That entire evening at a local bar, beers would appear in front of me, with someone, usually her friend Josh, shaking his head and saying, 'Trust me, you're gonna need it.'

We made it there well into the early hours of the morning. Indeed the rumors of the owner having altered his face surgically to resemble Elvis seemed true – at least, a very Elvis-looking man greeted us at the door of this ramshackle home, collected $5 from each of us, and then spent what felt like many, many hours talking at us nonstop, as he took us from room to room filled floor to ceiling with Elvis memorabilia, from stamps to books to albums to dolls to seemingly anything imaginable that was Elvis-themed. I remember at one point it felt like we'd never get out, but then somehow eventually we did. (The story had a strange end far beyond our imagination: In July 2014, McLeod was found dead on the Graceland Too porch, two days after fatally shooting a visitor who appeared to be a burglar.)

On the car ride back, I remember being in the backseat with

Josh, an Alabama grad student who seemed impossibly foreign to me, and resting my head on his shoulder as I fell asleep. 'Welcome to the South,' I remember him laughing. I must have snapped into consciousness and said something because I remember him telling me, 'And your adventure is just about to begin.'

I came to the adventure in the name of William Faulkner, but soon it was clear to me that Jimmy Faulkner was the real adventure. For the next 10 days, this man became a daily part of my life.

'Good morning, Pia,' he'd say at 7am, which felt late to him because he always got up at 5. (*Farmer's hours*, Bill explained to me, even though he was not a farmer and never had been.)

I became this Italian New York girl Pia who had a fancy job in publishing – he kept forgetting I was a student and instead focused on my magazine internship. As much as I'd tell him I was an intern and had no power, he'd insist it was an important job. At times, I worried he thought I was a key to him getting a potential book by John Faulkner published; I started to think that was why he was interested in driving me for hours all around the county, showing me 'secret Faulkner spots,' but Bill told me he'd occasionally take a liking to a visitor and give them the extended tour. Hearing that, I felt somehow relieved that I was not special, or less likely to be special.

We'd go to all sorts of places. One afternoon he drove us to the banks of the Tallahatchie River. Some of his friends were there and they looked like they were pacing, looking for something. 'Confederate gold,' Jimmy explained, and soon I saw several had metal detectors. 'They say there's something,' Jimmy went on, half-heartedly, like someone who maybe knew better or maybe not.

Another day we'd be in the cemetery, where he'd be telling me stories about obscure relatives. Or in his home, where he'd show me Confederate currency in a sock drawer and then make me an afternoon omelet. Or we'd be at a truck stop diner – a thing in the South, I realized! – where I'd listen to his endless stories while discovering the joys of collards and candied yams as my new favorite side dishes.

Often we'd go by Square Books right in the center of town, where Jimmy was treated as a celebrity, before the giant Faulkner displays. He'd show me all the fruits of the various annual Faulkner conferences and all his talks, with the pride of a man who, late in life, had become a scholar. Faulkner was still more popular than the other big writer in town, Jimmy seemed to proudly grumble, referring to John Grisham, whose massive compound seemed to look down on the city from every angle.

Another time he said he wanted to take me to a 'juke joint.' I had no idea what that was and played along. I remember feeling slightly uneasy after we pulled up to what looked like a tin shack off the side of a very green highway, with a bunch of cars crowding a dirt path. 'Here we are,' Jimmy said, smiling mischievously. It turned out that this was Chulahoma, 'Junior's Place,' built by the great Mississippi hill country blues legend Junior Kimbrough and now run by two of his sons (he was rumored to have 36 children) since he'd died a couple years before. I was familiar with Junior because Moby had recently released his album *Play*, and that had got me interested in the blues musicians on Oxford's Fat Possum Records – who had produced Kimbrough in his final years. I later learned that a 'juke joint' was both a lovely and a sad place – something created out of necessity, the refuge of plantation workers and sharecroppers after the Emancipation Proclamation, since there were still not public spaces that allowed black people to mix with whites. That sadness followed all the way: Just a few months later, the historic juke joint burned down.

But my best memory of all is an early one. In one of my first nights hanging out with him, Jimmy invited me to a family gathering at his favorite place, Taylor's Grocery. This was a strange sort of rundown mom-and-pop restaurant that had an amazing reputation in town, packed with families and music playing – a sort of cozy, cramped dining establishment full of red checkered tablecloths. Jimmy didn't ask what anyone wanted, but when the waitress came over, he ordered for all of us. I was too busy taking in the atmosphere to even notice, and soon sweet tea appeared before me and eventually a big plate of … fried catfish.

At that point I'd been a strict vegetarian for eight years, and I had snacks on me at all times for emergencies like this. I knew there was no way I could eat that fish and yet there was no way I could say no. I tried for a second to reach into my purse for a bag of nuts and explain to Jimmy, but he, hard of hearing, was yelling louder than ever in that busy dining room, telling me not to be afraid, I'd love it – he knew it was my first catfish (though not my first meat in ages – we'd never discussed vegetarianism). I realized I had no choice. Gingerly I cut into it and slathered it in sauce and took a bite, cringing. And then another and another. I didn't pause to think about the taste. Lost in that evening of music and laughter and conversation, I felt a part of Jimmy's world and so was that food.

I assumed I'd spend the night ill but instead when I got back to Robin's I lay in bed unable to sleep. I was full of energy, an energy unlike any I'd experienced in ages. This was the beginning of my pescatarianism, which would of course lead to omnivorism – but at least I could say a Faulkner did it to me.

Here was another piece of me. I was a person who could in the moment overstep my own beliefs, who could become someone else. Pia, Italian, New York Girl, fish-eater – none of those things held me back. They only reminded me that I, 22, could perhaps be anyone I wanted, and perhaps even one day in ways that I wanted.

We would sometimes spend eight-hour days together with only bits of silence here and there. Often I'd be asking questions and recording him, but other times we were just two friends hanging out, with no conversational agenda. One time he asked me about my family and I almost got into our years as immigrants and how I wished I could one day go back to Iran, when he cut in, 'Do they live in Italy still?' I shook my head, 'No, they're in California.' He looked sad for a second, as if he knew. But instead he said, 'We've all been from here – this land is all I've ever known and will know.'

Eventually it would be time to go home, the home that for me was not just New York but another step removed within it: college, where my time was dwindling, just a few weeks to go. Jimmy and Robin and pretty much everyone asked me what I'd do next and if I'd be back. I said I obviously would, but I didn't know if that was true. At that point travel seemed a confusing concept – all I knew was that I was moving to Brooklyn after graduation and there was no telling what would come of that, if I could even be the real journalist I felt I had experienced on that trip, the self I had gotten a sense of for a brief period.

Jimmy insisted on driving me to the airport in Memphis – he didn't mind the long trek, he assured me, as once I was gone his days would feel very empty. He insisted on carrying my bags, though I walked him back to his car. There he gave me the longest hug and leaned into a kiss, which missed my cheek and got to my lips. I laughed shyly then realized it wasn't a complete accident: 'I'm telling you, Pia, if you were older, and I was younger...' He left it at that, we left it at that. But it was a sentiment he returned to again in one of the many letters he wrote me after I was in New York, long letters in his beautiful handwriting, detailing his days, and only once in a while hoping that perhaps one day I could help to get John Faulkner's work published.

For a while I wrote him back, but eventually either he or I stopped responding, and the experience left my mind, as I was busy dealing with finding some sort of footing as an adult, now actually a real journalist in the city.

Years went by and then one day I found his letters again and thought I'd look him up online. What I found was sad, though not surprising: He had died at 79, just two years after my visit. It seemed hard to imagine, given his vitality. I felt crushed, remembering his letters. And yet I also felt lucky.

In 2008, my ex-boyfriend and I drove cross-country and stopped in Oxford for a couple nights. I remembered more than I thought even after eight years – 'Welcome to Lafayette County!' I announced, as if I had been a native. A couple of months before, the first Presidential election debate of 2008 had taken place there, and that was the only context my ex-boyfriend had. He was not a literary person, so I broke down for him my early love of Faulkner, and the Brother Will I discovered through Jimmy Faulkner, as we pulled up to the twin cedars of Rowan Oak.

'It's seems like you've lived here for ages,' he said. 'Like you've come home.'

There was a lot he did not understand. I had been Italian? I had broken my vegetarianism? (He was vegan.) I had just stayed with students? This had all meant the world to me?

But I didn't feel like explaining.

We walked into Rowan Oak, hand in hand, me shaking with so many emotions. Bill happened not to be there when we dropped by, but he was still the curator, an assistant assured us. This time I had a camera and took photos; the wallpaper on my computer is Faulkner's office wallpaper, taken on my camera from that trip. My ex patiently walked with me through it all, absorbing my enthusiasm though not emitting it.

And that was fine. We took a walk in the woods and I told him if he closed his eyes and breathed deeply, he could smell the mix of magnolia blooms and bourbon, but he couldn't. And there was something I loved about that – something that only I was able to channel, a portal that was mine, this universe that had in just some days shaped me, taught me who I was more than any other experience of my adult life.

'Not bad,' Professor Sizer had grinned, a rare expression of approval from her, as I handed her the 30 pages of my final assignment.

I didn't get it back until years later, when I returned to Sarah Lawrence to give a reading as a published author. Professor Sizer had apparently wanted to give my introduction, and she concluded her remarks with 'I have something for you,' then handed me my paper in front of a large audience. (It was an A-, with light pencil marks all the way through.) I thanked her and thanked her and thanked her in my head all through the reading, but also thanked everyone who I had encountered on that trip and especially Jimmy and of course, as sentimental as it might sound, Brother Will himself.

I also thanked that gray-skinned, frazzled, listless 22-year-old who lived with being so lost that there was no choice but to allow herself, on a most unlikely adventure, to be found again.

DBC PIERRE is known as much for youthful scandal as for books. Australian-born and Mexican-raised, DBC Pierre was an artist, photographer, and designer before writing his first novel in 2001. His debut, *Vernon God Little*, became the first book to win both a Booker and Whitbread prize, and went on to be published in 43 territories, leading to a further two novels – *Ludmila's Broken English* and *Lights Out In Wonderland*, in a loose trilogy of comedies. *Petit Mal*, a `picture book for grown-ups', followed in 2013, and the novella *Breakfast with the Borgias* in 2014. When not travelling, Pierre divides his time between the UK and a mountainside lair in County Leitrim, Ireland.

Hunting Nanda

DBC PIERRE

I strode over the tarmac at Dublin airport on a wind-lashed November day, trailing a glow of new authorhood. After two years of writing, five months of rejection, and a ten-day bender when I finally snagged an agent, one lunchtime brought a flurry of bidding, then sales to publishers. One of them was in Italy.

Now I was off to that book launch, my first.

The Italian publisher, from a prestigious old house, had decided to beat the English market to the post by hosting the novel's world premiere. Looking back, it was a risky first novel, a gamble for a publisher, and the premiere may have been meant as a hedge for its added publicity value. But I hadn't read so far into the situation. In fact, I hadn't thought about it at all. I was going to Rome full of the heady altruism known to first-time authors and astronauts, the feeling best described by Mario Puzo after selling *The Godfather* – 'almost like not having to worry about dying.'

I'd travelled before, to Rome as well, so it was nothing more than an exotic twist to what I foresaw as a celebration and fait accompli. Arriving in Rome, I was happy to be ripped off by the airport taxi, pleased to marvel again at just how wrong leather can be as a material for trousers, nostalgic to ask myself where the ancient Romans had really found the models for their statues. I checked into the Hotel Raphael beside the Piazza Navona, and after coffee went to meet my publisher.

'So here's the problem,' he said after pleasantries. 'This book will not be accepted in Italy unless we can get one lady in particular to write about it. We actually thought we had an appointment with her – but now we've lost contact and her trail's gone cold.' After a moment he shrugged in that Italianate, *che sarà* kind of way. 'She's very unpredictable. We'll just keep trying.'

So there was to be no fait accompli. No automatic celebration. Reality intervened at the first hurdle, making me calculate the power of this mystery person against Italy's diversity and size. It was some power.

Her name was Fernanda Pivano; everyone called her Nanda. She was the mother of American literature in Italy, and had famously been the muse – maybe more! – of Ernest Hemingway. She was an intimate of Kerouac, Corso, and Vidal, of Ferlinghetti, Burroughs, Bukowski, and Ginsberg. She had been imprisoned three times by Italy's fascist government for importing their liberal literature. And after such a formidable history she was now old – and grumpy.

'Well,' I ventured as she took shape in my mind, first as Helen of Troy, then Gertrude Stein, then Eleanor Roosevelt, 'in fact it's not an American book. I'm not American; I wrote the thing in London.'

'Forget it,' the publisher waved. 'In Italy it's American literature. We need Nanda or nobody else will take notice. For half a century she's been the patron and gateway for this kind of book. She has to meet you.'

And so the mythical doyenne ate the rest of the trip, became its tapestry. She roamed the shadow of every introduction, was behind the gaze on every face. She became the book's only chance. Pitched in my mind against visions of who she might be was a sober reassessment of this whole book game. It was more precarious than I'd thought. And failure here could only knock-on to the rest of the world. More weightily still, as the hours of my visit passed, a date with Nanda grew to imply much more than media approval; it became the approval by proxy of Hemingway and Kerouac themselves.

We had three days to find Nanda. In the meantime the publicity department spread her dust over every interview: 'Nanda is very interested, you know, she definitely wants to meet him. She's probably going to write something.'

But Fernanda Pivano, legend, keyholder of Fate, was nowhere to be found. On a rooftop overlooking Rome, I attended the first literary party of my new life, and her seed was already planted, her name travelled like a rumour of sex. She might even show up there! Why not? She'd been seen in Rome just that week, surely she could make an appearance. Looking around, it became clear that we were persons in waiting. Waiting for Nanda. All the assembled authors and publishers were not enough to carry the night.

They were only enough to ramp up the legend.

'She doesn't suffer fools, believe me. If she doesn't like you, forget it. If she doesn't like you, you may as well pulp the book and leave town.'

Day three approached and we not only had to find her but now she had to like me. All the intelligence I'd garnered was no help at all: it stretched to knowing who she really liked, and that was Hemingway, Kerouac, and Ginsberg. Hard acts to follow. What's more, unlike many salon legends, this wasn't bullshit. Nanda Pivano had translated most of her American friends into now classic editions in their own right, and had written, edited, criticised, and reported her own significant post-war and Beat works in step with them. She had not only been Hemingway's acknowledged confidante, she said she was the last person ever to hear from him.

Hemingway sought out Nanda before death.

'She was scheduled to appear at a venue on Thursday,' the publicity crew hissed. 'But she cancelled. Now she's not answering calls.'

'She was seen at an event! But she vanished.'

'We just heard she's moving house! But nobody knows where.'

'Someone answered her phone! Apparently she's not well.'

So came the cries from the jungle of my trip. Then on the day before the last, having enjoyed some old balsamic while adjusting to life as a reject of Hemingway: 'We found her – she's in Milan!'

I snatch an afternoon flight to Milan where I'm met by Chiara, my guide for the hunt's climax. She's a lively philosophy graduate from the publisher's local office, and presents with the right mix of realism, anarchy and hope.

'When's our appointment?' I ask.

'What appointment?' she smiles.

It remains a commando mission. Chiara has met Nanda before, and as we hunker down to strategize over coffee, she pulls a few more tales from the archive of Nanda's stubbornness, caprice, intelligence, and charm. And she repeatedly calls a local number, one we're assured is Nanda's, but there's no answer. Meanwhile information filters in that says the number connects to an apartment just around the corner – which must be the one Nanda is in the process of leaving.

Coffee turns into prosecco until the number finally answers. Its not Nanda but another lady, an assistant or friend, who says Nanda may or may not see us – but we can approach the apartment and take our chances. We walk to the address and try the bell, but no one comes. The building is an elegant low-rise over a gated garage with a restaurant built in alongside it. After loitering around the gate for a while, we retreat for more drinks and try the phone again.

Prosecco turns into grappa. Night begins to fall.

As a final shot within the hours of decency, we return to the darkened building and ring the bell. This time a lady comes to the gate and lets us in. Just like that, as if she's always there, and always lets callers in. She says Nanda is upstairs, and leads us to an apartment stacked high with boxes and furnishings. In one central room, once the living room, a sofa and an armchair still sit in place. And from deep in the armchair a pair of eyes sparkle up. They follow Chiara and me to the sofa. Behind the eyes a small round woman begins to smile. Her hair is short, still brunette, framing a Genoese face with the beaming cheeks and handsome radiance of a boy on the cover of a raisin box. She watches me for a few moments, then says in English, 'Take off your clothes.'

I grin. She beams. At eighty-five she has not only the face but the mischief of a schoolboy. Chiara, realising she's sat between urchins, flaps at me not to do it. She later tells me Nanda has used the gambit before, that it was a trick, because someone once actually undressed and she wasn't impressed. More playful gambits follow, and I roll with them until Nanda leans from her chair to say that she's read my book. That she loves it. This is the Mario Puzo moment I would've undressed for. In the buzz that follows, she invites us to invite her to dinner at the trattoria downstairs. Chiara and I take an arm each and manoeuvre her down to the place, settling at a large wooden table and ordering red wine. Nanda sits facing me, scrutinising. She wants to know about me, but my brief history – recent move to a forest in Ireland, upbringing in Mexico City, father running projects out of New York – makes her stop me.

'Do you keep animals, in this forest?'

'Not as in livestock. But there are creatures around the house, foxes and such. There's even a fox who comes to be fed every night.'

'And your father died in New York?'

'He didn't die there. Though he was treated for a time there, when he fell ill.'

'Foxes, New York,' her eyes glisten over my face. 'Listen to me: if you're going to write like this, you mustn't face the world as yourself. You need a *figura*. If you show them yourself, they'll destroy you!'

'But part of the soul of this work is that it's the first really honest thing I've done,' I say. 'It's not in that spirit to hide.'

'No, no,' she says. 'Don't show them yourself. Look at Hemingway, look at all his friends. Those were deeply strange men. If anyone knew how they really were, they would've destroyed them. Deeply strange, all those boys. Do you think they would've survived without their *figura*? I was imprisoned for some of their ideas. Imprisoned three times, under fascism. And let me tell you something – I can smell it coming again.'

The words settle heavily between us. 'Except, Nanda,' I start, 'it presumes that I'm also deeply strange...'

'Spanish liar!' she squeals. 'You're a Spanish liar! You need a *figura*! I'll make one for you, and I'll introduce you to all my friends in America...' and through my cigarette smoke, over wine by the light of her gaze, the night becomes a kind of arrival. A docking at the wharf of great spirits, hearts, and minds. Of human turmoil and its answers in art. That Trojan intellect empties me out and pumps me full of the substance of art and life, makes me feel for the first time like a writer. She gives Hemingway's blessing, speaks to me of him and his cohorts as of mutual friends we'd just been with. Then we kiss goodnight through the bars of her gate, and she is gone.

Sometime later a sketch of the article she was writing arrived at my place in Ireland. It was a poetic piece on me and my book, to be published in an Italian daily.

And there was my new *figura* – I'd virtually been raised by foxes in the wilderness, after my father's suicide in New York.

I wrote to Nanda about it. Raised by foxes is one thing; suicide was a little strong.

'Spanish liar!' she wrote back.

We corresponded in handwriting for a time before her death, her last letter to me from a summer house in Portofino. And thinking about it now, I should have taken her advice. She not only passed on secrets and tips, she handed me a baton and a challenge. Still today my mind hunts Nanda and her advice.

But maybe it's not too late to follow what she gave me.

After all, a suicide in the family can leave you confused.

And foxes are no example for a growing boy.

FRANCINE PROSE is the author of more than 20 books of fiction and non-fiction. Her most recent is a novel, *Lovers at the Chameleon Club, Paris 1932*. She is a Distinguished Visiting Writer at Bard College.

Swami Sand Castle
FRANCINE PROSE

Once, over lunch, I told an editor at a glossy travel magazine that I wanted to write a piece about the experience of not understanding a place, of being intrigued – but bewildered – the whole time I was there and leaving with no clear idea of what that place had been about. I'd said I'd noticed that the essays in his magazine were always written by travelers who seemed to know everything about their destinations long before they got there, or by writers who had a charming local friend who explained the region's many appealing customs and attractions, preferably over dinner at a villa, and provided introductions to nearby Michelin-starred chefs and gourmet-food providers. Was I the only person who had ever gone somewhere, been confused, and felt that I'd never figured anything out? From across his plate of micro-greens, the editor stared at me as if I'd suggested writing a piece about the nicest places on the planet in which to catch bubonic plague.

So here is a story about one of those mysteries of travel that has remained in my mind as a succession of somewhat dreamlike events, and a series of questions.

For years I couldn't remember the name of the village. I'd search for it on maps, but all I knew was that it was somewhere on the coast of the Arabian Sea between Cochin and Trivandrum, in the southern Indian state of Kerala. Then one morning, not long ago, I woke up and thought: Varkala! I googled the town, which turns out to have developed (surprise!) dozens of luxury and middle-class resorts along its gorgeous beach. But nothing remotely like that existed when Howie (now my husband, then my boyfriend) and I arrived in the winter of 1978.

Over time I have become the sort of traveler who likes thick towels, flat screen TVs, reservations made long in advance. But this is how we traveled then: We had an open-ended plane ticket back to the United States. We planned to spend four or five months in India and go home when we got tired or homesick or when our money ran out. We took the bus from Cochin to Trivandrum, with the plan of getting off and staying if we found a beautiful place.

Varkala was beautiful. We could see the palm trees and the clean white beach from the narrow road that ran through the peaceful little town. We assumed there would be somewhere to stay the night. After a day at the beach, we would continue on our trip across South India, through which I had traveled a few years before; I'd loved it and longed to return.

The bus left us in beautiful Varkala, where, as it turned out, there were no hotels. But a helpful man at the bus stop told us that a young fellow, very respectable, actually his nephew, was building some houses on the beach. One of these houses was nearly finished, and for a small fee the landlord-builder would probably let us stay there.

The house was easy to find, and the landlord spoke perfect English. He said we could stay on an air mattress in the mostly finished house, which had working plumbing, and he would bring us breakfast – some yogurt and fruit – and a vegetarian dinner, all included in the price. The fee, in fact, was amazingly small. We decided to stay for two nights.

That first afternoon at the beach we met some fishermen and their wives. The women gave me betel to chew, and tried to teach me how to spit, with something like panache, the red saliva that betel produces and that tourists in India sometimes mistake for blood, on the sidewalk. They laughed delightedly when red slime dribbled off my lower lip. The men tried to persuade Howie to go ocean fishing on what was basically a carved-out log, and when I begged him not to, they thought that was hilarious too. Anyway, they were probably joking. Testing us, I imagine.

For the rest of that day, and all the next, we sat on the beach near our house and watched a *sadhu* – a wandering holy man – perform a ceremony that was in more or less constant progress and consisted of various sorts of work on the beach, not far from where we sat. Because some of that work involved raking the sand and patting and piling it up into ceremonial circles and lingam-like sculptural shapes, Howie and I began referring to him as Swami Sand Castle.

The first thing that needs to be said about Swami Sand Castle is that he was extraordinarily handsome and that all his movements were assured and graceful, and fascinating to watch. He was tall and thin, and though he seemed to be in his early thirties – not all that much older than we were – his long hair had already turned silver. His eyes were so shockingly blue that we could see them from the polite and comfortable distance at which we sat. He was bare-chested, his skin was golden brown, and he wore the long wrapped white skirt the Indians call a *dhoti*, which gave him a Hindu Jesus effect. I liked the idea of a holy man who could have been a rock star back home.

For a long time he didn't notice us, or didn't appear to. And then he did. He nodded once and acknowledged us, and we smiled back. After that his manner changed a little and became, intermittently, a performance. He knew we were there, but he had work to do. Our watching gave the experience an ever so slightly voyeuristic edge, and – given how striking he was, and how young and in love and attractive we were then – an ever so slightly erotic aspect.

In addition to raking and patting the sand, he ministered to a steady trickle of people, men and women, old and young, families and solitary pilgrims, who came to him to receive a blessing, a dab of paint on their foreheads, and a packet wrapped in a leaf. They gave him money, then took the packets down the beach and threw them into the sea. When the stream of people slowed he would kneel and either make things out of sand or prepare more packets, small scoops of rice and spices wrapped in banana leaves.

That evening our landlord explained that it was a *puja*, a ceremony. Pilgrims traveled to buy a packet of food from the *sadhu*, food that the dead were known to like. Then they threw the packet into the sea, where the dead would somehow find it – and be fed.

By the second day we had developed a sort of relationship with the *sadhu*. When we got to the beach – on which, it seemed, he lived – he waved to us, and we waved back. Were we disturbing him? We didn't think so. Even if he didn't speak English, we reasoned, he could make it clear if he wanted us to leave.

Swami Sand Castle didn't speak English. Late that afternoon, he walked off the job and came over to us, and motioned for us to follow him. He pointed toward the town. He tilted an imaginary tea cup toward his lips. He said, *'Chai.'*

A cup of tea seemed simple enough. We'd go along and see where this went. We trailed Swami Sand Castle up the beach into the center of town and into a little hut. Maybe fifteen men sat on the floor or squatted at tiny tables drinking cups of the sweet milk tea that was boiling in a cauldron watched over by a sweating kid on a high stool up front. Every one of them looked up and stared at us, curious but not unfriendly. In pantomime, the *sadhu* made it clear that we would be buying him tea. He indicated the others: a round for the boys. Sure. This would still cost us next to nothing.

This is where my memory stops. Did we drink our tea in silence? Did we try to communicate in a simple language that involved pointing to ourselves and saying words that neither side understood, and nodding as if we did? Howie remembers that everyone smiled a lot. I remember Swami Sand Castle thanking us, pressing his palms together, and saying goodbye. We went back to our house, and I suppose he went back to the beach, to wherever he came from.

That evening, after dinner, Howie and I both got violently ill, first one of us, then the other; we took turns. When the landlord came to collect the tiffins, the metal containers in which he'd brought us dinner, he heard Howie retching in the bathroom. He asked me what was wrong, and though I felt sick myself, I told him the story of our day, all about the *sadhu* and the tea.

Cluck cluck. Our landlord said we'd made a grave mistake. This *sadhu* was from a very low caste, not a *harijan*, an Untouchable, but almost. The tea house he took us to was patronized by people of the same and similar castes. It was very dirty, very unclean there. No wonder we got sick! I remember feeling the particular embarrassment of travelers who have made a stupid tourist mistake.

Thanks to paregoric, an opium syrup one could get more easily those days, and which has a miraculously calming effect on the worst intestinal illness, we were able to get on the bus the next day and get out of town and go on to Trivandrum.

Do I understand what happened in Varkala? I have more questions than answers. Now that all the resorts have been built, are pilgrims still coming for packets of food to throw into the sea? Who was Swami Sand Castle? Where did he come from and what did he believe? What was he doing with the sand and what did he think about it? Who did he think we were? Was he as curious about us as we were about him? Who were the people who came to him for food to feed their dead? Why did I tell our landlord about the *sadhu* and the tea? Why were we so ready to believe our landlord, that the cup of the tea from the low caste cafe was what made us sick? Couldn't we just as likely have caught something from the yogurt and fruit the landlord brought or the vegetable curry dinner?

Even if we went back to Varkala, I would never find out. But I don't mind. I don't need to know the answer, and indeed I prefer that so much of what happened there remains unclear. For what is travel if not a confrontation with the mysterious, and why should we assume – or desire – that every mystery will be solved?

CHRISTINA NICHOL grew up in Northern California and received her MFA from the University of Florida. She has traveled widely, worked for nonprofit film companies, and taught English in India, South Korea, Kyrgyzstan, Kazakhstan, Kosovo, Russia, and the republic of Georgia, where her debut novel, *Waiting for the Electricity*, was set. Christina won a 2012 Rona Jaffe Writer's Award and a gold medal in the 2015 California Book Awards for First Fiction. She has been published in *Lucky Peach, Guernica, The Paris Review, Harper's, Subtropics*, and the *Wall Street Journal*.

Kazakh Flash Mob 2050!

CHRISTINA NICHOL

'**N**ext Friday, for International Women's Day,' Team Leader Franklin told me, 'we would like you to lead the shooting competition.'

'Shooting?' I asked him. 'As in shooting a film?'

'A gun,' he told me. 'AK-47.'

I knew they had a closet full of them. I had heard that the school principal could strip one down in twelve seconds, but only on that day did I learn that the Nazarbayev Intellectual School in Uralsk, Kazakhstan, the school where I was teaching, had a target practice range out in the yard.

I had already gotten used to the early morning aerobics routine where the students would be required to stand in front of the principal in North Korean-esque military lines and goose step to the pop music that the security guard/DJ chose. And now we were going to start shooting off guns? One definition of insanity is when meaning starts to break down. That was beginning to happen to me.

Before coming to Kazakhstan I had looked up Uralsk on Wikipedia. Located in Western Kazakhstan, on the banks of the Ural River, it was supposed to be an agricultural town that bred horses and camels. Unlike the other industrial towns along the northern border with Russia, which produced aluminum, chemical weapons, and Kazakh tractors, this region was famous for its medicinal herbs, and the town's biggest factory made licorice. They were even supposed to have a women's felt-making collective. I had come to Kazakhstan because I believed that they, like Kyrgyzstan where I had previously lived, had an ancient folk-telling tradition. I had read that every mountain, spring, and bush across their vast steppe contained a story and that these stories created a kind of a map that had once helped the nomads to navigate across the land. I actually thought that I was going to be living in a yurt, a nomadic round house, where everything was arranged with spiritual intent, in a land where it was virtuous to become one with your horse!

The Nazarbayev school, funded by and named after the current Kazakh president, claimed to be seeking Western educational reform, and I had fantasized that this could entail creating a digital storytelling curriculum where my students interviewed their grandparents (and the women at the felt-making collective) to learn the stories of the mountains, rivers, and bushes that surrounded them. I had imagined covering the country with story-maps. I believed that remembering these stories was one way to save the world.

On the eve of my departure to Kazakhstan, my aunt had told me that Thoreau, in the end, believed he hadn't lived his life extravagantly enough, but that unlike Thoreau, she said, I lived a spiritually extravagant life. Then she gave me some earmuffs and an orange knitted hat with a big flower on the side. I put them both on and said, 'This could be *our* tribal custom. I'll tell them that we reverse them when we get married. "You Kazakhs have your tribal traditions. We Californians have ours."'

Then my cousin gave me a bottle of JLo perfume, the bottle shaped like a sexy lady. And so – armed with JLo's Love and Light Perfume, my knitted hat, and eight photocopies of my favorite song from the musical score of *Finlandia*, 'This is my song,' about how the sky is blue not only in one's homeland but in every land, which I planned on teaching to my Kazakh students – I had set out to the great Kazakh steppe.

Air Astana, the Kazakh national airline, allows – in addition to the normal carry-on baggage – 'an umbrella, an overcoat, a cane, and a bunch of flowers.' They also, according to their webpage, had a dress code. I was charmed before I'd even arrived.

When I got to Germany and sat in the Air Astana waiting lounge, I looked around to see what that dress code might be. No one seemed to adhere to one. Most of the men were already seated and had soft paunches that they weren't trying to hide. These people were definitely not poseurs. Their black leather jackets and boots seemed to indicate a highly practical uniform: maybe they would have to ride their horses home from the airport. Some had soft, open, wondering expressions and were murmuring a gentle Russian. They all looked, to me, delightfully disheveled. I had half expected warriors, ancestors of Attila the Hun. But maybe the Kazakhs were just really cool, nerdy intellectuals from the '70s, the science types. Maybe I was about to enter my dream country.

When we flew over Uralsk, the autumn sun was setting

golden over the fields. A horse wandered across the runway. The place felt windswept and forgotten. The brown, frostbitten grass and the Soviet-era red and white striped airport hut gave the whole area a dune town feeling. All this vast space, where the imagination could soar, away from the flurry and urgency of consumer society, both excited and calmed me. When we descended from the plane, an airport worker ushered us through an old gate and we found ourselves in the parking lot.

Team Leader Franklin, long and lanky and from Wales, was waiting for me in front of an old car he had borrowed from one of the Kazakh teachers at the school where I would teach. I had been traveling for three days and frankly wanted to hug someone, but instead of saying 'Welcome!' he seemed to be sharing his own private joke with his assistant, a young Kazakh girl who regarded me scornfully. 'Don't you have a winter coat?' she asked.

'Yes, in my bag,' I said.

As we drove away from the airport, the horse from the runway crossed the road and a little boy ran after it. 'Village people,' the driver snorted.

While we were crossing the Ural River, Team Leader Franklin said, 'We are now leaving Asia and entering Europe.'

I was okay with that. I imagined tree-lined streets and streetside cafes. But 'Europe' consisted of some boxy buildings across a vast field of thigh-deep mud. 'That's where we teach,' Team Leader Franklin pointed out. Then the car ducked into a valley of old Soviet-style crumbling concrete block buildings. We stopped in front of one. 'Here is your home,' he said.

I am not an especially high-maintenance person; I have slept on old trains in both India and Siberia for days until my consciousness became part of the train seat. But these apartments looked like war-torn hovels in Kabul after a bombing. I actually had thought I was going to be living in a yurt! At my – what must have been – freaked-out face, Team Leader Franklin's assistant said haughtily, 'This is a very *prestigious* area of town.'

I gazed at her, looking for a crack in her armor, but found none.

Waiting for me on the kitchen table was a housewarming present. They had bought me an iron.

The school principal was my age but the weight of her stern expression gave her a matronly look. On the first day she proceeded to lecture me about how I must make the students love me, and then she gave me a little earring box in the shape of a yurt. I didn't know that this would be the only yurt I would see in Kazakhstan.

And thus commenced one of the most miserable winters of my life.

I had been expecting to find exalting nature in Uralsk, but the closest thing to a mountain in the whole region was the couch in the Information Center. The chemistry teacher, a Brit (though originally from Nigeria), and I would go there and lean our backs against the green couch mountain. He would complain about how the school had the highest-quality chemistry equipment he had ever seen in any school, but no chemicals. He spent the whole winter waiting for chemicals to arrive from the capital. All the classrooms had smart boards, as the school's promotional video had stated, but no one dared use them. If they malfunctioned, the teachers were responsible for replacing them.

And I soon discovered that educational reform did not mean developing critical or creative thinking skills. It meant teaching students technical skills so that they could replace all the foreign oil workers, so that Kazakhstan would become a world leader in 2050. On every holiday, fluttering banners promised this and in the public squares beneath them, people would celebrate with a giant flash mob. Even the traditional holiday, 'Emerge from Your Yurt and Greet Your Neighbor Day,' was celebrated with a giant flash mob. 'This country is going to flash mob its way through the 21st century,' the chemistry teacher groaned.

The licorice factory had closed down, along with the felt-making cooperative, and I couldn't find a single camel or horse, except for that one I had remembered seeing at the airport. My students weren't remotely interested in the stories of their grandparents. They only wanted me to teach them Rihanna songs or go with them to watch *Abraham Lincoln Vampire Slayer* in 6D at the super-hyper-mall downtown. (6D movies allow you to experience wind and blood in your face.)

A few weeks after I arrived, the principal ordered us to give dummy lessons to all the students. We were required to give them all the answers to the questions we would be asking them the next day when the Minister from the Ministry of Education came. We were supposed to make the school look good.

'What?' asked the chemistry teacher, incensed.

'Just do as they say,' Team Leader Franklin said and shrugged.

The next day, we woke up to find ourselves part of a Kazakh promotional piece, part of a Potemkin village. The water coolers suddenly had water, the bathrooms had toilet paper, and the chemistry labs finally had chemicals. The children ran through the halls straightening each other's ties, yelling, 'The Minister is coming! The Minister is coming!' But then, for some reason, the Minister didn't come. The water was removed from the coolers; so was the toilet paper. And, much to the dismay of the chemistry teacher, who was beginning to get so angry that I began to worry about him, the chemicals vanished.

I, too, was indignant. As far as I understood it, we had originally been recruited to bring ideas of educational reform. Our contract stated that we would be mentoring teachers in new teaching methods. Naturally, I had believed that the teachers would be receptive, especially since the Kazakh president was pumping so much money into this school. But then we found out that the Kazakh teachers hadn't been told why we were here. They saw foreigners entering their classrooms and they asked each other, 'What are *they* doing here?'

Team Leader Franklin took me aside and warned me not to become too political like the former librarian from Canada who had recently departed. She had ended up shouting at the principal and afterwards everyone had thought she'd gone crazy because she would speak only to the school plants. When I expressed dismay at this story, I was warned that I was being only 80 percent rational.

When the first snow fell it was like manna, like a blessing. The snow covered the ugly construction site across the street (the view out my window), and the strange tube-office that the contractor lived in was rolled away. The windows gleamed against the frosty sun. Sparrows pecked at the garbage. I took a walk and the thin, grey snow crunched beneath my boots.

I wanted to write in my journal. Because my hands were so heavily mittened, I used my teeth to take the cap off my pen, and when I did so, the freezing air caused my tongue to stick to the metal part. I had to hold it in my mouth to free my tongue. 'Numb knees, numb wrists, numb nose. -17°F and falling,' I wrote. 'But this is my main question,' I added. 'How long do I stay here waiting for the strange lessons that this land will inevitably teach me? How long will it take for this country to crack open and show itself? And at what point do I just give up, pack up, and go home?'

It was now the beginning of March, one week away from International Women's Day, and I still didn't feel that I had learned anything. In fact, my right arm had become paralyzed from stress. I could no longer use it even to unlock the door to my apartment.

Tonight was yet another enforced pedagogical meeting led by the principal, who had developed the habit of continuously abusing the teachers, calling them zeros. She lately had been telling us that, in nature, the head of a fish never rots, and that since she was the head, she had the superior moral consciousness. I leaned back on the green couch mountain to listen to what the topic would be tonight. She handed out paper and pens and told all the teachers to draw a picture of what they thought a leader was. With my left hand, I drew a flashlight to represent how a leader should shine light on people's potential, and a path between two cities, representing a leader navigating the way between realities. The chemistry teacher drew a jazz musician and said a leader should know how to improvise.

The Kazakh teachers drew pictures of crowns and microphones, said a leader must be strong, a good orator, and command her people, especially if they are weak. The foreign teachers and the Kazakhs looked at each other. We looked at each other again.

Miss Manners once wrote a column about how one should act when one finds oneself at a dinner party with a dictator. Confronting a dictator was not a skill I had ever developed. One of my team teachers told me that when Kazakhs get power, they become like wild horses and destroy everything in their path.

I had never felt this level of stress – the local teachers called it 'press' because, they said, it was a pressure from above pressing down on you.

The chemistry teacher and I leaned back on the green couch mountain and nostalgically remembered our drive from the airport the first day we had arrived. That had seemed like such a hopeful time. All those vast fields. Were we missing out on the real Kazakhstan at this Potemkin village school? How could we get back to that region near the airport? There had to be another Kazakhstan that we weren't seeing.

'I want to go someplace where there are just bushes and no people pointing at me, at the color of my skin,' the chemistry teacher said. 'I came to this country because I wanted to feel what it was like to be surrounded with so much vast space. For one day I just want to walk in that space, to only encounter a bush.'

When I would ask our fellow Kazakh teachers if we might be able to go to a village someday, they would look at me scornfully. 'Why do you want to go to a *village*?' they would say. 'They are not civilized there. They are only wild. We teach at a *presidential* school. We don't do such things.'

The chemistry teacher and I considered getting into a taxi and just telling the taxi driver to take us out into the steppe, but we were warned against this because the taxis weren't reliable when the weather was still -30°F. But that first weekend in March, when the temperature rose a little, one of the younger teachers, Gulnar, finally gave in and arranged to take us to a village. 'Just don't judge us,' she pleaded.

So on Sunday morning, Gulnar, the chemistry teacher, and I drove out into the steppe. There was nothing but white snow and white sky so that you couldn't see the demarcation of the horizon. 'Maybe we could just live out here, get a car, and commute,' the chemistry teacher suggested.

The door on the passenger's side suddenly flew open and the taxi driver pulled over to shut it. But when he started driving, it flew open again.

'Oh, I am shame, shame, shame,' Gulnar said, her head in her hands.

'No, this is why I came,' the chemistry teacher said, clenching his teeth with exertion as he held the door closed. 'I just want to hold the door closed. *Finally*, we are having a Kazakh adventure.'

The village was called Podstepnoy, which means 'the place below the steppe.' Gulnar had told the principal of Podstepnoy's school that we would be visiting. This principal had arranged, on a Sunday, for all her students to come to school and to greet us with bowls of homemade sour cream. Then she introduced us to the school's pets, a parakeet, a fish, and a frog, and then to the huge cucumbers and the herbs they were growing in the greenhouse. This school had a playground, not a target range. She brought us into their small auditorium and a young male teacher dressed in a maroon velvet jacket got on stage and sang us a Kazakh love song. As we were leaving, the students wanted us to write little prayers for them in their school notebooks. Then the school bus took us for a tour around the village. The bus driver took us to the cinema, where the locals showed homemade experimental films on a screen made of pieces of paper pasted to the wall. No Hollywood here. Here was a deeper sophistication.

The bus wound around the village and the driver pointed out the Friendship House and the Peace House and then dropped us off at the principal's house for a meal of fresh horsemeat. She had set the table with crystal and even invited our taxi driver in for the meal too. She introduced us to her son, a guitar player from a local alternative Kazakh rock band. He told me his name was

Nurlan. 'It means a real man,' he said. 'The actual meaning is Camel Hero.'

Camel Hero asked me why I had come to Kazakhstan and I said I liked to write about cultures. He admitted he had never met a person like that before. I said that I had found a soulful life in Kyrgyzstan and had wanted to write about the soul of Kazakhstan but I didn't know where it was.

'Really? I never imagined the West cared about souls,' he said, pondering. 'I never realized that maybe we are all the same.'

I turned to the principal and begged her, 'Can I just come and teach at *your* school? I'll volunteer.' She was shocked. 'But you teach at the *presidential* school,' she said.

'But the people in that school are so fake,' I said. 'Everyone just wants to watch that Hollywood movie *Abraham Lincoln Vampire Hunter*.'

'But that movie was made by Timur Bekmambetov, born in Kazakhstan,' Camel Hero said. 'He is who arranged that vampire movie. Maybe he revenged for *Borat*?'

Finally I was finding some humor in this place! We started joking. I asked him what he read. He said his favorite book was by Nurlan Abayev. I asked who that was. He said, 'Me!' Ha ha. Joke joke. Everyone at the table laughed. I said my favorite book was, *Beyond the Green Couch Mountain*. He said he had never read it. 'But you wrote it!' I said. Ha ha. Joke joke.

'Oh my god! You are one of us! You understand Kazakh humor!' Gulnar said. And I think I finally did.

Camel Hero asked if I had a husband and I said no.

'You should *joke* with him,' Gulnar nudged me.

So I said, 'I don't have a husband but I have a wife.'

'No! Not *that* kind of joke!' Gulnar said, scandalized.

'Okay, here is a joke,' I said. 'It's kind of dumb, though.'

'Tell me!' Camel Hero said.

'Once there was a fish and it hit a wall,' I began.

'A fish hit a wall!' he cried. 'Hahaha!'

'Wait! That's not the end of the joke,' I said. 'The fish said damn.'

'Hahaha.' He was still laughing. 'I understand the first part of the joke. I just don't understand the end of it.'

Camel Hero invited us to the new Kazakh cowboy bar where his band was going to be playing next weekend. It was called FOK Country Inn. Everyone there wore cowboy hats, he said, and they made TexMex food.

The chemistry teacher sighed and said, 'Why does everything have to be a joke here? Why do they have to call it FOK Country Inn?'

The principal then led us into a pillow-strewn room and told us to take a nap. The taxi driver placed a pillow on his knee, patted it, and motioned to the chemistry teacher, my rather proper English companion, to lay his head on it.

I'd finally found my Kazakhstan, for that one day in the village.

The next day at school, however, the teachers were shocked. How dare I go to the village! How dare I see how uncivilized their country was. Was I going to tell people in America about the Kazakh village, how they are all ruffians, hooligans, how they are just like the people at the ice skating rink who knock each other over and don't stand in line?

'But I love those kids at the ice skating rink,' I said.

That Friday, Women's Day, I prepared myself for the shooting competition. If I was really going to have to shoot an AK-47, so be it. But it turned out that they used only little cap guns in the gym and nobody really participated because everyone was so busy preparing for the main activity: the student dance performance.

As I sat there in the auditorium listening to the orchestra tuning up, the conductor showing off his Italian-speaking skills as he introduced the musicians, and the Kazakh violin players dressed up in their slightly shoddy light blue satin dresses that looked like they had been hand-sewn from curtains, I realized slowly that there was a bigger mind amidst all this. I mean, all the petty-mindedness was there, the power struggles, which you would expect would rise out of a presidential elite school vying for attention in the middle of absolutely nowhere. And yes, of course, some students were snoring, and some were talking on their phones. And there were still the suspicious neighbors: 'Why have you come here? What is here for you? You must be KGB/CIA.' And of course the chemistry teacher was still squirreling away his time in his lab, his lab without chemicals, googling 'Kazakh mentality,' trying to understand it here and becoming a little paranoid in the process. All that was here. But something bigger and more benevolent than all that was also here, some force that had invited us to experience their land. They didn't even want anything. They didn't actually even want reform. The teachers didn't want us to teach them anything. They wanted to teach *us*. They wanted to believe that we had come here to increase our knowledge of 'Stan' country mentality.

Our mistake was that we kept thinking we were supposed to *do* something. We kept thinking we were supposed to teach them how to be like us, how to be organized, how to plan ahead, how to make things work like we liked them to work, but the main ones suffering for it were us. All they really wanted was for us to come, observe them, and be happy. Wasn't the principal always ordering us to smile more? As I watched them dance, doing their flash mob, I realized they really just wanted us to look at them and say they were okay. They wanted validation that they were sophisticated too. And maybe there was something benevolent in us too. We came because we wanted to help. We would all go back to being petty and self-righteous, to feeling over-worked and under-effective, but there was something bigger. 'Come, valiant strangers!' they seemed to be saying. 'Come dance with us in our giant Kazakh flash mob.'

STEFAN MERRILL BLOCK is the author of two novels, *The Story of Forgetting* and *The Storm at the Door*. An international bestseller, *The Story of Forgetting* won Best First Fiction at the Rome International Festival of Literature, the Ovid Prize from the Romanian Writer's Union, the Merck Serono Literature Prize, and the Fiction Award from The Writers' League of Texas. Stefan's stories and essays have appeared in *The New Yorker*, *The New York Times*, *The Guardian*, *NPR's Radiolab*, *Granta*, *The Los Angeles Times,* and many other publications. Stefan grew up in Plano, Texas, and lives in Brooklyn.

And the World Laughs with You

STEFAN MERRILL BLOCK

Each morning that winter I woke to a routine: at five am, I slapped at the cheap digital alarm clock on the bedside table of my room at the Hotel Raysons, threw on a once-white t-shirt, and spent the predawn hour silently sipping a sugary cup of chai with my boss in the rear of a Range Rover as we shuddered through the tandoor smoke and motorbike exhaust of Kolhapur, India. Just before dawn – in hilltop parks, municipal gardens, and cricket pitches – we found them: Indians dressed in uniform, arranged in tight army formations. Someone happening upon one of these gatherings could have mistaken it for some sort of militia, but on closer inspection the uniforms displayed the faces of jolly Buddhas, clipart of bawling crowds, the words 'Ho!' and 'Ha!' hovering over crazed cartoon expressions like Pentecostal emanations.

'We are the healthiest persons in this world! We are the

happiest persons in this world! We are laughter club members!'
these groups' leaders addressed their ranks. 'Free Laughter! One,
two, three! Start!' And then the gatherings erupted, initiating
the forty-five minutes of their daily hysterics. My job was to
plant myself as deeply as possible among the manic throng, aim
the Canon XL2 video camera hitched over my shoulder, and try
to maintain the professional demeanor of a documentarian as
chubby, bearded men in jumpsuits reached out to tickle me.

'Hold the camera steady! Please!' my boss yelled at me, and
for good reason. At twenty-two, I was a nervous kid, with shaky
hands and distractible attention, but I had somehow lucked into
this first real gig in my supposed career as a cameraman. Back in
New York, serving an endless unpaid servitude as an intern for
a production company, I had met Neil, a fashion photographer
who had stumbled upon India's laughter club movement and
persuaded a few friends to fund the production of his first
documentary film. I still can't say why, other than my bargain-
basement rate, Neil might have hired me, but the source of his
fascination with the laughers of India seemed clear enough.
An exacting, impatient artist with a good taste for the absurd,
Neil was seduced by the devotion of the many thousands who
congregated each day to an idea equally joyful and outlandish.
By 2005, when we arrived, India's public parks were daily
jammed with the dozens or even hundreds who congregated to
laugh away the stresses of their modernizing nation.

There were no jokes told at laughter club. Instead, they relied
on a number of 'laughter exercises,' such as 'Bird Laughter,'
'Free Laughter,' and 'Tickle Laughter.' 'Laugh for no reason'
and 'fake it 'til you make it' were the two pillars of the laughter
club credo, and after a month of filming, I had seen how quickly
forced laughter, among fifty adults in an Indian park at dawn

or sunset, could become authentic. Dreamt up by Dr Madan Kataria, a physician from Mumbai, the laughter clubs called their activity '*hasya yoga*' – laughter yoga – and its members often rhapsodized about laughter's myriad health benefits.

'For God's sake! How hard is it to hold the thing straight?' Neil berated me, as I chased the laughers through the Kolhapuri dawn. Though I had spent my off-hours pacing the hallways of the Hotel Raysons practising a steady grip on the XL2, whenever I was confronted by the exuberance of actual laughter clubs, I still could not figure out where to point it, and so the camera veered wildly in my hands. Screening the smeary footage in our hotel rooms, Neil blinked furiously behind extravagant clouds of cigarette smoke. 'How can I use any of this?' he asked. It was my first job, in my first career, and I saw that my desperation to prove myself was precisely what doomed me.

The purported subject of our documentary might have been 'The World of Laughter,' but after a few weeks in Kolhapur, it had subtly shifted, at least for me. As it turned out, laughter, narratively speaking, was like a tulip or a sunset: nice to look at for a minute or two, but my interest quickly ran dull. '*Behind* the World of Laughter' was my new angle, and I set out to unveil the ordinary human aspiration, pettiness, rivalry, and self-deception that shaped the jolly dream.

The laughter clubs of India might 'laugh for no reason,' but the club culture we found in Kolhapur ('the laughter capital of the world,' its denizens proudly boasted) had come to use group laughter for purposes other than health. Kolhapur's clubs, populated mostly by the growing middle class, had become like de facto Rotary Clubs; I'd seen how the long walks to and from the parks offered an occasion for the city's upwardly mobile citizens to gather and chat about business. There was even a low-burning but perceptible rivalry between club leaders. After a day spent documenting a movement united under the motto 'world peace through laughter,' I was developing my own, less peaceable mottos. 'Stories are all about conflict,' I liked to say, and I did my best to capture whatever conflicts among the laughers that I could.

And conflict, I felt, was thickening in the humid Kolhapuri air. Our producers had spent a sizeable portion of the production money to help finance the first 'World Laughter Competition,' where the best laughers of each club would square off for the title of 'World's Best Laughing Human Being.' We invited rival laughter leaders for lengthy meetings to write the rules and plan the events for the big night. Upping the stakes, we paid the travel expenses for that laughter messiah, Dr Madan Kataria, to personally officiate the competition, where participants would be judged on the contagiousness of laugh, authenticity of laugh, and creative interpretation of each of the common laughter exercises. The grand competition's specifics were a good flashpoint for argument: occasionally, through the viewfinder of my XL2, I happily watched tiffs erupt. Just as often, however, the meetings would break forth into impromptu laughter sessions or dance parties. I liked to fancy myself a professional documentarian, but I was just learning my first lesson on the complexity of the relationship between storyteller and subject: their worst behavior was my very good news. But for the most part, the laughers of Kolhapur were behaving very nicely.

I might have spent my days in the epicenter of the world laughter club movement, but back in my hotel room, I brooded. Suffering the common gastrointestinal introduction of a first-timer to India, I sat in the bathroom worrying about our film. My own camera work might have been woeful and amateur, but each of my lousy videotapes seemed to me just a small example of the lack of focus that marred the entire production. Finding little conflict, no central drama, how could Neil possibly cut the ninety-minute feature film we imagined? And what would happen if this, my one absurdly lucky break, were to fail? Dreading my return to ungainful employment in New York, I felt how much I needed our film to succeed.

And yet, the camera continued to swing wildly in my hands, as Neil and I left behind our main characters to travel the red-brown Maharashtrian countryside, in search of better dramas. What we found were just more uncomplicated, triumphant stories: in one small town, we met a group of women in matching pink saris, whose laughter club provided many of its members their first occasion to leave their homes unchaperoned by men. We met a near-blind great-grandmother – doubled over with scoliosis in the packed asbestos shed in which she lived – who became a woman transformed when she laughed, standing upright and shaking the thin walls with her exuberant bellows. Building up to the night of the World Laughter Competition, I filmed stories of recovery through laughter – private triumphs over cancer, depression, substance abuse, loneliness, poverty, and repression. Despite my efforts, I seemed to be shooting a promotional video for the laughter club movement.

But my last best hope lay in the night of the competition. The event turned into something of a sensation, thousands cramming into the outdoor theater we had rented. The lead competitors arrived in grand fashion: that stooped nonagenarian came to meet her competition atop an elephant, preceded by dozens of laughers banging drums and waving tambourines.

And yet, despite a couple of instances of backroom drama, the competition itself was a frustratingly euphoric affair. None of Kolhapur's rival clubs was victorious: in the end, the leader of that small town women's club won the day, and everyone seemed pretty pleased with the result. Fireworks burst in the Indian night; the city of Kolhapur rocked with the thunder of five thousand voices laughing. I flew back to New York City, to a string of gigs filming bar and bat mitzvahs, until my career as a brooding guy videotaping other's joyful activities at last sputtered to its end. Neil and I fell out of touch.

And so it was a great surprise when, three years later, Neil sent an email to inform me that a short film he had cut from our footage would play as part of a new film festival called Pangea Day, a massive event sponsored by the TED organization, to be live-streamed to satellite gatherings all over the world. On the night of May 10, 2008, I sat in front of my computer, waiting for my first glimpse at our stunted laughter epic, which I still hoped Neil would someday complete. But – as far as I know – the culmination of our months spent chasing the laughers of India remains just that four-minute clip that I watched with all of Pangea that evening.

Absent all the behind-the-scenes drama I had tried so hard to capture, this film was a four-minute montage of men and women laughing into the pretty Maharastrian countryside as Dr Kataria, in voiceover, expounded upon his dream 'to bring the whole world like a family' through laughter. It was, in fact, precisely the promotional video for the laughter club movement I had worried we were making.

When the 240-second running time of our film came to its end, the live-stream cut to a shot of a stage at Sony Pictures Studios in Los Angeles, where the actress Goldie Hawn introduced Dr Madan Kataria. After describing his mission to 'connect the whole world' by establishing 'one million laughter clubs,' Dr Kataria spread his arms, drew his breath, and led the viewership of Pangea Day in one great, international laugh. And then, if only for thirty seconds or so, Dr Kataria's crazy dream came true: the live stream cut to masses in London, Rwanda, and Mumbai, united in laughter. Alone in my crummy Brooklyn apartment, the room lit only by the glow of my laptop, I was laughing too.

JACK LIVINGS' debut story collection, *The Dog*, was awarded the PEN / Robert W. Bingham Award. His work has appeared in *A Public Space*, *The Paris Review*, *Tin House*, and *Best American Short Stories*, and has been awarded two Pushcart Prizes. He lives with his family in New York.

Nothing Happened
JACK LIVINGS

In 2010, I flew to Lahore to help a publisher set up a Pakistani edition of the news magazine where I worked. My flight arrived at Allama Iqbal International Airport around midnight, and a customs officer ushered me into an office adjacent to the international arrivals hall. Inside were two paper-strewn desks, some chairs, a small couch, and sheaves of paper tacked to the walls – incoming flight manifestos, wanted posters, handwritten notes in Urdu and English. I had shown up with a letter of introduction but no visa, and the officer told me to have a seat and wait while he sorted me out. After a while, a clutch of timorous young men shuffled in, sat, and shifted nervously in their chairs until another officer retrieved them. By their silence I gathered they were in some kind of trouble. I was there long enough to begin to wonder if I was in some sort of trouble too.

I have a funny relationship with airports. I started flying

alone when I was six years old, done up in a blue blazer and clip-on tie, plastic wings pinned to my lapel that designated me an Unaccompanied Minor. I'd like to say the get-up was my mother's idea, but I was the one who maintained the sharp part in my hair and kept my shirt tucked in. Of course, I didn't always dress like that. At home, I was a normal kid: my jeans had holes in the knees and I spent a fair amount of my time traipsing around in the woods.

But I had learned early the transformative powers of travel. My parents were divorced, and I would leave South Carolina, where I was my mother's son, and arrive the next day in Frankfurt or Zurich my father's son. Perhaps that's why airports always felt to me like neutral ground, where I was no-one's child, and why even today I feel as though I exist in a quantum state when I'm passing through one, both myself and not myself. This belief that I'm not myself is a form of protection, I think, like the jacket and tie I wore as a boy to pretend I was older. An older boy – a man – wouldn't have been homesick or afraid of flying by himself. Whatever unrest I feel when traveling is mitigated by my belief that it's not me doing the traveling. It's someone else.

I was doing the usual identity calculus, then, wondering who the customs officer thought I was, and who I wanted to be. The letter I carried had been signed by the scion of a powerful Pakistani family – he was the publisher of the magazine I was there to advise – and I'd assumed his name would smooth my way. But the officer had been gone for a long time. I wondered if he'd seen through me. The letter stated that I was a journalist. By all appearances, I was. My employer was a news magazine, my business card had the appropriate job title, but there was an existential problem at work because I was not, strictly speaking, a journalist.

The man who'd hired me years earlier called it para-journalism, the mix of diplomacy and editorial work I practised. I was not a correspondent or a beat reporter. I was a desk jockey, an administrative lackey, a liaison between our overseas editions and the American home base. To call what I did journalism was to insult the people I worked with who ran into war zones armed with only a laptop and a satphone.

Eventually the customs officer returned with my passport and papers for me to fill out. I was relieved to see that he looked bored. He asked if I had brought a spare passport photo. I said no, and he frowned, but seemed to accept this as just another example of the incompetence I'd already displayed by showing up without a visa.

About half an hour later I was on my way to the hotel in downtown Lahore. It was bordered by a big lawn and hidden from the busy Mall Road behind fencing, barbed wire, and a stand of trees. In order to enter the driveway, our minivan had to execute a 180 off the main road and enter a narrow chute formed by concrete pylons. We were stopped by armed security staff who swept mirrors under the chassis, opened the back hatch, peered under the hood, shot flashlights into the cabin space, and then waved us forward to the front gate. Behind a hydraulic crash barrier, a crossbar extended across the driveway. On either end of the barrier were two yellow smiley faces. We were checked again, then waved forward. The barrier descended into the pavement, the crossbar rose. More armed security guards flanked the driveway within. The hotel itself was a gray modern fortress.

I spent the week ferrying back and forth between the hotel and the new magazine's offices, where I was set up in an air-conditioned room with a desk and a couch. The building had backup generators to cope with the electrical load shedding that

cut power in Lahore a couple of times a day. From my desk I
could see trees, a bus depot, and haze. Crows swooped in and out
of the trees. An employee in a white shalwar kameez delivered
Nescafe every hour or so. I worked on my laptop and met with
journalists. Once or twice a day my mobile phone rang, showing
a Pakistani number, and when I answered, the voice on the other
end said, 'Joe?' In the office it was generally agreed upon that
those calls were from one of the national intelligence services.
'They're just checking up on you', my Pakistani colleagues said.

'You're joking', I said.

They smiled and shrugged. 'Maybe it's just a wrong number',
someone suggested.

At the end of the week I was offered a tour of the Lahore
Fort, a Mughal-era edifice in the city's northwest. That Friday
afternoon, I said goodbye to the reporters and editors and
got into the back of the publisher's car, a chauffeured BMW.
The publisher stayed at the office, but sent along a reporter to
accompany me. We went first to a high-ranking government
official's office. I wasn't entirely sure what I was doing there, but
I suspect this audience was the publisher's way of paying for
the tours that were to come later in the afternoon. The official
complained to me about what he had deemed to be unfair
coverage of Pakistan by the US edition of the magazine. He was
still castigating me ten minutes later when the power went off.
The office fell into darkness and he kept right on talking. I could
hear my chaperone, the Pakistani reporter, shifting in her seat,
sighing loudly and, when she could take no more, she began to
take the official to task for his political failures. They went at each
other in the dark for some time, and when the argument lulled

I took the opportunity to thank the official for his time. We all walked toward the light of the door, shook hands, and a couple of army guards escorted us back to the car.

In the parking lot, a couple of more cars joined us, and then a police escort. We pulled out into the street, and motorcycle cops raced ahead to block intersections. We blew through red lights while rush hour traffic piled up on either side. If the reporter was impressed by our little caravan's display of authority, she didn't show it. She seemed not to notice at all, in fact, so deep was she into a diatribe about the rotten state of her country's government. She wasn't wrong – the government was a corrupt, feudal system presided over by a handful of elites who, for instance, granted police escorts to visiting American para-journalists.

We were making good time, and I'll admit I was enjoying myself a little. At that moment, was I not the embodiment of an American imperialist? Did I even care? I was in a motorcade, speeding unencumbered through a city of 7 million people, the sharp end of the spear of American empire. So be it. Then we ran into a protest.

In 2010, Pakistan's state of siege was its defining characteristic. In late May of that year, two Ahmadi mosques in Lahore had been bombed. Conservative estimates put the death toll at ninety-five people. Hardly a day in June passed without reports of a new terror attack somewhere in the country. The heads of police stations were targeted. Suicide bombers blew themselves up in markets. Militants ambushed Pakistani army patrols. Convoys were shot up. Vanloads of masked men opened fire on police stations. A group of Taliban had stormed a hospital, guns blazing, seeking to free a comrade who had been wounded carrying out an attack days earlier.

On 1 July, two weeks before I arrived in the country, a pair of suicide bombers killed fifty people and injured two-hundred more gathered at a Sufi shrine within Lahore's Data Darbar complex.

The driver braked smoothly, and we slowed to a roll as we caught up to the motorcycles. The car was surrounded by people. We pushed a little ways into the crowd and stopped. Not even the motorcycles, sirens blasting, could get through. The crowd, all men wearing shalwar kameezes, carrying signs, chanting, streamed around the car, which rocked as though we'd driven into a swift river.

'Where are we?' I asked the reporter.

She was craning her neck, trying to see through the windscreen past the crowd, exhaling with annoyance. It wouldn't have surprised me if she'd thrown open the door, climbed onto the roof, and yelled at the protesters to get out of the way. Back at the official's office it seemed that only the dark and the enormous depth of his desk kept her from physically assaulting him. I took some comfort from the knowledge that she could clear the crowd herself, if called upon to do so.

'So, where are we?' I asked again.

She mumbled something I couldn't hear.

'Sorry?' I said.

'Data Darbar', she said.

Yes. Up ahead, to my left, the two minarets, elegant, slender as a pair of arrows, stood against the sky. The crowd churned around the car. I slid down in my seat. It was a nice seat, cream-colored leather, engineered to be supportive, yet supple to the touch. The seatbelt was a wonder of delicate pressure – it moved with me, allowing my midsection to descend through the lap belt with little resistance. Though I am just over six feet tall, there was plenty of room for my legs, and with my eyes now just even with the base of the window, I noticed for the first time a copy of *Esquire* in the pocket affixed to the back of the driver's seat. Tom Cruise was smiling over the lip of the pocket. I could hardly tell the car was running. Even the climate controls keeping the cabin cool and dry were nearly silent. The chants from the protesters were muffled by sound-dampening window assemblies.

At no point during the week had I been afraid, despite everything I thought I knew about anti-American sentiment in Pakistan. One afternoon after work, I'd strolled over to the zoo and hadn't been regarded by the other visitors with kindness or unkindness as much I'd been disregarded entirely. I watched some children jab a long stick into a tiger's cage. The tiger swiped at the stick and the kids got into a fight over who got to hold it. I'd left the zoo and walked to a shopping area, where small storefronts were thrown open to the sidewalk, the merchants sitting just inside, out of the sun. Sports Shop, upon closer examination, was a dimly lit recess with floor-to-ceiling shelves bearing a couple of dusty soccer balls next to some cricket balls. I'd gone to a bookstore where Stephanie Meyer's vampire series took up most of the real estate on the English-language shelves. I'd crossed the Mall Road via an overpass, swarms of Honda CR-120 motorcycles buzzing beneath. On the other side of the road, I'd wandered back toward the zoo. In a store window, a sign read, No Guns Allowed Inside. It was the silhouette of an AK-47 that bore the circle and diagonal line. Not a soul spoke to me anywhere.

In the back of a German car, however, with a police escort, stuck in a protest at the site of a terrorist attack, I was a little worried. Again I was confronted with the question of who I was pretending to be. More to the point, what did I look like

from the outside? That's what mattered. The reporter huffed and
fell back into her seat, looked over at me where I was cowering
like a frightened rabbit, and resumed her monologue on the
government's ills. Maybe it's just another Friday afternoon in
Lahore, I thought.

The police escort began to make some headway and we inched
along behind them, eventually slipping out of the protest and
resuming our campaign to snarl traffic all the way to the Lahore
Fort. And that was that.

We arrived just as the site was closing to the public. It was
late afternoon, still light, still stiflingly hot, and we were met by
a photographer who would document the visit in excruciating
detail. I was pushed to the front of our little covey by a
businessman, a friend of the publisher's, and this man – let's call
him Sam – stayed on my elbow for the next two hours, steering
me in front of the camera, retrieving me when I lagged behind to
check out something interesting. No matter what I did to evade
him, he'd laugh and pull me back into frame.

It was dark by the time the tour ended, and Sam led us to a
table and some chairs that had been set up on a lawn just outside
the fort. We sat, about seven of us, and hot tea was brought out.
About thirty feet away was the entrance to the dungeon where
Salman Taseer had been locked up for opposing Zia-ul-Haq, the
military dictator who ruled the country from 1977 to 1987. By
2010, Zia was long dead in a suspicious plane crash and Taseer
was governor of Punjab Province. In January 2011, Taseer would
be assassinated by his own bodyguard.

Sam mercifully sat at the opposite end of the table, and a
friend of his took the seat across from me. He owned a business
that he claimed could deliver seeds anywhere in the country in
forty-eight hours. The day before, as we were barreling down a

main thoroughfare just outside city limits, the van I was riding
in had to swerve around a dead horse in the road. Its cart had
been pulled to the curb so as not to completely obstruct traffic.
I had the feeling that if this businessman could deliver *anything*
in this country in two days, he was destined to become very rich.
He was wearing a suit and tie, and gave considered answers to
my elementary questions about agriculture in Pakistan. He asked
about my family, told me about his, and explained thoroughly
but without drifting into dullness, the nuances of his business.
And then he began to talk to me about American foreign policy
and what the US owed Pakistan for its help fighting terrorism.

'You cannot expect us to fight the war by ourselves', he said.
'And you cannot simply send aid money. It vanishes. It all goes
to Dubai.'

'What's in Dubai?'

'The politicians' bank accounts', he said.

'Ok,' I said.

'You should write about this for your magazine', he said.

'I'm more of an editor', I said.

'America must send tangible things', he said. 'Weapons, food,
tanks, planes. This business of sending money is a guaranteed
failure.'

'I see', I said.

'Look at the British. Look at what they left behind! A railway
system. An education system. Tangible good deeds. Why does
America believe it can solve all its problems with money?'

If he'd been less gentlemanly, I might have asked if the legacy
of British colonization, partition, and the subsequent sixty
years of political strife, had been an even trade for trains that
run on time. But he was right, of course, to put these questions
to me. In 1982, Zia-ul-Haq took a break from tossing political

opponents in the dungeon to fly to Washington, where he met with President Reagan in the Oval Office. The US had been elbows-deep in Pakistan's governance, going back to the 1960s. The country was a protectorate of the United States, first as an outpost against communism, more recently against Islamic fundamentalism. As a citizen of the United States, I was therefore worthy of blame.

'I see', I said again.

And then he began to talk about India.

Earlier in the week I'd gone to Wahga, a border outpost along the Grand Trunk Road, an artery that ran from Afghanistan, through Pakistan and India, to Bangladesh. At sundown, Pakistan and India's respective armies performed a military ceremony culminating in the slamming shut of a massive gate, severing the connection between the two countries for the night. It was a bit like the flag ceremony at a NASCAR event: bombastic, militaristic, an orgy of patriotism performed before scores of screaming fans.

When we arrived at Wahga, our driver pulled into a shady lot next to a guesthouse. I slid open the door and was hit with a powerful smell. It was unquestionably organic, decomposition of some kind. Rotting flesh, I'd thought. It was the scent of dead deer I'd found in the woods when I was a boy, a smell that set off alarms in the central nervous system.

The driver was unfazed, and I didn't want to cause offense, but after we'd walked a little ways toward the border, I had to ask: 'What was that smell?'

'India', he said.

'I see, I see', I said. I mulled this while we walked some more.

'India', I said.

'Yes, India, this smell', he said, as if conveying tragic knowledge. He went on: 'They drive their cotton across the border but because it is Indian, it must be quarantined at customs, and then it rains, and the cotton becomes wet, and then you have this smell.'

'Ah, okay', I said.

In my brief time in Pakistan, I'd heard India blamed for everything from droughts to floods to electrical load shedding. Blaming India for its smelly cotton was the most logical defamation yet.

Now the seed-dealer across from me had invoked the name of the great scapegoat.

'India', he said, 'is funding most of the terrorism within Pakistan. It's a known fact.'

'Is that right?' I said.

'Tehrik-i-Taliban is *directly* funded by the Indian government. India wants to see us wiped from the map', he said.

I was completely unqualified to judge the veracity of this claim. If he was after an intelligent response to his statement, he'd have been better off addressing his cup of tea.

'I see', I said, which meant, of course, that I didn't.

He talked some more and I pretended to understand, and then Sam ushered us back into our cars. The police escort was long gone, and after dinner I was dropped at my hotel. It was nearly midnight, and I was in my room flipping through TV stations and eating crackers on the bed when I heard the bomb blasts. They were unmistakable, a pair of sharp, percussive booms. I turned off the desk lamp so I could see out the window, but there was nothing out of the ordinary: manicured lawn, flowers, the trees and barbed wire, a few motorcycles on Mall Road. I had a pre-dawn flight, and stayed up until it was time to leave for the airport, but there was nothing about the blasts on television. Reading a paper on the plane, I learned that a police station a few kilometers from the hotel had been bombed, and when the policemen came running out of the building, the assailants had opened fire on them. The story was deep inside the paper, and didn't warrant a photo, as I recall.

My plane was heading southwest toward Abu Dhabi, not too long after leaving Lahore, when we passed over the Sulaiman Mountains, a rumpled range at the southern end of the Hindu Kush. It was dark out, and I wouldn't have seen the mountains except that, out of the corner of my eye, I caught a bright flash of light, then another, popping across the wrinkled spines and valleys of the range. I turned off my reading light and peered out the window. The flashes kept coming. I was sure I was seeing shelling.

In the UAE I'd change planes for another business class seat on a flight to the US. There was a glass of juice on my armrest, a newspaper on my lap, and I could play Battleship on my viewscreen, unless I wanted to recline my seat into a bed and catch a nap. I watched the lightshow until we were out of range. Stripped of the volcanic rumble and the earth-trembling shock that accompanies heavy ordinance, it was as if the explosions had not quite enough meaning, and I tried to impose a sense of reverence on my voyeurism. I conjured up a heavy, solemn emotion and tried to hold onto it, the way one might at the funeral of a head of state. It faded quickly.

The pilot came on over the intercom to give us the details of our cruising altitude, speed, intended arrival time, and at the end of his speech, he said, 'You might have seen some heat lightning over the mountains a few minutes ago. It's nothing to worry about.'

DAVE EGGERS is the best-selling author of ten books, including *A Hologram for the King,* a finalist for the National Book Award; *Zeitoun,* winner of the American Book Award and Dayton Literary Peace Prize; and *What Is the What,* a finalist for the National Book Critics Circle Award and winner of France's Prix Medici. Eggers lives in Northern California with his wife and two children.

The Road to Riyadh

DAVE EGGERS

We are flying down an empty six-lane highway, on our way from Jeddah to Riyadh, a seven-hour drive, and I'm thinking of possible routes of escape. I'm in the passenger seat of a new Toyota sedan travelling at 140 km/h through the Saudi Arabian desert and I'm racing through the implications of opening my door and leaping free.

The driver is a stranger to me. He is young, no more than twenty-five, with a smooth face and a tentative moustache. His name is Shadad, but he is not a taxi driver, and this is not a taxi. This car and this driver were arranged hastily by my guide and friend, Majed, who helped me around Jeddah the previous week. Before this drive began, Majed and I considered it a decent, if necessary, idea to employ such a driver for this trip, but now I am pondering how I could leave this car. If I open the door and roll out, would I survive? And if I did survive, where would I go?

There's nothing but rocks and sand for miles in any direction.

But still. Vacating this car might be necessary, because though I want to trust this young driver, he is not really a professional driver, and he has no taxi licence, and most of all, moments ago, while he was talking to a friend on his cellphone, he looked over to me with a mischievous smile and said to his friend, 'Yeah, American, boom boom.' Then he laughed. He did everything but point his finger at me and pull the trigger. I'm not sure how many ways there are to interpret this.

It did not have to be this way. I woke up this morning ready to spend the day in Jeddah, having lunch with new Saudi friends, dinner with new Saudi friends, and then fly out of Jeddah in the late evening, heading back to the US on a red-eye through London. But it was soon after waking up that I looked closely at my itinerary to find that the flight I am booked on is not leaving from Jeddah at 10pm tonight; it's leaving from Riyadh at 8pm – five hundred and twenty-five miles away.

So I made a flurry of frantic calls back home, to airlines and travel agents, confirming that this was indeed the itinerary, and learning that there were no available flights that would get me from Jeddah to Riyadh in time. There are various reasons I need to get out of Saudi Arabia and back to the US this day, so I had no choice but to look into driving across the country, to Riyadh, to make the flight.

And I had to tell all this to Majed.

'How could this happen?' he asked. I told him I had no idea, that I was very sorry.

Majed couldn't do the drive himself, so he and I searched around Jeddah, looking for someone who could. We made our way to the outskirts of the city and through a brief labyrinth of small alleys. Finally we reached a dead-end, where about a half-dozen men sat outside on folding chairs. It was not a taxi stand or anything like it.

'This place?' I asked. 'Who are these guys?'

'Our only option,' Majed said, and got out.

I sat in Majed's car, thinking about what had transpired the previous day. Majed and I, who had enjoyed a fluid and friendly rapport for a week, had a strange exchange, which put in question if or why he should trust me. I made a joke about American-Saudi relations, and our military, their oil, various complicities and maybe even the CIA, and from then on, things went cold. It was as if he suddenly realised I was an American, and presumably participating in my country's various crimes, real or imagined. Since then, he had been visibly anxious to be done with me; we barely spoke, and he seemed to be counting the hours till he could be rid of me.

So I was in Majed's car, in this alley, watching him negotiate with the group, wondering if this could possibly be a good idea, getting into a car, for a six-hour drive across the Saudi desert, with a man we met in an alley.

Majed soon returned to tell me the price they'd arrived at. Because I trusted Majed's judgement, and because the price was far less than what one would pay for a six-hour drive in the United States, I agreed. He and the men and Shadad chose the car we would take, among a few of them parked outside, and I took my suitcase from Majed's trunk and put it in the trunk of this new car.

Majed and I said our goodbyes–which were far more perfunctory than I'd expected earlier in the week, when we were close – and Shadad and I took off.

And because I always trust people until I'm given a reason not to trust them, I was content. It was noon, and we had enough time to make it to Riyadh. And because I was sure we would make it in time, I relaxed and planned to watch the passing scenery and possibly take a nap. But then, ten minutes into the drive, Shadad was on his phone, talking to his friend, and while on the phone he looked askance at me, a bloated grin fattening his cheeks, and delivered the 'Yeah, American, boom boom' line into his silver cellphone.

Now I'm very much awake. And I'm contemplating my options. I want to roll out of the car, but the car is now doing 160 km/h. We pass a tanker truck as if it's not moving. At this speed I have no options. I'm going wherever this man wants me to go.

I want to make clear that I've rarely if ever felt in actual danger while travelling anywhere in the world. This could be dumb luck. It could be a combination of dumb luck, common sense, and the benefits of reciprocal trust: trust and you will be trusted. Give respect and you'll get it.

In any case, it's a result of a gradual evolution. When I first traveled, I was naive, sloppy, wide-eyed, and nothing happened to me. That's probably where the dumb luck came in. Then I began to read the guidebooks, the State Department warnings, the endless elucidation of national norms, cultural cues and insults and regional dangers, and I became wary, careful, savvy. I kept my money taped inside my shoe, or strapped to my stomach. I took any kind of precaution, believing that the people of this area did this, and the people of that province did that. But then, finally, I realised no one of any region did anything I have ever expected them to do, much less anything the guidebooks said they would. Instead, they behaved as everyone behaves, which is to say they behave as individuals of damnably infinite possibility. Anyone could do anything, in theory, but most of the time everyone everywhere acts with plain bedrock decency, helping where help is needed, guiding where guidance is necessary. It's almost weird.

But every so often I have the feeling that a certain guide or driver or boat captain or acquaintance has a powerful kind of leverage, and could kill me if they wished, and no-one would know, no-one could trace where or at whose hands I disappeared. This is one of those situations. Only Majed knows or cares that I'm in this man's Toyota sedan, and I am therefore at this man's mercy. But again, I was absolutely content with and trusting of this man before he made the 'Boom Boom' comment. And normally I would have shaken it off, giving him the benefit of the doubt. I would normally think, He's a young man, and he made a joke to another young man on the phone, and it has nothing to do with me.

But lately things have changed. There is new information. There are the State Department warnings in 2010, which say that Saudi Arabia is not so safe for Americans, and there are the many warnings made by hotel personnel not to get into random cars or taxis. And worst of all there is the fact that I have a friend who shared, I assume, my presumption of the goodwill of all those one might meet, and this acquaintance is currently in an Iranian prison. His name is Shane Bauer.

I've known Shane professionally for about three years, primarily as a translator. Back in 2008, I had just gotten back from what is now South Sudan, interviewing women who had been enslaved during the civil war, and I needed help transcribing both my interviews and some other interviews, many of which were in Arabic. So I was connected to Shane, a young man living in Oakland who spoke Arabic. He translated many of the tapes from South Sudan, and I later helped facilitate a trip he took to Darfur to make a documentary about the rebel movement there. Then, six months later, I learned that he had been imprisoned in an Iranian prison on dubious charges of espionage. And while I'm riding in this Toyota sedan, Shane is still in the Iranian prison, fate unknown.

This is all to say that something I would have previously deemed beyond the realm of possibility – that I would personally know someone being held captive in Iran as part of an internationally denounced power play on the part of the semi-sane government of Iran – has made me more realistic about the possibility that this young Saudi driver might try to do something nefarious to me today. And then there is Majed, who was my friend, but who now might think I'm some kind of enemy. My mind, alone in this featureless desert highway, creates grotesque possibilities. Could Majed have set me up? Because he came to believe I was some intelligence agent, could he have handed me to someone who would profit from my kidnapping? These thoughts are shameful, embarrassing. But if Shane Bauer can be jailed for hiking near the Iranian border, is it so improbable that I could be disposed of in some way here in the Saudi desert?

I look at the car's gas gauge. I have the thought that if the driver is running low, and needs to refill, I'll be able to escape. I assume there's no way he could stop me. I have half a foot of height and thirty pounds on him. Then again, there could be a secret rendezvous point where he'll fill up his tank and hand me to someone who will pay some bounty…

The gas tank is full. At the very least, it will be a while before we stop for that particular reason. Looking around the dashboard, I notice that the car's interior is still covered in plastic. This is a different way of going about things, and I've seen it before in other parts of the world – the reluctance to take the plastic off new cars, new furniture, and bicycles. I notice that though the car seems new, there is a cassette player, and that the driver has many cassettes; I haven't seen this many cassettes in one place in a decade or two. On the mirror itself is a simple sticker that says SAUDI ARABIA, lest he or any other driver of this car forget where they are. I notice, most of all, a blue sign hanging from the rear-view mirror that says HELP. Below it is an arrow pointing to an ISBN code, as if that help might come via checkout scanner.

We continue to pass other cars and trucks so fast that they seem stationary. Could he be in a hurry to bring me to his receivers, those he's sold me to? Now he's smoking. I try to roll down my window but it's locked. The driver sees me trying and unlocks it. I lower the window an inch. He looks at the window disapprovingly, and I realise the effect is the opposite as desired: the smoke is crossing the car to exit above my ear. I close the window. He opens his and looks to me.

'Smoke no good?' he asks.

'Smoke no good,' I say.

'Smoke good!' he says, and smiles. He's making a joke. This is promising, I think.

Sensing the beginnings of a human connection, I open my backpack. He seems unconcerned that I might be taking out something dangerous – another good sign. I take out a folder, where I have my itinerary and tickets and other documents, including a photo of my wife and two kids, which I had printed on an ink-jet printer before I left. In what now seems like prescience, I figured I might need such a photo, to show to a man like this, if such a man had ill intentions toward me and might be dissuaded by seeing me as a human, as a father; who might even find my children cute and want these children to grow up with two parents and not one.

So I take the photo out and lay it facedown on my lap. And then I ask him if he has kids. He doesn't understand, so I mime the cradling of a baby, then point to him.

He scoffs and says, 'No. No baby. I am the baby!'

It's a good joke, and we both laugh. This is good.

I turn the photo to face up, and point to it and to myself. He looks at my two children, both very young, two and five years old, and he looks at my wife, and then he sees me in the picture, and he puts it all together. He smiles, nods, and I feel like showing the photo has come off as natural, as a logical enough thing to do during a long drive. And maybe I've put a thought in his mind: that I am a father, that my children are young, that I seem like a regular person, probably not a spy or Halliburton contractor or collaborator with the network of government officials and oil and defence contractors who might be the target of his opprobrium.

I leave the photo on my lap for a few miles as we continue driving. He asks no questions about my family – not that he could, with the language barrier, but still, something, I hope, has changed between us. I very well could be imagining it all, but I have no choice but to hope. He flips the cassette in the tape player and lights another cigarette.

I made no decision to be an American, made no sacrifices to be called an American, did no work to be born into the place and time and conditions that the United States enjoyed in 1970 and my family enjoyed in 1970. It is chance, blind luck, random. And it's random that this Saudi driver, now hitting 175km/h, was born into a Saudi vessel – both countries are so new that identifying too strongly with their names and flags is a psychic stretch – and it would be absurd if this man, this soul-in-a-Saudi-vessel, were to harbour any antipathy toward me, a soul-in-an-American-vessel. So it makes it difficult to take a situation like this, the possibility of danger in this car hurtling through the Saudi desert, too seriously for too long.

I have the frequent thought that if the worst came to the worst, a man like this and I could together recognise the absurdity of our nationalities. You are not a Saudi, I would say, referring to a country that has only existed since 1932. I am not an American, I would say, referring to a country that has existed for 240 years. You are not a driver. I am not your passenger. We believe so little of what we would be expected to believe – we believe nothing of the foundational evil of our nations assumed by many – but we do believe that it feels good to be trusted; we believe in the constant movement of souls, the restless nature of the spirit, the profound game of make-believe necessary for either one of us to assume a set of values or motives of the other based on our passports; we believe that we are tired, so tired, of being asked to distrust or hate the people of this country or that culture, the people wearing this uniform or that one, the people who worship this prophet or that god; that we can do better than our fathers and grandfathers and forgo the pretence of rivalries and suspicions; that what we really want are not inherited antagonisms but only some measure of human and material comfort; some frequent stimulation and delight of the mind; some sense of progress for the rights of people; some possibilities and choices for our progeny and the progeny of our neighbours; the ability to love who we want to love; the ability to move freely around the planet as time and means allow.

And right now, driving with this man, what I want is to make this interaction work. I want him to feel good about having met me, and I want to feel good about having met him. One thing you learn after twenty-odd years of random travel is that the people you see along the way – the cabbies, the vendors, the hoteliers, the fellow bus passengers, the man who rents you the kayak on the Isle of Skye – you're unlikely to see again. So you want to get it right. To get it right you have to make it right.

But I didn't make it right with Majed. I run the incident through my mind a dozen times during this drive, watching the desert go by. What did I say that was so wrong? Some joke about the American military. Some joke about unnecessary wars. It was not so wrong. He shouldn't have been offended. Not just offended – he changed his mind about me completely. Had our friendship been on this razor's edge from the start? One wrong phrase and I'd fallen into league with all US foreign policy wrongdoers – that couldn't be fair. And then I was offended that he was offended. I was finished, too. I could spend hours trying to convince him I wasn't some agent of imperialism, or I could wait out our last day or so, allow him to put me in some random car with some random man, and be done with it. Which is what I did.

Hours have passed since the 'American, boom boom' comment. Shadad has made various other, uneventful, phone calls since then. I have felt comfortable enough to even take a few photos out the window, and even a few inside the car, including the one opposite. Shadad didn't seem to mind.

And now we're stopping for gas. The station looks like any gas station anywhere in the world. Shadad stops and unlocks the doors.

He gets out, stretches. I open my door and look around. I could run this way, I think. I could make a phone call at that shop over there. I could hide over behind that shed. I could appeal to that truck driver over there.

But instead I ask the driver if he wants a snack or drink. I mime drinking and eating. He shakes his head.

I walk over to the shop next door to the gas station. Inside, there is a solitary man, in his sixties, behind the counter. He nods to me and says, *'Salaam.'* I nod back, return his 'Salaam'.

In the shop, I think again about escape. I could stay here. I could find a way to call Majed, and ask Majed for his guidance and his help, and maybe along the way apologise for my unfunny jokes about Saudi-American relations. I would miss my flight. I would have to stay overnight in Riyadh. Majed would have to drive out to get me here, four hours away from Jeddah and into the desert, to get me to Riyadh, or back to Jeddah, or–? But what's the alternative? Should I really get back in the car with a man who seemed to have promised some terrible threat to my person?

Travel is about great and illogical leaps of trust, though, so I find myself buying a soda for myself and one for the driver, and a box of crackers big enough that we can share it. And then I'm walking back to the car. Shadad is already inside, a new cigarette filling the car with a toxic cloud. I offer the soda to the driver, but he smiles, confused – *Didn't I tell you I didn't want a drink?* – and puts the car in gear, and we're off. He doesn't touch the soda the rest of the drive.

Night comes on as we approach Riyadh. The city's lights overtake the darkness. I look at the clock and see that because we've been travelling so fast we're almost two hours early. I want to believe that Shadad was devoted to making sure I was on time for the flight, but it's just as likely that he wanted to be finished with me, with this long silent drive, so he can get home.

I get out at my terminal, and he helps remove my bag from the trunk. 'We made it in good time,' I say. I point to my wrist and give him a thumbs-up. He nods and almost smiles. We stand outside and again we stretch.

I take out an envelope of cash and try to give it to him.

Looking confused, he refuses.

'You friend?' he says. 'He pay before we leave.'

I should have known. Majed, a young man of no great means, paid for the whole ride when he met Shadad in that Jeddah alley. I think of Majed now, and I want to embrace him, to tell him how sorry I am. But now I have only Shadad, so I shake his hand, my two hands around his one hand, and he adds his second hand to mine.

FIONA KIDMAN is the author of more than 30 books that include fiction, poetry, non-fiction, and memoir. Her latest novel was the bestselling *The Infinite Air*, based on the life of the famous aviator Jean Batten. Fiona has been a passionate traveller, as circumstance allowed, preferring little company and out-of-the-way places. She has been honoured with several prizes and awards, including the French Legion of Honour (*Chevalier de la Légion d'Honneur*). She is a Dame Companion of the New Zealand Order of Merit (DNZM). Her home is in Wellington, New Zealand, overlooking Cook Strait.

The Road to Lost Places

FIONA KIDMAN

Some of my most memorable adventures have begun so benignly, with the seemingly harmless preoccupations of a writer at her desk. All my life I've been interested in the places where writers lived and the journeys they took. Not those of my contemporaries, which seems intrusive, but, rather, those seen from the distance of a life in its entirety. I've been especially drawn to the dark moral dilemmas that stalk through the work of Graham Greene. *The Quiet American*, set in Vietnam, is one of my favourites among his books. I knew that for a time he had forsaken Roman Catholicism and embraced the Cao Daist religion, a unique sect founded in 1926 and based in South Vietnam, and that its temple in Tay Ninh Province had provided one of the prime settings for the novel. In 1991, I innocently decided that I would go there.

Tay Ninh province is northwest of Ho Chi Minh City,

bordered on three sides by Kampuchea, or Cambodia as it is known these days, Kampuchea being the name bestowed on the country by the Khmer Rouge. Now, when I close my eyes and recall Tay Ninh, I see a great plain dotted with brick kilns crouching like red igloos against a cobalt sky. Beyond lies a mountain range known as Black Lady Mountain. In 1991, the little township was a collection of makeshift dwellings, mostly open to the elements, many of them surrounded by rusted barbed wire. Its distinguishing feature was the Great Temple of the Cao Dai Holy See, home to a religion that had been formed through a fusion of secular and religious philosophies from both the East and the West, including those of Roman Catholicism and Buddhism.

I can picture all this now, but when I arrived in Vietnam in 1991, when the country still had a wild and dangerous feel, and you might go all day without seeing another European, I had no idea what I would find at Tay Ninh – or where that journey would end up taking me.

My husband and I were staying at the Rex Hotel in Ho Chi Minh City. The hotel was a strange hybrid of East and West, occupied by the Americans before the fall of Saigon. You could tell it was a place meant for men, with twisted wooden racks for holding uniforms at the doors and no mirrors in the bathroom. Carved wooden animals crouched in the dim passageways and more amongst the topiary work on the rooftop garden. A huge crown, twice our height, rotated on a pedestal. Giant orange and black cichlids floated in shoulder-high tanks encrusted with china decorations.

We were visited at the hotel by a guide whom we had hired to escort us to the Củ Chi tunnels. When I told her that I also wanted to go further into the countryside, beyond the tunnels, she was doubtful. 'I have never been to Tay Ninh,' she said. 'You would have to pay extra.'

She said that she was a poet, but that poetry didn't pay very well, although she had won the Grand Prize for Young Writers in Vietnam. Her name was Pham Thi Ngoc Liên, she told us. Liên meant lotus flower. In order to pay the bills, she had learned English so that she could guide people like us.

I told her that I was a writer too, both a novelist and sometime poet. I explained my mission to follow in the footsteps of Greene. She would talk to the driver of the car, she said. After some time, she came back, nodding. She had talked to the driver, who turned out to be a dour former tank driver called Nuan. It was agreed that both destinations were possible and there was no particular danger in such an excursion. He had been to Tay Ninh during wartime combat and knew the area. All the same, she shook her head and muttered what I took to be 'crazy New Zealand writer'.

So, the following day, after we had been to the tunnels, we set off for the temple at Tay Ninh. I was glad to leave the tunnels, for I don't care for confined spaces. The road we took was crowded with stray ducks, children riding buffaloes, and, in some places, rice that had been laid out to dry on its clay surface. Clay from the surrounding area was used to make bricks and tiles; smoke drifted from kilns.

Then we came upon the enormous sprawling temple. It reared up against the sky on the flat plain, and it was not unlike coming upon Chartres Cathedral in the French countryside, astonishing, sudden, vast – although there the comparison ends. The Eye of God at the entrance to the temple stared at us across a brick and beaten-grass causeway from under its portico, a wide unrelenting eye with a heavy fringe of lashes. The temple was a cross somewhere between the castle of the Wizard of Oz, Notre Dame Cathedral, and a pagoda. Lattice-work balconies trickled over the walls, snakes and dragons curling up its pillars, and Christ-like figures were embedded amongst pink plaster, carved lotus flowers, and six-sided stars.

Midday prayers had just ended, and shadowy figures were sliding away to a compound of smaller buildings. But on seeing us, the group turned back and beckoned us towards them. These were *huong*, or nuns, and *thanh*, or priests, dressed all in white, although the men wore little flat pleated black hats. We followed the group and came face to face with a mural depicting Victor Hugo, holding a quill pen, alongside the Chinese statesman and revolutionary leader Dr Sun Yat-Set, who was holding an inkstone, and the Vietnamese poet Nguyen Binh Khiem (he died in 1587), depicted writing with a brush. These were the three signatories of 'The Third Alliance Between God and Man'. Revelations, I was told, arrived during séances through the medium of poets, philosophers, and political leaders.

Some English was spoken. A nun told me she taught herself from books after her nightly prayers. Liên and I were taken by the hand and led in one direction, and Ian, my husband, in the opposite direction by the men.

'We women will walk clockwise, the men anti-clockwise,' explained Liên, who had been talking to the nuns. This was how it was, men and women walked in the opposite direction to each other. Before us lay the dim interior of the temple, built on nine levels, with nine fifteen-metre-high domes, each dome representing the starry heavens. On the roof of one, Christ exposed his bleeding heart, but Buddha and Confucius also appeared. Under the furthest dome stood a colossal blue globe speckled with what I was told were 3072 stars, but I wasn't counting.

And then, when the tour was almost complete, we began to rotate anti-clockwise towards the men.

'Why is this?' I asked. 'Why are we allowed to break the rules?'

There was a concerted sigh from the *huong*. They had been in conversation with Liên. 'You are a writer, the rules do not apply to you. You will write us a poem. You will both write us a poem.'

So there, in that strange temple, which ultimately Greene would dismiss, some garbled messages that passed for poems were written by me and the young Vietnamese poet. Liên's writing was that of a fine calligrapher. Perhaps the poems are still there.

And that is where the day should have ended, with the photographs and smiles that followed. Only, on the way back, we spotted a signpost pointing down a road which the usually taciturn driver indicated, via Liên, was the way to the Kampuchean border. It was full of bullet holes. 'Take us there, please,' Ian said.

'No,' said Nuan, finding some English.

'That's not possible,' Liên said.

'Boom boom, you die,' said Nuan. An uneasy memory flashed past me of a young man back home in Wellington who, when we had said we were going to Vietnam, had held two fingers to his forehead. I had dismissed this as scaremongering. The war in Vietnam was over.

Ian is rather deaf. He has said, since then, that he didn't really hear what was being said. He suggested a further fee of a hundred dollars. The car pulled over. There was a silence, and then a reluctant agreement. The road we followed led to Cho Huu Nghi, loosely translated as The Friendship Market. I believe it is now a tourist destination called the Moc Bai Border gate. Hundreds of cyclists were hurtling towards us, laden with enormous packages on their backs, on the handlebars, in trolleys pulled along behind them. The bicycles were not ordinary vehicles, but consisted rather of two bikes lashed together, their cargo so heavy that the riders teetered from side to side.

The marketplace was a huge squalid area, filled with mosquitoes. Makeshift bamboo dwellings were huddled as far as the eye could see, in ankle-deep mud. Thousands of people were camped out there, the men bare-chested, wearing rolled-up trousers, the Cambodian women colourful in their *krama*, the big scarves serving as headdresses, sarongs, and bags. We could see what was being traded, items such as Marine Saigon brandy going into Cambodia, Western clothes and toiletries and tobacco coming into Vietnam. The whole scene was seething with movement and a sense of urgency. Ian, who was teaching Vietnamese and Cambodian refugees then, was enchanted. He began walking through the crowds. At first the people were merely curious, smiling slightly at our presence. A man asked Ian to take his photograph. Liên translated the tattoo above the stump of his arm – Pol Pot wound, 1979. But after a few minutes, she retreated to the car. I felt exposed, sensing a tension around me.

By then, our guide and driver were both sitting nervously in the car, the doors hanging open, the engine idling. Ian raised his camera to take pictures. And suddenly I understood what a terrible risk we had taken. We were seeing what no Westerner was meant to see. We smelled of Western money. I know now that people were being traded across those borders too. I remembered the year before when I had had a child offered to me for sale in a Cambodian market, and the shock and revulsion I had experienced.

The crowd began a pincer-like movement towards Ian, cutting off his retreat. Liên and Nuan shouted at us to jump into the car, which had begun to move slowly away from us.

I saw at once what would happen: we would disappear over the border and nobody would ever admit to having seen us.

I screamed, 'Ian, get in the bloody car. Run!' He heard me and understood. We both ran, with the crowd in hot pursuit, jumping into the car as it speeded up, the doors swinging wildly. A shot rang out behind us. We came to a checkpoint, manned by military police whom we had not properly taken into account on our approach. A barrier fell across the roadway. There was not a glimmer of friendliness in the faces of the men in uniform. 'Get out,' they indicated, and we stood there in the Vietnamese afternoon, with our hands raised and guns pointed at our heads. Our guides were quivering with fear as they spoke rapidly to the soldiers. Nuan's movements were slow and careful, his voice low and insistent, sounding as if he was pleading with the men. Lifetimes seemed to pass. I thought about our children and how they worried about us on their travels, and, as I remember it, I said their names to myself, trying to visualise them for what might be the last time. I looked up at the roadside signs with their bullet holes. We were nothing in the scale of carnage that had occurred along this road.

Nuan continued his intense murmuring conversation with the police. Perhaps three or four minutes passed. We must have looked worthless after all, foolish nosy tourists, nothing more, because all at once, the barrier arms lifted and we were allowed to go. We all climbed back in the car, and it barreled away, weaving between the steady stream of loaded bicycles. The rest of the journey back to Ho Chi Minh City passed in silence. We said we were sorry, and asked our guides to accept a gift of money.

We could think of nothing else; at least they would be spared working for people like us for a month or so.

We wandered over the road that evening to the turn-of-the-century Hotel Continental, more Graham Greene territory, where other parts of *The Quiet American* had taken place. Beneath the ornate ceiling there was a hollow air. The famous 'Continental Shelf' where war correspondents used to hang out was deserted. When it got dark we walked back to the Rex, watching lizards weaving across the lemon-coloured walls of City Hall.

We had planned to go to Hanoi, but we heard there was a cholera outbreak up north and suddenly the thought of a beach in Thailand was very appealing. It would take us a day or two to organise early tickets out of the country. There were all kinds of documentation and paperwork required, explaining what we had done in Vietnam and why we were leaving before the expiry date on our visas. We lay low at the Rex until we were able to go. We didn't hear from our guide, and who could blame her.

But news travelled in the city. When we got to the airport, suddenly Liên appeared. She had come to wave us goodbye and give me a copy of one of her books. She waved as we disappeared into the terminal. 'Crazy writer,' she called, 'come back!'

That was nearly a quarter of a century ago. I go back when I can, and some of the most vivid experiences of my life have occurred in Vietnam. But I haven't been back to Tay Ninh.

M. J. HYLAND is an ex-lawyer, a lecturer at the University of Manchester, and the author of three multi-award-winning novels: *How the Light Gets In, Carry Me Down* (which was shortlisted for the Man Booker Prize) and *This is How*. She is also the author of dozens of essays and short stories and works for The Guardian Masterclass Programme and BBC Radio. In 2013 she was appointed to the Academy for the £40,000 Folio Fiction Prize.

How I Evaded Arrest on a Train Platform (Somewhere in the North of England)

M. J. HYLAND

I was on my way home from a literary festival in the southeast of England and I took a seat in a first-class 'quiet zone' carriage. In a complicated act of willful blindness, I conned myself into believing that the festival (which was no more than a circle of tents in a wet field and which didn't pay me a fee) had paid for a first-class ticket so I could read and rest during the five-hour journey home.

Before the trouble started, I was disproportionately happy: I love trains and stories and films set on trains, and one of my dominant daydreams goes like this:

> I buy a coat from a charity shop and in the inner lining, there's an 'open' first-class ticket for the Trans-Siberian Railway, due to depart in December. After a few phone calls, I track down the owner, and he says: 'Please

keep the ticket, my dear, I don't have any use for it.'

Not long after boarding, the meal was served (smoked salmon with capers) and the inspector came to my table. Less than an hour later, she called the police and asked to have me 'forcibly removed for failure to carry a valid ticket.'

'Madam, your ticket isn't valid for travel in first class.'

'I'm sorry. I didn't realise.'

'You need to purchase a valid ticket.'

She was squat and square with the orange teeth and fingers of a heavy smoker. And yet, she was beautiful, had the kind of implausibly blue eyes I'd seen only once before when I met a Serbian boy in Starbucks.

'Can't I just move to standard class?' I said.

I didn't want to move and lose this rare mood of peace and privilege, the feeling that an oubliette on the Orient Express would no doubt bring.

'You can't move seats whenever you feel like it, and you've already eaten half the meal.'

'How much is first class?'

She pushed buttons on a dusty machine strapped to her belt. '£179.73.'

I had about £20 in my wallet and less than £300 in my credit account. I couldn't afford first-class silence, this soft wide seat far from businessmen with mobiles who are fond of saying, 'Moving forward… We need to drill down… To be fair… I think you're boiling the ocean on this… At the end of the day… We need to get our ducks in a row…'

There'd be no silence now, no chance of sleep or reading undisturbed by gangsters drinking beer and eating KFC from buckets, probably boneless banquets – all the chicken, none of the evidence.

'I haven't got enough money,' I said. 'Can't I just move?'

'Madam, as I've repeatedly said, you can't just eat the meal and what-have-you and then change carriages whenever you feel like it.'

I wanted to reason with her but she'd likely hate me more if I said that my desire for first-class train journeys started around the time I lived in a council estate and first read *Strangers on a Train*, *La Bête Humaine* by Zola, and Chekhov's stories.

'What happens now?' I said. 'I can't pay and you won't let me move.'

'You'll be fined and escorted from the service by transit officers.'

Transit officers? This puffer-fish hated me for reasons of an order more perverse than professional and when she left me alone to check tickets in the next carriage, I read some Chekhov for comfort:

In a second-class smoking compartment five passengers sit dozing, shrouded in the twilight of the carriage. They had just had a meal, and now, snugly ensconced in their seats, they are trying to go to sleep. Stillness. ('A Happy Man')

She was back. No chance of stillness now. No chance of sleeping with my head on the bath towel I'd taken from the motel room (which had no biscuits) and no looking out the window at howling winds buckling fences, security lights flashing on and off in porches of empty houses; no chance now for watching scenes sucked back at speed with just time enough to notice that sheep aren't in the habit of running.

I put my books in my suitcase and stood.

'You can't leave,' said the inspector.

'This is so fucking bloody-minded.'

'Please don't use that language at me, madam.'

'I'm swearing at the situation, not you,' I said.

A man sitting a few rows behind came to my table, sat, introduced himself and, as though the inspector wasn't there, chatted a while about overzealous and officious ticket collectors.

'I've seen trouble like this before,' he said, 'and I've written several letters of complaint.'

The man was Mr W, a semi-retired solicitor, mostly conveyancing law, but he knew (he said) that this inspector was 'out of bounds both legally and ethically' and he asked for her name and rank.

'I'm the train manager,' she said. 'Satisfied?'

'Well, then, you should know that I happen to agree with the young lady here that this situation is ludicrous.'

She coughed.

'And,' he said, 'I'd like to pay for the young lady's ticket.'

This wasn't the first time I'd encountered an extraordinary act of kindness. My life has been spiked by regular bouts of obscene luck: in early childhood neighbours and relatives willing to rescue me, in school a teacher who took me from my cruddy home and let me live with her while I finished my final year of school, and later, a professor who part-funded my scholarship to study law at the University College Dublin.

I refused Mr W's offer. He insisted.

'You can't buy her ticket anyway,' said the inspector.

'Why on earth not?' said Mr W.

''Cos she's not the valid ticket holder, is she?'

'You're being unreasonable,' said Mr W, 'and you're on very thin ice legally speaking.'

She shrugged. 'Let's see what the transit police have to say about that,' and went to the vestibule and called for 'immediate reinforcement.'

I put my head on the table, like a child might: If I couldn't see her, then she couldn't see me and I might stay this way and not lift my head till I was home.

Before the second bell, while Podtyagin is standing at the refreshment bar, drinking seltzer water, two gentlemen go up to him, one in the uniform of an engineer, and the other in a military overcoat.

'Look here, ticket collector,' the engineer begins, addressing Podtyagin. 'Your behaviour to that invalid passenger has revolted all who witnessed it.' ('Oh! The Public')

The train pulled into the next station, a transit cop boarded, came to my seat, and stood so close that the winter came in a gust at my face.

'That's her,' said the inspector, and then she left.

'I'm officer B.L.,' said the transit cop. 'Madam, do you understand why I've been called at this time?'

'I just want you to know,' I said, 'that I'm sorry for this waste of your time.'

'That's not at issue here and we need—'

'But you shouldn't have been dragged out in the dead of night in the middle of a freezing blizzard.'

'No need to apologise, madam. Just a touch of wind and hail.'

'Okay, but could you please write that down.'

He frowned. 'Write what down?'

'Write down that I've made a full apology.'

'Madam, can you confirm that you've refused to purchase a valid ticket?'

'I'm not refusing. I can't afford it and I offered to move as soon as I realised I didn't have a first-class ticket.'

'At what time was that?'

'We were no more than ten minutes into the journey,' said Mr W. 'Just a mile or two beyond M station.'

'But you aren't holding a valid ticket. Is that correct?'

'Officer,' said Mr W, 'did that overzealous inspector happen to inform you that I offered to buy a ticket on this young lady's behalf, and that I was refused and furthermore—'

Mr W was interrupted by an announcement: *'N Trains apologises for the delay which is due to the matter of a passenger in violation of the requirement of travelling with a valid ticket during transit who is presently in the rear carriage of the train being escorted from the service by transit police. On behalf of N trains I do apologise for this unforeseen delay. Our estimated arrival time…'*

The inspector came back, her shoulders higher, her hair brushed and a badge pinned to her black jacket: N Trains Manager. She stood beside the transit cop and said, 'So, where do we stand?'

'The customer says she can't pay and made a mistake and back near M and that she offered—'

'She still needs to be removed immediately, or—'

'I'm not going anywhere,' I said.

Mr W said there were 'no grounds whatsoever' for my removal.

(A few weeks later, Mr W sent a letter to N Trains – copied to me – alleging, among other things, 'maltreatment of elderly and infirm passengers' and 'the appalling conduct by the train manager' and then I understood that what he did that night was an act of kindness and a certain enjoyment in taking revenge.)

The inspector and transit cop chatted in the vestibule and the cop came back alone.

'Madam, the Metropolitan Police will alight the service at the next station and—'

'This can't be happening,' I said.

'You will then be processed, fined, removed from the service, and taken into custody.'

I needed to urinate.

The transit cop left and Mr W gave me his business card, and said, 'Don't hesitate to call me if you need advice.'

'Thank you.'

We were silent a moment. I was nervous and he offered me a drink.

'The cop forgot to ask for my ID,' I said.

'That's right, and since you're not in an allocated seat, you're a person unknown. Even to me.'

I smiled.

'Maybe I should make a move while I can,' I said.

Mr W shook my hand, wished me luck, and, as he stood, said, 'Do what you need to do, young lady, but if it comes to it, I'd advise you not to resist arrest.'

I packed my case and went to the bathroom in the next carriage. The cops would be on the lookout for 'a Caucasian female, approximately five-foot-seven, thirty-to-forty-years-old, long dark hair, red lipstick, wearing a green poncho and …'

I stuffed the poncho in my case and replaced it with a dark jacket; wiped away my make-up and tucked my black hair inside a grey beanie. When the engine slowed, I moved to the final carriage – the caboose – and when the doors opened, I stepped into the darkness and pelting rain.

There were three Met Officers on the platform talking to the inspector who pointed at carriage B – at my table. Two cops got on the train and the third stayed outside on watch. There was no cover on the platform, the Northern night was deep in dark, and hard rain flew sideways, all of which made identification tricky, though not impossible.

Running would give me away, but I had to move, and fast, and so I did. About a half-dozen passengers moved toward the exit and the coffee shop where an awning gave the only shelter on the platform. I merged with these passengers and asked a man for the time and smiled for no reason and asked him if his watch was waterproof, for the illusion we might know each other, might be man and wife.

As I walked, I passed within a body-length of the cop 'on watch,' but he did no more than slackly gaze at the rainy windows. The cops inside must have known that I'd done a runner, or maybe not. Perhaps they thought I was in the buffet-car buying a snack, or fixing my lipstick in the bathroom. Maybe they hadn't counted on a person like me doing a runner – not a well-dressed woman in her mid-thirties who read 'literary' books, spoke in a posh voice with an accent hard to pin down, of no fixed address or nationality.

I stood under the cafe awning and a woman said, to nobody in particular, 'This bloody weather. I need to pick up my youngest from her granny's.'

'I'm in a mad rush too.' I said. 'And I hate being late.'

She didn't ask where I needed to be.

'It's so cold,' she said. 'I just want to go in there and get a hot chocolate with piles of those mini marshmallows.'

I looked at the cop 'on watch' and though he hadn't moved, he was on his two-way, and that could mean trouble

'I know what you mean,' I said. 'Being cold to the bone makes you hungry for sugar.'

She smiled.

'Oh, this rain's infernal – when will it ever stop?'

I didn't tell her I love rain; that I like living in the North because it rains often, and rains all ways and most days, sideways, up-ways and hail-ways.

'It's so icy,' she said. 'It better not start snowing.'

I didn't say that I love snow in the city, or that I like storms and howling winds, how the air smells at 3am when I wake early; how strange it is that I don't feel sleepy, but more alive.

The woman moved away from me to stand under the light so she could fix a broken spoke in her umbrella. I stayed close to her but didn't mention all the reasons I love the snow, how things mostly ignored are noticed when it snows: a dormer window on the sixth floor of those flats by the newsagents, the troughs and chains outside a pub where horses were tethered in the 1800s. And how laughter is louder in the wake of snow, and cats leap and twist as though in fright when they see that their small paws make wide dark holes and for a while they're confused, or think they might be bigger than they knew.

The train steamed rapidly out of the station, its lights soon disappearing, and a minute later even the sound it made was silenced, as if everything were conspiring to bring this sweet oblivion, this madness, to an end as quickly as possible. ('The Lady with the Dog')

Being alone made me conspicuous, so I kept talking to the woman.

'Can I help you with the umbrella?'

'Thanks, but I think this one's for the graveyard.'

'Then we're doomed,' I said. 'Stranded.'

She laughed. 'No. We're not bloody stranded.'

She shook the rain from the umbrella and put it on the

window sill, gently, as though it still mattered and somebody else might like to have it.

'Come on,' she said, 'let's me and you make a run for the taxi-rank.'

She laughed again.

'Let's get ourselves soaked as a pair of socks and never care.'

STEVEN HALL is a writer working in books, TV, audio drama, and digital/interactive storytelling. His first and only novel, *The Raw Shark Texts*, has been translated into 30 languages and has successfully avoided becoming a film on several occasions. In 2013, he was named as one of *Granta* magazine's Best Young British Novelists.

The Hotel Whose Name We're Not Going to Mention in This Story

STEVEN HALL

In the summer of 2000 I spent six weeks backpacking around the Greek islands with my at-the-time girlfriend. Like anyone who makes this sort of trip, I have stories – trekking up to the discovery site of the Venus de Milo at dawn, then sitting in a quiet, grassy, old amphitheatre to watch dolphins swimming in the bay below; trying to stay calm as a death-or-glory bus driver threw his ageing vehicle – complete with stickers of fighter jets on the windscreen – around the tight, narrow bends of the road that zigzags up the thousand-foot cliffs of Santorini; the discovery that pelicans are really, really large creatures. All these stories, as important as they are to me, are pretty usual. If you've ever been backpacking around Greece, you'll probably have at least some of them yourself. There's one story from this trip, however, that is not at all usual. One story that is odd and unsettling. This is the story I'm going to tell here.

We arrived into the port of Heraklion, Crete, at dusk.

We'd picked a hotel in the city and, because we were tired, we decided to blow some of our dwindling funds on the luxury of a taxi to get us there.

We chose a taxi driver carefully from the many trying to get our attention on the dock – he was young-ish, professional-ish, though what can you honestly know about a person in those circumstances; you have to just go with your gut – and followed him to his cab, jumping in the back.

'Can you take us to the-hotel-whose-name-we're-not-going-to-mention-in-this-story?' my girlfriend asked. He nodded and fired up the engine.

We guessed it'd take about ten minutes to get to the hotel in a cab, up from the docks and into the heart of the city. We probably could've made it on foot but, as I said, we were tired and didn't want to think about navigating a strange city in the failing light. We just wanted to get to the-hotel-whose-name-we're-not-going-to-mention-in-this-story, check in, and fall asleep.

Ten minutes later and the lights of the city were starting to disappear behind us.

Shit.

I leaned forward in my seat. 'Is this the way to the-hotel-whose-name-we're-not-going-to-mention-in-this-story?'

'Yes,' said the driver. 'Relax. It's fine.'

Fifteen minutes and the city was well and truly behind us.

Twenty minutes and we were in the countryside, driving through what looked like an abandoned quarry in the fading light.

Oh *shit*.

We looked at each other, neither of us quite believing that this was happening and yet all too aware of how badly it could play out.

'This isn't the way to our hotel,' my girlfriend said. 'Where are we going?'

'Somewhere better,' the driver said.

'I think you should take us back now,' I told him.

'Relax, please. I'm helping you,' he said to the road ahead.

We considered our options, which were limited.

After a tense, thirty-minute drive, we found ourselves sitting in the bar of a tiny deserted little hotel in the middle of nowhere, as the driver and the hotel owner whispered in one corner.

'They don't look like killers,' said my girlfriend. 'We could stay. Get out of here in the morning.'

By this point, night had fallen. Outside was pitch black.

Getting out of here tonight would mean another cab, or the same cab. It would mean the cooperation of at least one of the people currently whispering about us at the other end of the room.

'I think we should go,' I said. I was scared, but I'd found the edges of something hard inside myself that I'd never noticed before. 'I don't want to be here and neither do you.'

At that point, we forced ourselves into some rational thinking. Nobody was going to be murdered. The driver was probably related to the hotel owner, or picking up a little cash on the side from bringing paying guests here. These weren't psychopaths. At the very most it was a scam, a little strong-arming, but not much more than that. We just needed to show that we weren't going to be strong-armed by anybody.

The driver and the owner came over to us.

'We asked you to take us to the-hotel-whose-name-we're-not-going-to-mention-in-this-story,' I said to the driver. 'Why are we here?'

Steven Hall

'Stay here,' said the driver. 'This is a good hotel. It's better for you.'
The hotel owner didn't speak any English, or he wasn't joining in.
'We don't want to say here,' said my girlfriend.
'Yes,' said the taxi driver. 'You do.'
'No. *We do not.*'
What followed was a fair amount of back and forth until I played what I hoped was our best card and flat-out demanded that he drive us to the offices of the transport police in Heraklion *right now*. I might even have banged on the table. It was impressive stuff.
And it did the trick.
'Fine, of course, if that's what you want. I'm just trying to help you,' said the driver as we followed him out to his car, as if this had been his attitude all along.
Here's what I did next. Under the advice of the recently discovered hard thing inside me, I sat behind the driver for the return journey. With what seems now to be a disturbingly icy and detached sense of clarity, I positioned myself so that I could quite easily get my arm around his neck to restrain or strangle him if I felt that to be necessary, and from there could go on to kick at the steering wheel and run us off the road if I needed to. I should say that I was completely prepared to do these things, and wasn't panicked. It felt like there was a current running through me, but I was focused, still, practical. I'd never found myself functioning in this mode before, and have never experienced it since. I remember assessing the situation, not like a chess player but like something with a mouth full of sharp teeth. The driver had to face forwards, operate the car, keep his eyes on the road. I was behind him. I had an overwhelming advantage. I remember thinking that – *I have an overwhelming advantage.* Thinking about it now is still unsettling.

Thankfully, the driver did take us exactly where we wanted to go, all the while explaining that he was only trying to help us out. He pulled up in front of the transport police building in Heraklion and then offered to drive us to the-hotel-whose-name-we're-not-going-to-mention-in-this-story, as it was just a couple of blocks away.

'Okay, yes. You should do that. Thanks,' said my girlfriend, struggling to find the right words for the situation.

A minute or two later, we were standing on the pavement outside the-hotel-whose-name-we're-not-going-to-mention-in-this-story, catching our breath and being pleased, more or less, with how we'd handled things. It was our first real challenge, and we'd asserted ourselves, come out the other side feeling like seasoned, capable travellers.

We went inside.

My girlfriend began to notice it straightaway, but it took me a little longer. At that point, I was still preoccupied with what had happened, and still thinking over the scary operating mode I'd found myself running in on the return journey. Its existence went against a lot of the things I'd always thought about myself, and I could see there would need to be some time and thought to integrate it into the overall picture.

Preoccupied as I was with these thoughts, it took me a few moments to pick up on the look my girlfriend was giving me.

The look said *what the fuck?*

I raised my eyebrows. *What?*

She tipped her head towards the receptionist.

At first I didn't understand what she wanted me to see. The young woman looked normal enough, though she gave us a couple of nervous glances while trying to do something

with the check-in computer. Moments later, it became clear
that she couldn't get it to work. What was that look? Was she
embarrassed? Finally, she gave up and began searching around
for what eventually turned out to be a cupboard full of room
keys.

Why couldn't she find the room keys?

That's when I saw what my girlfriend was trying to tell me.

My stomach lurched a little – the realisation was so strange.

This woman was dressed as a receptionist and standing at a
hotel reception, but she *wasn't a receptionist*. She was pretending.
She'd been standing here, in uniform, pretending to do a job that
she didn't actually do.

Why?

I looked around the lobby seriously for the first time.

We were standing in a large, grand building. Opulent. Faded.

Dotted around the place in small groups were perhaps a dozen
older Greek men in suits. They were all staring at us. Staring a
little aggressively, I thought, but much more than that, staring
with surprise and incomprehension. The way you might stare if a
pair of zebras wandered in off the street.

And another thing, when I turned back to the reception, I saw
that it wasn't just clean and orderly as I'd first supposed; it was
sparse, under-dressed – it looked like a set.

This might sound crazy but my now ex-girlfriend and I have
talked about this a lot in the fifteen years since it happened
and we're both of the same opinion: the-hotel-whose-name-
we're-not-going-to-mention-in-this-story had put a lot of effort
into appearing to be a hotel, but it wasn't a hotel at all. It was
something else entirely. What? We still have no idea.

Various people have suggested all the obvious things – a
gangster hang-out or some sort of front for a criminal operation,

a brothel – but none of these feels right; these explanations seem too straightforward, too recognisable, and this wasn't that at all, this was something *other*.

Imagine wandering into a David Lynch movie, or into the Overlook Hotel during the Jack-Nicholson's-losing-his-mind part of *The Shining*. That's the closest I've ever been able to come to describing the experience. It felt unsettling; it felt all wrong.

After the not-receptionist had found us a room key, a not-porter – equally confused and horrified – had shown us upstairs, through empty, silent, shabby corridors, to our room.

The room was about as convincing as the reception.

We slid a chest of drawers in front of the door and didn't sleep very much.

In the night there was a series of loud bangs, but no sounds of movement, no mumbled voices of any other guests. For a hotel, it was very quiet indeed.

Early the next morning, we headed into Heraklion to cash in some travellers cheques.

'And what hotel are you staying in?' asked the cashier.

'The-hotel-whose-name-we're-not-going-to-mention-in-this-story,' my girlfriend said.

The cashier stopped writing. I can still see this so clearly – she stopped writing and looked up at us slowly with barely disguised alarm.

'The-hotel-whose-name-we're-not-going-to-mention-in-this-story?'

'Yes,' said my girlfriend. 'Why? Is there something wrong?'

'No, no, no,' the cashier backtracked with a nervous breeziness. 'Of course not. It is a very nice hotel.'

We wandered through the streets in silence for a little while after that.

Eventually, my girlfriend said, 'I'm trying to help you.'

'What?'

'I'm trying to help you. That's what the taxi driver kept saying over and over to us yesterday, wasn't it?'

It was.

Oh shit. It really was.

'I think we should get our bags,' I said.

'I think so, too.'

And reader, that's exactly what we did.

MANDY SAYER'S first novel, *Mood Indigo*, won the Australian / Vogel Award for writers under 35. Since then she has been named one of Ten Best Young Australian Novelists by the *Sydney Morning Herald* and has published five further works of fiction. Her first memoir, *Dreamtime Alice*, won the 2000 National Biography Award, Australian Audio Book of the Year Award, and New England Booksellers' Award in the US. It was published to critical acclaim in the US and UK and was translated into several European languages. Her second memoir, *Velocity*, won the 2006 South Australian Premier's Award for Non-Fiction and the 2006 Age Book of the Year (Non-Fiction). Her third memoir, *The Poet's Wife*, was published in Australia in 2014. She has also edited the anthology *The Australian Long Story* (2009) and *In the Gutter, Looking at the Stars* (with Louis Nowra), a collection of literature set in Sydney's red-light district, Kings Cross. Sayer has two degrees from Indiana University, and a Doctorate from the University of Technology, Sydney, where she was the 2014 CAL Non-Fiction Writer-in-Residence.

Sleepless in Samoa
MANDY SAYER

I t was supposed to have been a romantic week in the tropics, all expenses paid. My boyfriend, Louis, was researching Western Samoa for a screenplay he was about to write, commissioned by an Australian film producer. We hadn't been together long, about nine months, and were still swimming in the early waves of lust. I packed vintage pornography and a satin bag filled with recently purchased sex toys.

On the plane I was introduced to some of the more unusual aspects of Samoan culture: a native returning home was so morbidly obese, due to an unhealthy Western diet, that he could not fit into the toilet cubicle. Two resigned attendants came to his rescue, holding up blankets around him in the aisle while he dropped his trousers and aimed his piss through the open door and into the bowl. Beside us sat a perfectly coiffed female impersonator, replete with false eyelashes, heavy make-up, and bee-stung lips. Louis later explained to me that the person was a *fa'afafine*, a boy who'd been raised from birth as a girl, not unusual in Polynesia, especially if a family has no daughters. Most of them made a living in Samoa by performing in cabarets.

We landed on the island of Upolo late at night. Through the open windows of the bus from the airport, I glimpsed traditional thatched huts, bamboo pavilions, and market gardens. The air was cool and fragrant with the scent of frangipani. No wonder Robert Louis Stevenson had chosen to live and write here, I thought. The place was an exquisite paradise.

At the registration counter of the famous Aggie Grey's Hotel, we were the last to check in, and were assigned the final available *fale*, or traditional hut, in the complex. It was so far away from the main building, however, that we were unable to find it on a map, a piece of paper so riddled with circles and squiggly paths that it looked like an Aboriginal dot painting. After returning to Reception, perplexed and confused, we were assigned a teenage porter who led us on a ten-minute walk along labyrinthine tracks until we reached the chain-link fence that bordered the property. Here, at the end of the very last row of huts, was our very own *fale*, built in the shape of a hexagon and thatched with palm leaves. I didn't mind being so far from the hotel's restaurants and swimming pools; the distance would be a bonus, I reasoned, and would provide us with even more privacy and peace.

At dawn the next morning, I was awakened by a loud, industrial throb that sounded like a semi-trailer idling beside the hut. As I crawled out of bed, I could sense the *fale* and the floorboards beneath my bare feet vibrating. Was it an earthquake? I wondered. I opened the door and stuck my head outside: in the light of day, on the other side of the chain-link fence I could see a rudimentary building made of corrugated iron and a sign that read Bottling Factory.

Louis pulled on a pair of trousers and a shirt and went to complain at the front desk. Twenty minutes later, he returned wet with sweat and told me he'd been fobbed off by the staff, whose ability to speak and understand English had mysteriously escaped them. One attendant, however, had managed to explain, in halting pidgin, that the bottling plant only operated between 6am and 6pm every day, and so shouldn't interfere with our sleep at night. The relentless revving grew louder, combined with the occasional din of shattering glass. We showered, dressed, and fled the *fale*. After breakfast in one of the hotel pavilions, we took a stroll downtown, following the curve of Apia Harbour. Curiously, for such a hot climate, and in such glare-filled light, there were few awnings or trees to shade the streets. I'd forgotten to bring a hat and yet every store we entered had none in stock. And then I realised that the obese man on the plane the night before had not been an anomaly: just about everywhere I looked, I saw islanders so overweight that some were hyperventilating and finding it difficult to walk.

We bought some local newspapers and retired by the pool back at Aggie Grey's. I read that the city was experiencing a feral dog problem, with mongrels roaming the streets and attacking pedestrians in packs. I also read that recently there'd been a series of unsolved murders on the island and that local authorities believed the fatalities were linked. While I cooled off in the pool, Louis made another complaint at Reception about the infernal noise filling our *fale*, again to no avail.

After dinner that night we decided to have a cocktail in the hotel bar. We hadn't drained our first martini glasses, however, before another two were promptly delivered to our table. I glanced up at the waiter, puzzled. 'Those men over there wanted to buy you a drink', he said, and nodded toward three smiling young men a few tables across, obviously islanders, with broad, sinewy shoulders and necks as thick as palm trunks. We raised the glasses to them and nodded a thank you, and they nodded back. Louis immediately told the waiter to deliver another set of cocktails back to them, whatever they were drinking. Minutes later, the men walked over with their drinks and joined us, shaking our hands and introducing themselves. Originally from Samoa, they were cousins who now lived in Sydney, but who'd travelled back to Apia to settle a land dispute. One man, Paul, was set to inherit his father's side of a particular mountain, a parcel of land that had been passed down in his family, from generation to generation, to the first-born male, for hundreds of years. The only problem was proving it to the Western courts without the benefit of written deeds. Paul also told us that in Australia he lived in Frederick St in Sydenham, and that he worked in building scaffolding for a man called Tom Domican. Paul bought us another round of drinks and then insisted that we come and stay with his family and experience the true Samoan culture. His grandmother would cook for us and he'd take us to some secret beaches that weren't on tourist maps. He pressed his phone number, written on a coaster, into my hand and made me promise to call him the following day. Louis bundled me out of the bar and into the cool night air. 'Well, wasn't he nice?' I remarked, weaving tipsily along a path beneath flowering vines. 'I'd rather stay with his family than in that noisy hut.'

Louis linked his arm in mine and drew me closer to him. He explained that he, too, had once lived in Frederick St in Sydenham, on the same side of the road as Tom Domican's boss, Neddy Smith, who was a notorious Sydney drug trafficker, thief, and murderer. 'When Paul says he's into scaffolding with Tom, it doesn't mean he's in the construction business.' I paused and asked him what he meant. '*Scaffolding* is a euphemism. Paul's one of Neddy's standover guys and does his dirty work for him. We're not ringing him tomorrow. We're staying the fuck away from him.'

At dawn the next morning I was rudely awakened again by the industrial throb of the bottling plant. I thought of Paul's generous offer to stay with his family, but quickly dismissed it, particularly after a wave of nausea rose through me and I ran for the toilet to throw up. I felt my face flare with fever; sweat rolled down my temples and cheeks. I wiped my face and retched into the toilet again. My elbows and knees began to burn. Had someone slipped a mickey into my drink the night before or was my unexpected illness merely a coincidence? I groaned and staggered back to bed.

'Fuck this,' said Louis, after he'd risen, showered, and shaved. Since we'd arrived, he'd complained about the bottling plant noise several times, but the staff at Reception had continued to pretend that they did not understand him. He swept out the door and returned twenty minutes later with two male porters, who proceeded to collect our luggage and convey it along the winding paths and narrow lanes, with Louis and me following, until we came to the main building of the hotel complex. We trailed the porters up a flight of stairs and onto the second floor. One unlocked a door and we were ushered into a huge suite with floor-to-ceiling windows. There were separate living and dining areas, a kitchen, bedroom, modern bathroom, and, most importantly, air conditioning. A wide terrace ran the length of the apartment, affording stunning views of Apia Harbour. 'This best room in hotel,' assured one of the porters. 'This best room on island.' Before they left, Louis palmed them each a tip.

By this time I was so dizzy and disoriented that I staggered into the bedroom and sat on a sofa. Louis sat beside me and rested a hand on my forehead.

'How the hell did you manage this?' I asked, gesturing vaguely around the apartment. 'A bribe?'

Louis grinned and shook his head. 'I told them I was writing a travel article for the *Sydney Morning Herald* about Samoa and their hotel. Suddenly, for some reason, they could understand my English perfectly.'

The cool air and silence were a blessed relief. Louis returned to the living room and I decided to take a nap. I pulled the satin bag of sex toys from my case, popped them into a bedside drawer, and collapsed onto the queen-sized four-poster. There would be no love-making today or tonight, or even the following morning. I was still wracked with nausea and my joints were on fire.

The next four days passed in a hallucinogenic spiral of sweating, spewing, and shitting. I was unable to eat and so began subsisting on martinis and Panadol. The only reception I could find on the TV was a cable channel that showed one movie repeatedly on a loop. Called *Pay it Forward*, it was about the karmic fortune gained by committing good deeds to virtual strangers. I continued to read the local papers daily, following updates on the feral dog epidemic, and the recent spate of unexplained murders. A wife and mother of two had been discovered the day before, stabbed to death on her kitchen floor. The woman had had no known enemies and the police, perplexed, could find no motivation. A concerned neighbour, however, had seen a blonde-haired woman running from the crime scene and escaping on a child's bicycle.

Louis spent most of his time in the living room, researching

Samoan history. The screenplay he was writing was an adaptation of Robert Louis Stevenson's novella *The Beach of Falesa*, which Stevenson had written in his home, only a few miles away. The story was about a European man who gets conned into marrying a local girl who secretly is cursed. Louis, too, read the papers each day and discovered an advertisement for a cabaret show, featuring the local *fa'afafine* exotic beauties, at one of the nearby hotels. We hadn't experienced any Samoan culture since we'd arrived five days before and so that night I forced myself from bed, showered, and dressed, and accompanied him to the event.

The show was to take place inside a long pavilion with a stage at one end. We sat at a bamboo table at the front and ordered martinis. Curtain Up was advertised for 8pm sharp, but by 9.05 the black velvet drapes remained unmoved. After ordering our third cocktail, we heard some yelling from the back of the pavilion and presently a drag queen in her mid-40s, wearing fishnets and a sequined miniskirt, came clacking in high heels down the aisle, calling to someone behind her, 'Fuckin' hurry up!' We turned to see a chubby white man in his late 20s, wearing cargo pants and runners, struggling to carry all of her luggage and equipment: a 1950s beauty case, a cassette player, several garment bags trailing feather boas. They both ran up the stairs and disappeared backstage. Five minutes later, music began to swell through the pavilion and she appeared from behind the curtain and introduced herself as Fifi. She was wearing a red satin gown, her black beehive sitting like a turret on her head, and holding a microphone. But when she recognised the opening trumpets to Shirley Bassey's 'Big Spender', she lifted the mike and yelled backstage, 'Not that one, you stupid cunt! The other one! My opening!'

Suddenly, the song stopped. We heard a rattle backstage and the sound of glass breaking. She rested a hand on her hip and waited, rolling her eyes to the thatched ceiling. After a minute or so, another song was broadcast, and she launched into lip syncing 'Black Magic', by Ella Fitzgerald.

The chubby man returned from backstage and sat at the table next to ours with an older woman. Fifi dedicated most of her songs to 'my man in the front row', or to the woman next to him, whom she referred to as 'my mother-in-law.' By this time, however, we were more interested in watching the boyfriend, who knew all the words to Fifi's songs and would mouth every lyric back to her.

It was during the interval that Louis told me that he recognised him. He'd been in the newspapers back home recently. Apparently, two years before, he'd been appointed by the Australian government as a diplomat to Samoa, and had caused a scandal by having fallen in love with a *fa'afafine* and requesting to marry her. Such arrangements are common in Samoa, but not in Australian Foreign Affairs. The man had been given an ultimatum: give up the *fa'afafine* or resign from his position. He'd obviously made his choice, preferring to carry the bags of a demanding diva than a job for life in the diplomatic service. In some ways, I thought, the story sounded like a contemporary corollary to the screenplay Louis was attempting to adapt. When we arrived back at our hotel room, I threw up again, swallowed two Panadol, and flopped back onto the bed.

The following morning – our last – I was still nauseous and burning with fever. Louis and I sat up in bed, drinking tea and reading the local papers. There'd been two new developments in the series of murders: firstly, the American FBI had been called in to investigate the serial homicides; secondly, the murderer of

the wife and mother who'd been stabbed two days before had
been apprehended. The female suspect who'd been seen by a
neighbour escaping the crime scene on a bicycle had turned out
to be the woman's husband: he'd managed to disguise himself by
donning his wife's kaftan and one of her blonde wigs.

Louis had one landmark to visit in order to complete his
research: the final home of the Scottish author, Robert Louis
Stevenson, a five-minute taxi ride from our hotel. Having been
a fan of Stevenson for years, especially *Treasure Island* and *Dr
Jekyll and Mr Hyde*, I insisted upon coming along, in spite of
my vertigo.

It was late afternoon by the time the cab pulled up on a grassy
rise. We climbed out into the sunshine to see a large white,
two-story home with wide verandahs, surrounded by palms
and tropical flowers. I climbed the stairs to the main entrance
unsteadily, with Louis' hand on the small of my back guiding
me. A young Samoan woman, with an American accent, met
us in the airy foyer to act as our private tour guide. Ceiling fans
revolved in lazy circles. Louis pointed to framed photographs
on the wall of Stevenson and dark skinned local natives from
the 19th century – all slim, healthy, with fine, sharp muscles
skeining their shoulders and arms. 'That's what they used to look
like,' he remarked, 'before the Westerners got to them.' Louis
added that Stevenson had been highly critical of the European
officials appointed to rule the Samoans, and had bonded with
the local natives well, adopting the name Tusitala, meaning
'storyteller' in Samoan.

Our tour guide was clearly bored with her job. She showed
us through the home that Stevenson had built for himself and
his family, gesturing casually at paintings and ornaments. In
a monotone she explained that the author's wife, Fanny, ten

years his senior, had been married twice before and had been a widow with two children at the time of their marriage. Due to the author's failing health, he and his family, including his now-widowed mother, made several peripatetic journeys throughout the Pacific in search of a new home. It was thought the climate of Upolo would be efficacious. His decision to marry the older widower, however, and to settle in the tropics, had turned out to be a disaster. While he may have written such important works as *The Beach of Falesa, Catriona,* and *The Ebb-Tide* on the island, the guide explained that Mrs Stevenson had a rapacious taste for the finer aspects of life, demanding expensive extensions to the house, sumptuous furniture and ornaments imported from Europe, and all the best china and cutlery. As the guide explained Fanny's extravagant tastes, I felt my stomach flip with nausea. 'He worked himself to death,' concluded the guide. 'He couldn't keep up with all her demands.'

It always disturbed me to hear stories of talented writers and artists who'd married the wrong partners, partners who cared little about the effort required to produce the work, but who were happy to exploit the results. Pausing in an open doorway of his study, gazing at his wooden writing desk, I felt bile beginning to rise in my throat.

'Where exactly did he die?' I managed to ask, leaning against the doorjamb.

The guide's eyes grew wide. 'Well, this is a coincidence. Right on the spot where you're standing now!'

We returned to the hotel to pack our bags. Even though Louis had secured a late checkout, when we walked into our suite we discovered four maids variously vacuuming, sponging the bathroom, sweeping the terrace, and polishing the furniture. They didn't want to rush us, they explained, but they needed extra time to prepare the suite for some very important guests who were about to arrive. As the maids swarmed around us in a frenzy of cleaning, Louis and I threw our belongings into our suitcases and zipped them up. We ended up leaving the suite at the same time as the maids, who locked the door behind them. 'Hey?' I asked one of them, as she dropped the key in her pocket. 'Who are the very important guests taking over the suite?'

'You know about all the murders lately on the island?' she asked. I nodded and told her I did. 'The FBI, they coming from America. They stay in this suite for all of the week.'

The shuttle to the airport wouldn't leave for another hour, so we stored our luggage at Reception and repaired to the bar for final drinks. We'd barely ordered our first round, however, when I heard a man's voice shout from one corner, 'Why the hell haven't you called me yet?!'

I turned around to see standover man Paul striding towards us. He was frowning, fists balled, as if he wanted to have a brawl with both of us right there and then. I felt myself paling and tried frantically to think of an excuse. 'I've been really sick,' I blurted. 'The whole week.'

'She's been ill,' added Louis. 'Vomiting, fever, diarrhea—'

Paul narrowed his eyes and looked me up and down. 'You've lost weight,' he added. 'Are your joints aching?'

I nodded and leaned on the bar. 'They feel like they're being roasted over a fire.'

Paul nodded and bustled us back to a couch where four of his mates were sitting. They made space for us both and Paul made an announcement. 'These are the guys I was telling you about. They didn't ring because,' he pointed to me, 'this one's got dengue fever.' The men all glanced at me, shook their heads, and groaned.

'What's dengue fever?' I asked, as Paul handed me a martini.

'It comes from a mosquito bite. Like malaria. But the strains on this island are strong enough to kill a man.'

Three hours later, as we were flying southwest over the Pacific, Louis broke out in a sweat and developed a fever. His knees began to burn and he writhed in his seat like a man possessed. As I reached into my backpack to find some Panadol for him, the bag seemed curiously empty. I placed my hand on a familiar paperback novel, a spiral notebook, my toiletries. But something was missing, and as I pulled the Panadol from an interior pocket, I realised with horror what I'd left behind.

'The sex toys!' I said to Louis. 'I left them back at the suite. They're still inside the bedside drawer!'

I expected him to be angry, or at least frustrated, by such an obvious oversight. Clearly, in those early days of love, I didn't know him well.

He wiped the sweat from his brow and burst into laughter. 'Well, the FBI are going to have a good time tonight!'

LILY KING is the author of four novels, *The Pleasing Hour*, *The English Teacher*, *Father of the Rain*, and, most recently, *Euphoria*, a finalist for a National Book Critics Circle Award and the winner of the Kirkus Award. Her short fiction, essays, and reviews have appeared in many publications, including the *New York Times*, *The Washington Post*, *The Los Angeles Review of Books*, *Ploughshares*, and *Glimmer Train*. She lives with her husband, Tyler Clements, and their two children in Maine – when they are not traveling.

Peru, 1996

LILY KING

I was dating a guy who was hard to read. The first real sign that he liked me, apart from the fact that he asked me out on dates, came when he pulled away from a kiss in his car and said, 'I want to go on a road trip with you.'

We were in our early thirties, with jobs and rents to pay, but we were nomadic in spirit. Neither of us had ever bought a piece of furniture. What little we owned had been acquired from other nomads on their way out of town. We both wanted to be writers. We wrote in the mornings, and in the afternoons he coached crew at Boston College and I waited tables in Harvard Square.

Our first trip was to Provincetown, at the tip of Cape Cod. It was early spring, cold. We stopped at a beach and he pulled a fishing rod out of his trunk. We pawed at each other in the sand, everything brand new. That summer we drove to Maine to see my family, Cleveland to see his. Then, in October, we decided to go to Peru.

I had a good friend in Lima, someone I'd taught with in Spain a few years earlier. Marcy was teaching at the American school there and living with her Peruvian boyfriend, Leo. She'd been urging me to get down there for a while.

It was a good time to get away. I'd just finished another draft of my first novel. I needed to leave it behind and clear my head. When I got back, I'd have to decide if it was finally ready to try to publish. It was also a good time to figure out this relationship with Tyler. We'd been going out for eight months by now, but our feelings were nomadic, too, hard to pin down. Or at least hard to talk about. We were very similar. We were wary of commitment. We ached for new experiences. We feared routine, conformity, and, most of all, the end of our youth. Of course we didn't say any of this – we didn't know how. We barely knew it ourselves.

We took an overnight flight to Lima. Though there is only a one-hour time difference, it felt like six. My memories of Marcy's and Leo's apartment are dim: white walls, busy street. Tyler and I slunk off to our fold-out couch in their living room any chance we got. Neither of us had traveled in a while. We were out of practice.

They showed us all around the American school and took us to a few casinos. Marcy had many guidebooks. We plotted out our trip at their kitchen table.

On Monday they went back to work and we flew to Cusco, the Incan capital. When the flight attendant opened the door and depressurized the cabin, my lungs sucked up air in a desperation I'd never felt before. I could not get enough oxygen. Everything sparkled, grew gray, then slowly went back to normal. My heart was pounding. We're at eleven thousand feet, Tyler told me.

We walked around Cusco slowly, pausing to gather strength at the bottom of the steep hills, stopping to catch our breath halfway. We drank *mate*, which was supposed to help with altitude sickness.

In the States I was broke. All my savings had gone into this trip. But of course I didn't know broke, real broke. The poverty in Cusco was extreme. Children aproned us wherever we went, pleading with us to buy their packages of Chiclets or Kleenex. Once we stopped in an alley to look at a furry rug then moved on, and the woman folded it up in her arms quickly and followed us. *No, gracias*, I said. *Lo siento*. But she didn't stop. She followed us moaning and weeping until we bought it.

We found a guide named José to take us to Pisaq, a town in a valley beyond the mountains to the north of the city, and to some ruins nearby. In Pisaq it was market day, with rows of tables of alpaca hats and paper fans, vegetables, fruits, and poultry. Small children in traditional clothing flocked to us, each with a puppy or two under bright cloaks. They wanted to pose for photos. José told me to buy a big bag of wheat muffins instead of giving them money. They took the muffins one at a time, gingerly, then disappeared. Tyler and I ate at a table at the back of the market: noodles with hot aji sauce and salty potatoes and stuffed peppers. Tyler drank *chicha*, a beer made from corn. José laughed as he explained that one of the ingredients of *chicha* was saliva, which served as an enzyme to break down the starch.

Amid the ruins José spoke passionately about the Incas and their beliefs. He told us they had symbols for time: the serpent for the past, the puma for the present, the condor for the future. On the way back to Cusco he pointed out the face of a mountain with Inca terraces and paths that formed the shape of a condor. People, he said, went to the foot of this mountain to die, to be closer to the talons of the condor which would carry them off.

From Cusco we took a train to Aguas Calientes. The seats

bounced like mini trampolines. Tyler got into a conversation
with a German woman about spirituality and the unconscious.
Villages flashed past. We went inside a mountain and came out
again. Enormous ice peaks appeared. Tyler and the German
woman scrambled for their cameras but it vanished and we were
inside a mountain again. I could hear the German woman tell
Tyler that now was not the time to discuss her past lives.

Thoughts of the novel I'd written came to me in waves, like a
disturbing scene I'd witnessed and could not forget. That novel
had been my life for nearly six years. In that time, I'd moved
from New York to Spain to California to New Hampshire to
Massachusetts, but the novel had been my home. I'd had nine
jobs and a few boyfriends, but the novel had remained steady.
I didn't know who I was without it. And yet I didn't know
exactly what *it* was. Was it any good? What if it stank and no
one wanted to touch it? Would I do it again? Would I keep
moving from place to place, keep switching jobs and boyfriends,
keep waiting tables, smiling for tips, kowtowing to managers,
overdrawing my bank account every month? My friends were
starting to have real salaries. They were starting to send me
wedding invitations. Some were even having babies. Their
choices were incomprehensible to me. But my own were starting
to feel incomprehensible, too: I was tying on a black apron every
afternoon; I was sneaking mushroom soup and crème brûlée
from the kitchen to the wait station when no one was looking.

Leaving your life, leaving the country, cracks you open. You
start hearing a voice inside that you haven't been listening to,
or that you've been listening to so long that you no longer hear
it. Mine was, I want. *I want* I want I want. I wanted so much.
I wanted my own life of my own design. I wanted my own

apartment (I couldn't afford it – I lived with my sister and her boyfriend) and a dog. I wanted a relationship that worked, that lasted. I only half-believed that existed, and if it did, I wasn't sure I was capable of it. I wanted to publish my novel. I wanted to begin my life as a writer, whatever that meant.

Tyler was struggling with the same questions. He was having similar thoughts about his writing, his job at BC, his future. But we didn't talk about this. We were writers but we didn't yet know how to say the most important things out loud. Since we'd arrived in Peru, we seemed to be not coming closer, not bonding as nomads, but moving apart from each other.

On the train I felt him getting dreamy and abstract, drifting farther away. If I weren't there I wondered if he would go off with the German woman, learn about his own past lives.

Aguas Calientes sits at the bottom of a gorge. Mountains, the eastern edge of the Andes, bear down on the small village from all sides. We got off the train and I felt some sort of pull. I could instantly imagine staying here, teaching at what must be a tiny school, giving children more than change or wheat muffins. It was just a tourist spot, the only place from which to catch a bus to Machu Picchu, but I was entranced.

But within a few hours Tyler was sick. Very sick. The *chicha*, we decided. The saliva beer. All evening I went back and forth to the little store, for water and Gatorade (he was dehydrating from all the vomiting and diarrhea), for Tylenol (he was burning up), and anything else the woman at the counter told me would help. At one in the morning, I woke up the man in the room behind the front desk to ask for a doctor. I was scared. He'd gotten so weak so quickly. He was lying on the tiles beside the toilet bowl, pale green and slick with sweat. The doctor never came.

By morning the crisis had passed. He was not going to die.

I was not going to have to call his mother from a payphone in Aguas Calientes and tell her that her son had died from drinking a foamy beer with spit in it.

At breakfast when the food came, the anxiety I didn't feel the night before flooded through me and I had to leave the table. I walked around the square several times to get my heart rate down. The sun couldn't get past the mountains. The whole town was cast in blue-black shadow. These mountains seemed sinister to me now. They seemed nearly alive and knowing.

We took the bus to Machu Picchu. We climbed the fifteen hundred steps slowly, both of us sapped of energy. At the top the sun was bright and strong, while all around us, on every other peak, clouds darkened the trees and patches of bare rock, moving in a great wheel. It seemed like this was the reason the Incas had chosen this spot on which to build their city of stone. I couldn't feel the Incas' presence, but I could feel their strength, and their desire to be left alone.

We went back down to Aguas Calientes to wait for the afternoon train. The mountains seemed to be rising. I began to panic that this train, the last train of the day, wouldn't come. But it did, and the same German woman got on with us.

The train rattled loudly as it turned around the mountains. The German woman talked to Tyler about love, but I couldn't hear all her words. Then it quieted down and she said she liked to travel because everyone was a stranger, which felt right to her because we were all strangers on Mother Earth.

The couple facing us on the train were Peruvians from Arequipa. They were in their early forties, and tender with each other. He stroked her fingers, one by one, and the two of them seemed to fit together like pieces carved for that purpose. To sit together on a train.

Peru, 1996

A moon rose over the mountains, just past full. We flew by chipped stucco houses, squat windows, small, ribbed dogs. People stood in doorways and windows and watched the train pass. Tyler was writing. I was writing. The train seemed to speed up in the growing dark. We looked up at the moon, at each other. We were separate. We did not fit together then like carved pieces of wood. But we were sharing the same exhilaration, and it was exactly what we'd come for.

And then that connection slipped away. From Cusco we went to Paracas, a fishing town on the coast. After a few days we met up with Marcy and Leo and their colleague Barbara and flew northwest to Iquitos.

We checked in at Hotel Safari on Calle Napo, then walked down some steps at the end of the street. Beneath another, smaller moon we found the Amazon. I couldn't see it well in the dark but I could hear voices coming up from the shacks down at its edge, and long croaks and gasps of animals I didn't know. The river was just a streak of light. I barely knew what I was seeing or hearing. After a while everyone else went back up to the bar for a beer, but I stayed there, just above the smell of the water and the raised shacks and the noises that made no sense.

In the daylight the river was narrower than I had imagined; the jungle closed in on either side. We took taxis to explore the city: Belén market, Casa de Fierro, Plaza de Armas. The taxis were two-seater open carriages pulled by motorcycles. Marcy and Leo always went together. Tyler would sometimes go with me, sometimes with Barbara, and sometimes alone so that Barbara and I went together. He didn't want her to feel like a fifth wheel. Each time he chose to go with Barbara or alone, I was absurdly devastated.

But much later, after we have been married sixteen years, this

191

will be one of my strongest memories of Peru, and one of the stories I tell our children, how kind Tyler was to Barbara, how sensitive he was to her situation and how at the time I could not see it through my own insecurity and selfishness.

We found a guide, Guido, which in hindsight probably wasn't his real name, who took us in a small motorboat four hours up one of the many tributaries of the Amazon. His camp, he said, had showers and three bedrooms.

Away from Iquitos the river thinned, the air thickened. When we got there, it was impossibly hot. Irrationally hot, like it was a joke, a machine that someone would soon shut off. But it didn't shut off. It was hard to breathe. We were slathered in sweat. And Guido had lied. There were no showers, and the 'bedrooms' were five narrow mats tented with mosquito netting on a screened-in porch. So much for sex, private conversation, reconnection.

In the back of this shack there was a kitchen where people were making dinner. Being a server, I was always aware of service, of being served, and it shamed me. It was a cheap tiny rickety camp with a lying guide, but I felt I had come all this way and paid the last of my savings to feel like a lazy, rich American.

There was a baby inside crying and chickens chortling out back, and insects sawing with what sounded like slivers of steel. Further out, there were birds cawing and whooping, hundreds of them, loud and garrulous, with none of the reserve of the New England birds I was used to.

Guido and his partner, Enrique, took us through the jungle, informing us of the medicinal value of every plant and tree, and of the poison in certain ants, snakes, and spiders. They led us on a paddle down the river in dugout canoes to a tiny village on stilts. It was the dry season so their houses were two stories high until the rain came and the river rose. A few women were out in their yards combing the dirt with homemade brooms. There was a volleyball net in the center of town and Guido arranged a bet between us and some of the village women. Marcy was an excellent player. Tyler and Leo were strong, too, and they poached every ball that came in my direction, but we still lost.

Guido took us the next day to a larger village, with an infirmary and a school. We looked up at the school from the ground. Long blackboards hung on one wall and wooden desk-chair units stood in rows. Maybe I could teach here. I wanted to climb up and see what was written on the board, on scraps of paper, but we moved on.

The next night we went back to Puerto Miguel for their Saturday night dance. It was in the bodega, the only hut with a generator. They had cold beer and a disco ball. They were playing Latin pop music. We bought beers and sat at a long table. Marcy and I made friends with the teenage girls sitting on a bench nearby. With them were a few younger girls. The tiniest of them was bawling. When I asked why she was crying, a girl told me that she was scared. Scared of what? I asked. Scared of you all. I told them not to be scared of us, and two of them asked Tyler to dance. The three took to the dance floor, smiling madly the whole time. An eleven-year-old boy named Johnny asked me to dance and, after a while, even the way cool older boys, in their button-down shirts and high tops in the corner, shuffled out onto the floor under the disco ball.

On the way back, Guido drove the boat full throttle. The only light was a flashlight Enrique held, indicating with quick jerks the place Guido should go, making sure the path was free of caimans, then shutting it off so we could see by natural light. The stars exploded above us, every inch of sky lit.

·

On our last morning on the Amazon, alone in my little tent, I wrote in my journal. I wrote about how much I missed writing. I made pledges to send out parts of the novel to literary magazines, to start volunteering, to start saving for more travel. 'It has been a good trip,' I concluded, 'if only for making me want what I already have.'

We packed up and got back in Guido's motorboat. We would fly to Lima the next day. But in a basement hotel room in Iquitos that afternoon, alone with Tyler for the first time in six days, I broke down sobbing as hard as the little girl at the bodega, and we finally said so many of the things we'd been feeling but not saying for so long. It was an imperfect conversation, unskilled as we both were at really expressing our emotions. But it was a beginning.

From Lima, Tyler and I continued on to Boston, where the condor took us up in his talons and carried us swiftly into our future.

Peru, 1996

SUZANNE JOINSON is a novelist and travel writer. Her first novel, *A Lady Cyclist's Guide to Kashgar*, was translated into 16 languages and was longlisted for the International IMPAC Dublin Literary Award. Her second novel, *The Photographer's Wife*, will be published in April 2016. She lives in Sussex, England, and travels regularly, writing for a range of publications.

In a Caucasian Wonderland

SUZANNE JOINSON

'**A** man is hiding out at the Swiss Embassy at the moment. He was tipped off that he is "next for assassination", so if you see men in black coats eating sunflower seeds they are security police waiting in case he runs for it.'

My friend Alice speaks in her soft English voice as she pours Azerbaijani tea. It is minty, medicinal, delicious.

'Okay,' I say, as if this is perfectly normal.

Our maps are spread across the table in Alice's flat in old town Baku. The minaret outside the window is a thousand years old and beyond it fog folds over the Caspian Sea. Steamboats from Turkmenistan come in and out of sight. I run my finger along the blue thread of road we are about to drive along, officially the M4, known locally as Sheki Road. It runs from Baku to Mingacevir, following the course of the Southern Caucasus Mountains. We are leaving in ten minutes, but I am having an internal crisis: I am not sure I want to go, but I don't know how to confess this to Alice.

My visit to Azerbaijan has coincided with Novruz, the celebration of New Year and spring. Outside, flutes play and children run around in traditional hats, but I am far from festive as I do my final bag check: phone, iPad, charger, camera. What is it I am feeling? I know: fear.

Everything in Alice's flat is beautiful. The carpets are antiques from Kashgar and Kazakhstan. The books on the shelves are in seven different languages and yet, despite this luxurious comfort, there is an odd atmosphere. The Azerbaijanis like to know what she is doing. Her phone is tapped, emails read, surveillance maintained. I keep checking corners of her rooms for cameras.

'Are you ready?'

I zip up my rucksack. It's now or never: tell her that I don't feel safe. But she is at the door, patting her pockets, checking that she has keys, ready to go.

Alice, I say. Although I don't; I pick up my bag, walk behind her.

It was a confusion of geography. I thought I knew where Azerbaijan was, but I only looked it up on Google Maps the day before flying and it showed me something different. It wasn't nestled against Kazakhstan as I'd thought, but instead was *this* side of the Caspian. It had a border with Russia and a contested war zone with Armenia, both of which I knew about, but also two other significant borders: Iran and Iraq. As if telepathic, my dad texted at that exact moment.

Do you realise where you are going a few hours drive miles from Mosul in Iraq?

I examined the distances; he was right. I was heading straight towards the strip of the globe regularly shown in the media as full of lootings, war, fighting, kidnaps, beheadings, uprisings, jihadi brides, and death cults. In short: terror. On the other hand, I was thinking, Azerbaijan: isn't this the land of glamour, oil, songs, and Eurovision? My head awash with stereotypes and nerves, I looked again at those borders. Close to Kirkuk. To Baghdad.

I considered pulling out, but as is the way with trips, the momentum was stronger than me. To bail on Alice the day before would be mortifying, but more than that, what I couldn't shake was the feeling that *forces* told me I should not go to this part of the world, and the question was: did I believe them? Before I knew it, I was buying supplies of water from a tiny shop and walking down the cobbled steps of Baku's old town towards Alice's dust-covered 4X4.

'The thing about a road trip,' Alice says, as she swerves to avoid an oncoming Mercedes on the wrong side of the road, 'is that we are free. We can do what we like.'

'That's true,' I say without conviction. Alice's car has diplomatic plates so she can park anywhere. This is handy, but it also means people peer in to see who we are. Alice insists on smiling and speaking to everyone, whereas my instinct is to shuffle down in the seat and be as invisible as possible.

I take out my camera and video the passing blurred world to calm my tension. The oil-slicked glitz of Baku city quickly transforms into ramshackle bungalows squatting at the feet of electricity pylons. The sky clears, the sun is with us. We turn on some music. Soon there are no more houses, no trees, instead a moonscape, desert swells of land with speckles of green.

'In a few months, it'll be parched and barren,' Alice says.

I write down the names of the places we drive through: Mushvugabad, Gobustan, Jangi, Sabir. We cross the river Agsu, a trickle in the middle of a dry bed of stones. Along the roadside people wave, trying to get us to pull up and purchase things. Sheep are penned in cages with carcasses hanging next to them. There are violets for sale, spring hyacinths. We stop and buy a bunch and the powerful hyacinth smell overpowers the car. I smile at one teenage boy holding up a bag of anonymous green herbs but, as we drive on, he throws a stone and it hits the rear of the car.

In the dip of a valley, a deserted amusement park sprawls along the edge of the road. The unmoving Ferris wheel and shuttered-down cafes remind me of my home and I have a pang, missing my kids, who might be walking along the seafront now.

'So is it very Islamic where we are going? Should I have brought an abaya?'

'It's practising Muslim, of course. In Baku it's a fairly relaxed version; in the mountains, it's more Caucasian.'

I have no idea what this means. Alice looks at the clock. We are meeting one of her friends for lunch in the town of Shamakhi, which is, I am told, famous for divine carpets and tin roofs and carpentry.

'Perfect timing,' she says as we roll into the car park of an unassuming cafe that has the pit-stop look shared by roadside diners the world over: dodgy toilets, tired-looking families, adequate food, smokers smoking.

Alice's friend is a writer named Ayten Caravanshaz and we three chat about books, life, travel. We eat eggs scrambled with tomatoes and drink chai. We are the only women in the cafe aside from a couple of babushkas with tiny children on their knees opposite. Men sit in small groups talking quietly. Our conversation turns to Iraq, Syria.

'You realise,' Ayten says, lighting a cigarette, 'that many here think that Isis and terrorism are created by the British to make trouble.'

'Really?' I say. 'Is that how you see it?'

She nods. 'How do you see it?'

Alice looks carefully at me.

'Somehow the world feels hysterical. More unstable than ever.' I want to articulate how strange it is to be overwhelmed with fear like this. I've crossed borders between the Palestinian Territories and Israel, I've travelled through Mongolia and Northwest China, across the whole Middle East. I don't know why I am nervous here. Is the world more hostile than it previously was? Or have I changed, become fearful?

'If I listened to the UK Foreign Office advice, I wouldn't go anywhere now. I ignore it because I want to travel, but I'm not a brave foreign correspondent or one of those camera guys taking pictures with bombs flying around their heads.'

Alice scoffs. 'You certainly are not.'

'What am I, then?'

'You are a writer,' Ayten says. 'You travel in a different way.'

In my head I picture a real travel writer, not an imposter like me: a person endlessly drawing maps on napkins, catching buses instead of taxis, hitchhiking, speaking obscure languages, unaffected by borders or politics. Not sliding down the seat of the car to avoid eye contact with men on the streets. Alice and Aytan begin to discuss a trip they are planning in the summer to cross the Iranian border.

'Really?' I say. 'Iran?'

Alice looks at me with surprise. 'Yes. I believe that people are friendly, if you just speak to them. It helps if you have the language of course and my Farsi isn't great, but you do your best. Doors open. They really do.'

I listen to their plan to visit Lankaran, the Azerbaijani region that borders Iran and the excursions they will make across what sounds like a final frontier, the very definition of inaccessible other-land. I excuse myself and go in search of toilets. As I navigate my way through a scrub-land behind the cafe occupied by chickens, I try to work out my anxiety: it is true that the logistics I need to put into place before I go anywhere these days are complicated, with kids and the pausing of life. Neither Alice nor Aytan has children, does that give them additional courage? I'm not sure. I can imagine both of them packing a child into a rucksack and heading off into remote hills.

When I emerge from the toilets it is as if a switch has been flipped. The weather has changed into sleeting rain, the sky a despondent grey, a low cloud trying to snow.

Aytan bangs her fist on the bonnet of the car and then waves. 'Enjoy *Mabrouk Novruz*! Jump over the fires!'

'Are you really going into Iran?' I say as we trundle along the road towards worsening weather.

'Definitely.'

I can't decide if she is the sane one or me.

I have brought only one book with me on this trip: Knut Hamsun's *In Wonderland*, a description of a journey he took through Russia and the Caucasus. I read passages out to Alice as we drive. *An almost sleepless night on account of the Caucasian fever and Caucasian bedbugs...* I like the way he writes about travel. He describes a powerful need to be in fantastical strange places but, once there, he is full of an unwanted homesickness and the journey itself triggers memories of the past. When in Baku he yearns to reach Iran, Persia generally, but he never gets there.

'By the end,' I tell Alice, 'it is not the Caucasus he calls Wonderland, but his home, Nordland. He went in a big circle and ended up home.'

The sleet is now real snow.

'How annoying,' Alice says, as the road climbs and twists. 'It had to start snowing just as we get to the higher, thinner bits of the road.'

Up on a higher plateau, our visibility is now perhaps two metres. We are inside the cloud and on Alice's side there is a steep drop into a ravine. We stop talking to concentrate; she is hunched over the wheel, both hands gripped. Cars creep towards us with hazard lights flashing and I remember something I read once by WG Sebald: *If you are travelling along the road and things come in from the sides to offer themselves, then you are going in the right direction. If nothing comes you are barking up the wrong tree.* What, then, does it mean if you can't even see the sides of the road due to terrible weather? We edge along and then, in that mountain way, everything lifts. The flurry is behind us. We turn off the Sheki Road, into an unsigned mountain road which heads upwards into the Ismaili region of the Caucasus range.

The road follows the valley for some time before climbing properly. My ears pop, we turn a corner, and the mountains are grey slate-creviced scars, volcanic, dreamlike. The river bed below us is mostly stone, but the view is deceptive; the water must be wider and fiercer than it looks because the sound of it resonates across the slate and quartz. I write down the name of the river, Girdimanchai, and on we climb. Each twist of the road reveals Tolkien-like mountain passes more dramatic than the last. I can hardly breathe with the beauty of it and for the first time, I relax. I let go of home and worry, remember why I travel. The road is so high now that I can't bear to look down. We drive past a terrifying footbridge over the ravine that surely nobody would use and then we come to the end of the tarmac. Our destination, the village of Lahic, is 1376 metres high, but we are not there yet.

'Where's the village?' I say.

'Up there.'

From here on the road is a track, but there is a problem ahead. There has been a landslide, chunks of the mountain have fallen and blocked the road. Alice turns off the engine. We get out. I glance up to see if more rocks will fall, but for the moment all seems steady. The road at this point is too narrow to turn the car. Alice would have to reverse all the way back, on the twisty-turny road. We look at one another and even calm Alice is frowning.

As if answering a wish, we hear a clip-clopping noise behind us. A man on a pony comes towards us. Alice shouts out, 'Salaam!' The man puts his hand on his chest and answers with a formal, 'As-salamu alaykum.' Alice speaks to him in Azerbaijani, whispering to me that he speaks Tat, although they have found a way to communicate.

'Tat?'

'An old Persian dialect. There's no alphabet.' Alice, language geek, turns back to the man.

'He says these landfalls get moved very quickly, but it won't be today now.'

'What does that mean?'

'We have to leave the car for now and climb over the rocks,' she says. 'We'll walk up to the village and sort out the guesthouse, get the car in the morning.'

It takes us an hour and a half to complete the walk to Lahic. We are greeted by chickens clucking and cockerels crowing. The guesthouse is a welcome place: warm, a fire glowing, a great relief, but without the car our only way of getting out of here is to walk. What if the weather changes? We have tea and the ubiquitous plate of sugary baklavas and then as the sky darkens we head to the village square to check out the Novruz celebrations.

Lahic's square is flanked by a mosque, stables, a building with a sign above a door that Alice translates: 'Man's Club'. Music blares and people are gathered around a pile of tree branches waiting to be lit. The tradition is to jump over the fire. Small boys run around setting off bangers, and every now and then a firework is released by a child, directly into the air above, or simply thrown onto the ground in front of the fire so that everyone ducks and covers their ears. Health and safety measures are not remotely considered.

I stand near a wall as Alice wanders into the middle. It occurs to me that we are the only women, certainly the only foreigners. Presumably the village women and girls stay away or are kept inside. The fireworks and bangs make me jumpy. There is a cheer when the fire is lit, and more fireworks are let off at dangerous angles. A boy is looking at me. He takes a firework canister and points it at me as if it is a gun, makes a mock firing gesture. He is about six, the same age as my son; confident, cocky, he entirely belongs here, thinks he is a man already. He disappears.

Alice is close to the fire, taking photographs, talking to one of the older men. The boy reappears, this time holding a rifle. Being British, I'm always shocked by guns because I rarely encounter them – but I have never before seen a child with a gun. I push myself against the wall hoping it is a toy. He waves it in the air, runs towards the other children, all wearing matching woolly hats, thick jumpers. Then he turns towards me, puts his rifle to his eye, trains its viewfinder on me. Somehow I know it is not a toy. I look over for Alice, still near the fire, laughing, her face lit up and pretty. The men here don't scare me, they seem reserved, private, cautious, but that boy does.

Perhaps there is some truth to Alice's theory that people are friendly if you just talk to them, but does this extend to children? To wild-eyed boys with no perspective to bring them caution? The bonfire is full-blaze and a man pokes a pitchfork into it, pushing it down into a manageable size. The kid still has his gun pointed at me. The music is loud and begins to be interspersed with a strong wail of the call to prayer. Young men jump the fire, leaping stags, each hop raising a cheer. They are burning away the troubles of the last year, cleansing themselves for the year ahead.

I don't belong here, it's true, against the mosque and the mountains and the men, this isolated community who do not even mix with Azerbaijanis let alone the British, but I am so blessed to visit and see it; I could at least be friendly, non-judgemental. Alice turns and waves. Because she shows no fear, she is part of the scene. I am the one cowering at the edge unable to find a way in, jumping out of my skin every time a firework is lit. It is easy to be scared: snowy ravines, mountains collapsing, terrorists behind every boulder, but I need to shake away the feeling that the planet is pure danger. If I believe that, then it will be.

I walk towards the boy with the gun. He does not change his position. It is a real rifle, but I choose to believe it's not loaded. I smile at him. He gives me a blank-dead look and then, as children do when an adult takes control, he is more comfortable, he shrugs, flings the rifle over his shoulder, and runs away to throw bangers at his friends.

I don't jump over the fire, I can see that women aren't supposed to do that here, but I hold my hands out and feel the heat from the flames. Men jump, and then rush to the mosque, and in an instant the square has entirely emptied as all the men have gone to pray. The craggy mountains around us are black triangles and shadows. Alice comes towards me.

'Time for a tasty plate of *plov*?'

'Sounds good.'

We return to the guesthouse. Objectively, it's true: I am in the bad-lands where anything could happen, but this is something I have come to believe: the world would be a much darker, more misunderstood place if it weren't for wandering types willing to cross over into parts of the map that politicians tell us are no-go. The further I travel, the dearer my home is, the Wonderland I return to from faraway places, but without the different perspectives travel brings me, I would never remember that safety is not necessarily staying at home. The fire has been stoked inside the guesthouse and two glasses of the best Georgian wine are waiting for us.

ALEXANDER McCALL SMITH is the international bestselling author of more than 100 books, the latest of which is *Emma*, a modern retelling of Jane Austen's *Emma*. His beloved, bestselling No. 1 Ladies' Detective Agency series, the Isabel Dalhousie series, the Portuguese Irregular Verbs series, the 44 Scotland Street series, and the Corduroy Mansions series and numerous children's books have been translated into 45 languages. He is the recipient of numerous awards, including the Crime Writers Association's Dagger in the Library Award, the UK Author of the Year, the Saga Award for Wit, and the 2015 Wodehouse Prize. He is professor emeritus of medical law at the University of Edinburgh, has served with many national and international organisations concerned with bioethics, and holds honorary doctorates from 12 universities. He was born in what is now known as Zimbabwe and taught law at the University of Botswana. He lives in Scotland. Visit his website at www.alexandermccallsmith.com.

A Trip to Some Islands

ALEXANDER MCCALL SMITH

We have a house in the Highlands of Scotland, underneath a mountain, at the head of a long finger of sea that feels its way into the land. It is a wild and beautiful place, made all the more dramatic by the weather that comes at it directly from the Atlantic. There is rain just about every day – soft, warm rain that falls in shifting white veils, obscuring the dark shapes of the pine trees, the sweep of heather and bracken. From the window of my study I look up to a waterfall that traces a line of white down the mountainside, loud and throaty after prolonged rains, otherwise wispy and quiet, disappearing here and there behind rocks and vegetation. From the front of the house we look out across the sea loch to the next peninsula, Ardnamurchan, to where Ben Hiant rises to make a jagged, irregular horizon. Ben Hiant means *Holy Mountain* in Gaelic, the language that used to be spoken so widely here, but which now is reduced to small clusters of native speakers and those outsiders who master its liquid vocables because they cannot bear to witness the death of yet another language.

Few live where we have this house, *more deer than people*, as they say in that part of Scotland. The peninsula was once home to almost four thousand people; now there are just over three hundred. The Highland Clearances, one of the great tragedies in Scottish history, saw small farmers – crofters – cleared off the land in the early years of the 19th century. Large landowners used their muscle to drive out their tenants, getting away with it, as one Scottish historian puts it, because the poor had no lawyers. They acted with callous ruthlessness: houses were burned and livestock dispersed as the Highlanders were shifted to make way for sheep. What had once been a land of small farmers, living on such livestock as they could raise and such bounty as the sea would yield, now became a depopulated wilderness, largely forgotten by the rest of Scotland, haunted by the ghosts of its vanished community.

This journey started at that house. It was not a long trip – just under two hours on the way there and slightly less on the way back – but it led to a most extraordinary consequence. Of course that can happen: the start of one journey may conceal the beginning of a much bigger one. And that bigger journey may be something you never expected, however experienced you may be in the ways of the world.

It was midsummer, and we had left our main home in Edinburgh to spend some time in our Highland house. I was looking forward to a few weeks during which I would do all the things that people who go off to a summer cottage like to do: walking, some fishing, catching up with some of the reading that the busy world stops you from doing. My wife, Elizabeth, was hoping for good weather to spend time in the vegetable patch she had set up – a small square of uneven hill land protected by a high deer fence. Where we are, the deer will determinedly eat anything you plant; they have as little respect for flowers as they have for anything else that manages to grow – it is all fair game to them.

Peter, our neighbour in this bucolic spot, has a small estate on which he grazes cattle and hopes to generate hydro-electricity. He lives for most of the time in Northern Ireland, but he and his wife make their way over regularly in his own boat to spend time in Scotland. It was he who suggested the trip. 'It's weather for the Cairns of Coll,' he said. 'We could go out there together – you in your boat, us in mine.'

I consulted Elizabeth, who agreed that we should accept the invitation. She made flasks of tea and prepared buttered rolls. 'Where exactly are we going?' she asked.

Although I had a boat that I used regularly to make the journey to Mull, I had not at that time done much exploring of the coast. 'The Cairns of Coll. I've looked them up on the marine charts. They're just north of Coll.'

As it happened, Coll itself was an island we had visited before. It lies in the Hebridean Sea, some fifteen miles off the coast of mainland Scotland. Beyond it, across the stretch of sea known as the Minch, are the Outer Hebrides – the line of islands that marks the very edge of Europe. There is nothing further out, apart from the St Kilda group, forty miles or so off the Isle of Lewis – an astonishing cluster of tiny islands from which the last remaining inhabitants had been evacuated in the 1930s.

We set off at eleven in the morning and were back on the mooring in the late afternoon, not that it would have mattered had we been much later. In the middle of a Scottish summer, especially at those latitudes, it barely gets dark, even at midnight: white nights, as the Russians call them.

There were two boats. Peter, his wife, his teenage children, and a couple of the children's friends were in his boat, and Elizabeth and I were in ours. The boats were both *ribs*, open craft with engines capable of propelling them through the water at thirty knots or more if one was in a particular hurry. Peter's boat was more powerful than mine but we kept more or less together as we made the crossing. The sea at that stage was in one of those states that go with high pressure – a flat blue field, almost glassy, only moving slightly, as if there were a heart beating gently somewhere deep beneath the surface. Here and there sea birds sat upon the almost imperceptible swell as if it were their private counterpane.

Our route took us across the top of the Sound of Mull, that long channel that runs down between the island and the Morvern Peninsula on the mainland. As we rounded the point of Ardnamurchan Head, the most westerly tip of the British mainland, a cluster of distant islands appeared to the north. The grandest of these was the Isle of Skye, with its great mountains, the Cuillin, dominating the far horizon. The mountains were of a delicate, attenuated blue, as distant mountains might be in a well-worked watercolour. In front of them, much closer to us, were the Small Isles, the beautifully named Rhum, Eigg, Canna and Muck. The island of Muck is the smallest of these, a tiny patch of green inhabited by only a handful of people but much loved by them and by the visitors who make their way out there.

Our destination, though, lay to the west rather than the north. There was Coll, now visible on the horizon – a long smudge of land with a ridge of small hills to give it salience above the flatness of the sea. And just above Coll, separated from the main island by a channel of half a mile or so, was a small group of islands, some no more than rocky islets. These were the Cairns of Coll.

Not far from our destination we saw a small fishing trawler, and stopped to ask the skipper whether he had anything to sell. He did. A few hours earlier he had hauled up his creels and he had as many prawns as we would care to buy. These were what many would call large shrimps – the size of the jumbo shrimps served with Caesar salad in a thousand hotel dining rooms. In these parts they are called prawns and we bought a good bucketful of them before setting off again to complete our journey.

As we drew closer I was struck by the beauty of the Cairns of Coll. If one were to imagine an archetypical romantic island, complete with lagoons, pristine white beaches, and crystal-clear water, one would dream up something like the little island that we now approached. I could barely believe that such a place existed outside the doctored Caribbean travel brochure. But here it was in Scotland, made golden by the sparkling sunlight of that day – a place of such utter perfection that it seemed almost wrong to set foot upon it.

But we did. We secured the boats to rocks with grappling hooks and waded through the last few feet of water. And then, against a rock further up the beach, we laid a small fire of driftwood and cooked the prawns for our lunch. As we ate, inquisitive seal heads popped up in the water behind us, watching our moves with undisguised curiosity. There were more than ten of them – and others of the colony could be seen further out.

The teenagers swam in a lagoon concealed behind a flower-embroidered hillock. They allowed the outgoing tide to carry them round a small point and then swam back onto the beach. The seals accompanied them like friendly lifeguards, interested in rather than resentful of this intrusion upon their world.

There was not a soul about – apart from us. Nor was there any sign of the works of man, other than an unattended lighthouse on the most northerly of the islands, a human structure than seemed utterly right in its setting.

After our picnic we explored the island on which we had landed. From the tops of the highest hillock, one could look out over the other islands in the group, all very small, some with patches of white where there were beaches, some very rocky, with the merest covering of vegetation. On the far side of the outer islands, the sea had begun to break, white against the black of the rock: a wind had come up and, with it, waves.

We began our journey back. The waves that had sprung up were not high, and they were rolling in the direction we were following. We rode them easily and they aided us in our passage home. Off to the south was the coast of Mull, seeming so large after this pocket-sized universe on which we had spent the last few hours. Before us, stretching out, were the mountains of Ardnamurchan and Morvern, the landscape I have come to love so much.

Over the couple of years that followed, we visited the islands occasionally, landing in the same place as we had landed that day. I enjoyed showing them to friends who visited us, and they were usually delighted by the discovery of what struck most people as an enchanting – and enchanted – place. Then, one morning in Edinburgh I opened my copy of the *Scotsman* newspaper and read that the Cairns of Coll were for sale. I had never really thought of them as being owned by anybody, but they obviously were, for here was the owner putting them on the market. I took the newspaper into Elizabeth's study.

'The Cairns of Coll are for sale,' I said. 'And …'

She looked at me. 'And?'

'And I want to buy them.'

There was a silence.

'I have to,' I said.

They were not too expensive – around about the price of a modest flat in Edinburgh. I was in the fortunate position of being able to acquire them, and I did, phoning my lawyer immediately and asking her to set the transaction in motion. I spoke to the seller, who lived on one of the outer islands. The Cairns had been in her family for three generations. I assured her that my motive for wanting to acquire them was to protect them. I promised her I would look after them, which is exactly what I intend to do.

They are there for people who pass by in boats to wonder at. They can go ashore if they are able, as long as they are careful of the wildlife, the birds and seals who are the true owners of these astonishingly beautiful little gems. I go there myself a few times a year and stand under that high sky and let the breath of the Hebridean Sea envelop me. I shall not allow anything to be done to them. They shall never be built upon or spoiled.

Sometimes we make journeys that seem at the time to be small and unimportant ones. But these journeys may turn out to be ones that lead us along a surprising road, the outcome of which may be unsuspected, unknown, and wholly magical.

MARINA LEWYCKA was born of Ukrainian parents in a German refugee camp after WWII and now lives in Sheffield, Yorkshire. Her first novel, *A Short History of Tractors in Ukrainian*, was published in 2005 when she was 58 years old, and went on to sell a million copies in 35 languages. It was shortlisted for the 2005 Orange Prize for Fiction, longlisted for the Man Booker Prize, and won the 2005 Saga Award for Wit and the 2005 Bollinger Everyman Wodehouse Prize for Comic Fiction. Her second novel, *Two Caravans* (published in the US as *Strawberry Fields*), was shortlisted for the George Orwell prize for political writing. She has also published *We Are All Made of Glue* and *Various Pets Alive and Dead*. Her short stories have been broadcast on BBC radio, and her articles have appeared in *The Guardian*, *Independent*, *Sunday Telegraph*, and *Financial Times*. She is now working on her fifth novel. In her spare time she used to enjoy walking and gardening.

A Miracle in Luhansk

MARINA LEWYCKA

We started out from Kiev on the morning of a fine autumn day; the sky was a perfect blue dome pierced by the gilded crosses of the Lavra monastery, the trees a golden-leaved cascade tumbling down the steep banks towards the silver Dnieper River. Most visitors to Ukraine never get beyond Kiev with its lovely onion-domed churches, or the picturesque formerly Polish town of Lvov in the west. But our destination was Luhansk in the industrial rust-lands of eastern Ukraine, where tourists never go, and our road trip was also a journey through the past, through the heart of the country's vast little-known rural hinterland, and through our family's history. This is a journey that would be impossible today; this pastoral region has become a war zone and my cousin Volodya, who was my driver and companion on this trip, has become a refugee. Recalling our road trip together has a particular poignancy now.

Volodya was in a pessimistic mood as we set out; his Cossack-style moustache drooped as he informed me that the starter motor of his seventeen-year-old BMW was playing up and we had 800 kilometres to go. But at least the CD player was working, and Stella Zubkova was warbling songs of yearning as we crawled bumper to bumper on the traffic-choked Poltava Highway.

At last we left behind the dismal suburbs and the turn-off to Borispol Airport. 'Bye-bye, Kiev! How do you do, Luhansk!' cried Volodya, putting his foot to the floor. The ancient motor leaped like a stallion over the potholes in the road. Thumb on horn, foot on gas, he kept up a running commentary, waving one hand in the air to illustrate his points. Sometimes, for a particularly complicated point, he had to use both hands. Each time we overtook another vehicle, Volodya triumphed, 'There they go, those fool Belorussians in their stinky Lada – Lukashenko! Ha ha ha! There go the insolent Russians in their mafia Volga – Putin Schmutin! Bye-bye! There go those Franczooski in their showy Peugot 406 – au revoir! See! Seventeen-year-old Beyemvey beats all!'

Through the open roof, the sun poured in and the songs poured out. Stella Zubkova's voice was throbbing with passion. 'Ha! Now who is this idiot trying to overtake us?' A tank-like land cruiser with darkened windows glided by. Volodya accelerated briefly, then pulled back and shook his head. 'Go, fool! Go! Biznessmyen!' I smiled weakly and hung on to my seatbelt. Volodya thought seatbelts were for cowards.

Despite the mechanized terror on the road, the countryside we drove through was lush, drowsy, stuck in a time warp. Locals with time on their hands sat behind roadside stalls selling apples, pears, berries and cherries, freshwater fish, plastic buckets, bits of dead Ladas, and mysterious cloudy fluids in plastic bottles. As we sped by, Volodya greeted them all. *Beep! Beep! Beep!* We passed wooden cottages surrounded by hollyhocks, and willow-fringed streams where sun-burned kids splashed about in their knickers. We passed dozy cows sleeping off their lunch in the long grass, a hay wain straight out of Constable, and a child wobbling behind it on a bike. *Beebeeep!*

At Kurenka the road forked and we headed south towards the city of Poltava, which was close to the village that our grandparents came from. It was time to think about lunch. We stopped in a village with a market, where people from the surrounding countryside had brought their produce to sell. I had gotten so used to uniform pre-packed supermarket apples and tomatoes that at first these seemed misshapen and too full of life – literally. A small maggot poked its head out of a blush-red apple, looked around, then disappeared again. Volodya bought a kilo. 'Better taste,' he said.

Volodya was a connoisseur of Ukrainian fast food and made a beeline for an open-air food stall where salads, boiled eggs, sour cream dumplings, meatballs in tomato sauce, curd cheese, red cabbage, and an abundance of beetroot in various guises were on display in plastic boxes that would probably have failed a hygiene test. But it tasted like home, fresh from the garden and delicious. And for dessert there was another of Volodya's favourites: *Napoleonka*, a stack of thin pancakes held together with cream, jam, berries, and custard. Delicious. Volodya flirted shamelessly with the pretty stallholder, and got an extra portion for free. I was hoping he wouldn't be tempted by the liquor stall – his driving was already giving me the jitters – and happily he had only one shot. Then we were off again.

After a few kilometres we turned down an unmarked side road. I don't know how Volodya knew where to go, but he wove confidently between wide flat fields, a chequerboard of blue linseed flowers and golden wheat. This was the heart of the black earth country – the blood-soaked loam that armies marched through, that once fed a vast empire, where our family had survived Stalin's famine in 1932 when corn and seed-corn were commandeered to feed the workers in the cities; it still seemed eerily unpopulated.

Khutr Mikhailevka was little more than a scatter of thatch-roofed cottages along a dirt road, which had been commandeered by a cockerel strutting with his harem of chickens. Nearby was a pretty blue-washed Orthodox church. Once upon a time, long before the civil war that followed the Russian revolution, before the famine that depopulated this countryside, before our grandfather was murdered in prison, before the Nazi armies marched through here on their way to Stalingrad, long before all that, two little sisters, who became our mothers, must have knelt here side by side and prayed for whatever little girls pray for, along with our grandfather, Mitrofan, once a handsome army officer with twirled moustaches that were Volodya's envy, and our grandmother Marina. As we stood in the incense-scented silence, I noticed a tear leaking from Volodya's eye, and truth to tell, I was feeling quite sniffly, too.

There was no trace of our former family home, which we believed had been rather grand, in the village, but we met an old lady in her nineties called Evgenya who remembered the family, and even had a drawing done by my artist great-uncle hanging alongside the icons on her walls. Her two-roomed thatched cottage was damp but surprisingly warm – she showed us the gas pipe that ran through her garden, above ground between the sunflowers, dahlias, rows of beans, and maize, bringing cheap domestic gas all the way from Russia. She plied us with sugary black tea and talked about her childhood, the candlelit parties, fishing on the lake, the feasts of carp, the country dancing, the cattle, the vodka. 'Ah!' she clasped her gnarled hands together. 'Those were the happy days!'

It was late afternoon by the time we got back on the road. We had a nervous moment when the starter motor, which had obeyed at first command after lunch, took three or four tries to get going. Dark storm clouds were rolling in over the horizon, and by the time we were back on the main road raindrops were splatting on the windscreen. There was another nervous moment when the wipers took a few attempts to start, but soon they were conducting a frenzied tempo as Stella Zubkova sang of love and war and we cruised at full speed into a treacherous spray of blurred car lights and streaming water, overtaking everything, drenching cyclists and pedestrians. Volodya confided, 'Imported tyres for Beyemvey cost sixty dollars each. But I got two front tyres for sixty hryvni [about £4 at the time]. Ha ha!' I hung on to the seatbelt and closed my eyes.

Poltava, when we got there, was a dismal rain-grey town, and the huge hotel where we were booked for the night, though classed as a tourist hotel, seemed to be a bleak relic of a pre-tourist era with dingy rooms, broken bathroom fittings, thin lumpy mattresses, and sporadic hot water. We were the only guests in its one-hundred-plus rooms, and frankly, if we had known what it was like, we too might have chosen to stay somewhere else. However, Volodya unerringly tracked down an excellent fast food eatery, and after a couple of vodkas even the thin lumpy mattress didn't seem too bad.

The next day, we got up early in order to visit the Korolenko National Pedagogic Institute, where one of our ancestors had been a teacher. It is a fine Art Nouveau edifice in the style of the famous Glasgow School of Art, and Vladimir Korolenko, after whom the Institute was named, was a writer who must have been known to our great-grandparents. A Populist exiled to the Siberian wilderness in 1881 by the tsar, he wrote vivid accounts of nature and climate in the ice-bound regions. We were thrilled to find our family name painted in gilt on one of the oak panels in the Institute, and we toasted him with an extra glass of celebratory vodka over lunch.

Then it was time to move on. The car started at first go, and Volodya put its earlier tantrums down to empathy and emotional blackmail. Our next stop was to be Kharkiv, halfway between Poltava and Luhansk, the second largest city in Ukraine, an important city of the Russian Empire and a major industrial centre even today. My parents lived here in Soviet times; my father wrote poetry and my mother learned to operate a crane. There were some lovely churches dating back to its 17th-century origins, but it was mostly built up in the Soviet constructivist style. The traffic was horrendous, and we didn't deviate for sightseeing. Besides, Volodya was keen to show me a 'miracle' before we reached our destination.

Some miles west of Luhansk, following a hand-painted wooden sign, we veered off the main road again and took a track that meandered between wide fields of sunflowers and wheat, past groves of chestnut trees, suddenly opening out into a makeshift parking area where a collection of antique Ladas were parked alongside a vintage tourist bus bedecked with faded plastic flowers, Ukrainian flags, Orthodox crosses, and images of saints. Volodya pulled up proudly between a rusty Zaporozhets and a camouflage-green-painted motorbike with a sidecar, possibly a war relic: his BMW definitely put all the other vehicles to shame.

A footpath led along the edge of the field down into a woody hollow where a crowd of people were gathered beside a stream with their heads bowed. There was a low murmuring sound halfway between humming and chanting.

'They are praying for a miracle,' he said.

A moment later a black-robed priest stepped into view, carrying a blue plastic bucket and a washing-up brush. As we watched, he dipped the brush into the bucket and splashed water over the onlookers, including us.

'Holy water,' whispered Volodya as I backed away. 'Look, the water comes out of the rocks. It never goes dry.'

I looked where he was pointing. Below the trees was a cave where water burst out between the rocks and trickled down into a clear stream that wound away into the wood. As I glanced at the people beside us, I noticed a man on our left with a horribly weeping eye; the emaciated old lady beside him had hands twisted with arthritis; another man had a stump for a leg and several people were on crutches. A little boy with Down's syndrome held the hands of his parents. A girl in a wheelchair was pushed forward to receive an extra drenching. My secular heart contracted with pity. In a country without a functional health service, they had to make do with a priest with a plastic bucket and a washing-up brush.

The ground underfoot was boggy, we were standing on slippery wooden planks, and mosquitoes were whining around our ankles. Volodya pointed to a wooden hut a few metres away that housed a bath where the more seriously afflicted could immerse themselves totally.

'Would you like to try it?'

'No. NO. Thank you. Really, I feel fine.'

I felt a moment of gratitude remembering my clean, efficient, if somewhat over-crowded local hospital back home. This display of hopelessness and credulity made me depressed, but my cousin filled a plastic bottle at the source to take home some holy water for his mother, my aunty, who was in her eighty-ninth year, and feeling all the usual aches and pains of old age.

We made our way back to the car and Volodya turned the ignition key. Nothing happened. Uh oh! He tried again, and again, and again. Still nothing. A kindly Lada driver tried to help us out with jump leads, but to no avail. The war-relic motorcyclist saluted us with a gauntleted hand and roared away, a pair of crutches poking out from his side car. Dusk was drawing in and the car park around us was gradually emptying, as the faithful, healed or not, were heading home for their beetroot soup and sour cream dumplings. Feeling hungry and emotional, we munched on wormy apples as we contemplated our possibilities. At last, only the Zaporozhets and our BMW were left in the car park.

'We need a miracle,' said Volodya.

I was all for tipping the whole bottle of holy water into the radiator, but Volodya demurred. While we were arguing, a whiskery young man wearing a leather jacket and carrying a holdall and a blue bucket climbed the footpath from the spring and made his way over to the Zaporozhets. As we greeted him, we recognized the priest who an hour ago had splashed us with holy water.

'Can you help us?' Volodya asked.

The priest rolled up his sleeves and got under the bonnet. His face was shiny and optimistic, but the German-made BMW was too complex. Still, there was a time-tested fix for all such problems. He opened up his boot and pulled out a coil of heavy-duty rope with which he attached the bumper of the BMW to the Zaporozhets. Volodya took the wheel of the BMW, I sat beside the young man in the Zaporozhets, and we took off with a lurch. It seemed incredible, but the battered two-stroke Soviet car was actually pulling the BMW along a track between the sunflowers.

The priest was charming, educated, and serene, despite the burden of suffering he dealt with on a daily basis. He told me that this place, Kiseleva Beam, had been a shrine since the 18th century, when a boy was cured of blindness by these waters and a vision of the Holy Virgin appeared among the twisted tree roots above the spring. In fact there were two springs here that flowed together, one sour and one salty, to cure afflictions of the body and mind. Holy water played an important role in the spirituality of the Orthodox Church, he explained, and thousands of people came here every year to be healed. It was a privilege to serve them, he said.

As we turned off the field track onto the main road and picked up a bit of speed, there was a sudden jolt on the rope behind us and a loud insistent beeping from Volodya. We pulled over and went to see what was happening. And before Volodya could even wind down his window with a joyful grin, we could hear that the old BMW was back in business.

'See!' said Volodya, keeping his foot on the gas as the priest and I uncoupled the rope. 'It was a miracle!'

We thanked the priest from the bottom of our hearts, beeped a few more times, and then we were away.

In Luhansk, at the door of a grand but crumbling flat, we were greeted by my Aunt Oksana, whom I had never met before. I was glad we hadn't squandered the holy water on the untrustworthy car because the frail old lady looked as though she needed every drop of it. Yet meeting her here for the first time was a different kind of miracle. I clasped her in my arms and we wept as we talked about the long separation, the travels and travails of more than sixty years, the hardships, the people who had died whose sepia photographs still hung on the walls of that flat where my mother and her sister had once lived, where our grandmother Marina, after whom I was named, had died of pneumonia in 1952. Volodya was weeping too as he opened the door of the cabinet where the vodka and glasses were kept. He poured three generous measures, and topped each one up with a dash of holy water.

NATALIE BASZILE'S debut novel, *Queen Sugar*, is soon to be adapted into a TV series by writer/director Ava DuVernay, of *Selma* fame, and co-produced by Oprah Winfrey for OWN, Winfrey's cable network. *Queen Sugar* was named one of the *San Francisco Chronicle's* Best Books of 2014, was longlisted for the Crooks Corner Southern Book Prize, and was nominated for an NAACP Image Award. Natalie has a MA in Afro-American Studies from UCLA, and holds an MFA from Warren Wilson College's MFA Program for Writers. Her non-fiction work has appeared in *The Rumpus.net*, *Mission at Tenth*, *The Best Women's Travel Writing Volume 9*, and *O, The Oprah Magazine*. She is a member of the San Francisco Writers' Grotto.

The Boudin Trail
NATALIE BASZILE

It's two o'clock on a Thursday afternoon in early May, and the air inside the New Orleans airport smells like fried shrimp, mildew, and a hint of the Gulf. It's a comforting smell, at least to me, and every time I fly down here from California, the first thing I do after stepping off the plane into the terminal is inhale deeply.

If I were here by myself, I'd be on the road by now, easing into the Crescent City or flying down Highway 90 towards New Iberia where my friends live. But this trip is different: I'm on a mission. I'm meeting my mother, my dad, and my sister, Jennifer, to whom I just started talking after a two-year estrangement. I'm taking them on a drive along the Boudin Trail.

We have a lot to heal on this trip.

Jennifer's flight from Connecticut is scheduled to arrive twenty minutes after mine. We've agreed to meet in baggage claim. The carousel has just lurched to life and suitcases are sliding down the black conveyor belt when I spot Jennifer at the top of the escalator. For years we both wore short afros. People assumed we were twins. Three years ago, Jen decided to grow pencil-thin dreadlocks, and now they cascade across her shoulders. I can't help but stare. Even in jeans and a V-neck t-shirt, she looks downright regal.

It's odd to think of my mom and my sister being here in this place I've laid claim to. Louisiana is mine and I'm not eager to share it. I cringe at the thought of having to show them around the city, taking them to the restaurants and shops I frequent, the out-of-the-way spots most tourists know nothing about. I'm being selfish, I know. If my Louisiana friends had been this closed-hearted with me, I'd still be a tourist, wandering down Bourbon Street with a fishbowl filled with green alcohol hanging from a cord around my neck.

My dad is the person I should really thank for introducing me to Louisiana. He was born and raised in Elton, a tiny town one hundred ninety miles to the west. And even though he hated almost everything about his life down here – hated the humidity and the grass growing up between cracks in the sidewalks; hated how every man in his family was the pastor of a storefront church; hated Louisiana so much that he left the night of his high school graduation, set out for California and never looked back – he returned every spring to take his mother on a road trip: Grand Isle, Holly Beach, Natchitoches. Any place they could get to and back from in four days – which was all the time he could stand before he started remembering why he left in the first place. When I was in college, he invited me to tag along, and even after my grandmother died, I kept coming back.

Unlike my dad, I loved the heat and the crumbling buildings

overtaken by kudzu. I loved the endless hours my aunts, uncles, and cousins spent in church. I loved Louisiana's earthiness, her accents and her twisting bayous. I loved it all.

So while I wait for my bags, I give myself a little pep talk – *Come on, Baszile, lighten up. This will be fun.* By the time Jennifer steps off the escalator, I'm feeling generous.

'Hey, Wench,' I say and hug my little sister.

'Hey, Wench,' Jen says, hugging me back.

This is our standard hello, the way we've greeted each other since we were teenagers. But we haven't used the greeting at all lately and I can tell Jen is as nervous and relieved as I am to say the words. We used to be close. Used to call each other every day, sometimes *two or three times a day*, and then suddenly, two years ago, we stopped speaking. At the time, I was struggling to write my novel, going to grad school, and raising kids. Jennifer was divorcing her husband, writing a memoir, and leaving her university job. I don't remember the details of the argument, only that one day, neither of us picked up the phone. Days stretched into weeks. Weeks stretched into months. We didn't speak when her book was published or when my oldest daughter delivered her middle school graduation speech. We didn't speak when my dad's cancer came back a second time.

It was only after my dad landed in the hospital with failing kidneys that we finally reconciled. *It would be a shame if you two reconciled over your father's deathbed.* That's what my husband told Jen when he called to intervene. She called me a couple of days later to say she was coming to San Francisco for a conference. She asked if we could meet. I drove to her hotel near the airport and saw her through the plate glass windows in the lobby. Before I could park, she was outside, standing beside my car.

An hour later, my mother arrives dressed in pleated pastel slacks and white patent loafers, a black quilted carry-on slung over her shoulder. She greets us with her signature beauty contestant wave and flashes a toothy smile.

'Here they are,' she says, standing on her toes to kiss us. 'My two girls.' She runs her hands through Jennifer's dreads, fingering the tiny cowry shell dangling from one of them.

'Where's Dad?' I ask.

Jennifer massages her temples. Her tone is somber. 'I can't believe we're doing this.'

'Got him right here,' Mom says, and pats her carry-on conspiratorially.

A trip along the Boudin Trail was my idea. Three years ago, a friend sent me an article listing all the boudin – the mix of seasoned pork, beef, or crawfish and rice all stuffed into a sausage casing – in South Louisiana. The article linked to a website showing every grocery store, restaurant, gas station, and roadside stand along the two-hundred-mile strip between New Orleans and Lake Charles. If you planned right and had the stomach for it, the article said, you could hit every establishment in a single weekend, three days tops. The moment I finished the article, I called my dad.

'How'd you like to take a trip along the Boudin Trail?' I asked.

My dad was into slow food and 'nose-to-tail eating' decades before the lifestyle became fashionable and trendy. *Black folks practically invented slow food*, he liked to say. As a kid growing up in South Louisiana, he hunted raccoons, possums, and squirrels in the woods behind his house, then brought them home to his mother who cooked them in stews. Sometimes, he shot an animal just to see how it tasted. Once, he shot and ate a crow.

'Let's do it,' he said. 'I'd like to get home one last time anyway.' He'd just been diagnosed with Leiomyosarcoma for the second time.

Instead, he spent most of the next two and a half years cycling through hospitals and rehab centers, growing frailer every month. Until the cancer, he'd never spent a night in a hospital, never broken a bone. By the end, he couldn't walk from the family room to the kitchen, couldn't hold a fork.

Now, it's just the three of us: my mother, Jen, and me. Mom transferred some of Dad's ashes from the urn she has at home into a small wooden container no bigger than a pack of cigarettes. That container is now safely zipped in a plastic Ziploc sandwich bag. We're going to sprinkle his ashes along the Boudin Trail.

We've just tossed our suitcases in the trunk when Jennifer notices my food bags – two oversized, insulated empty totes with heavy-duty zippers and straps wide as seatbelts.

'You've got to be kidding,' she says.

'What?' I sound defensive. 'Someone has to do it.'

Dad always brought his food bags on our road trips so he could stock up. He bought boudin but also crawfish and the andouille sausage he used in his gumbo. We'd stop in a handful of towns on our way back to my grandmother's house, and by the time he purchased what he needed, we could barely zip the bags, each of which – between the food and the ice packs – weighed nearly fifty pounds. Dad treated his food bags like they were his children. He requested hotel rooms closest to the ice machine, monitored the bags' internal temperature to make sure the contents stayed cold, and carried them on the plane rather than check them as luggage.

Jennifer looks at me skeptically. 'Do you even know how to cook gumbo?'

'That's not the point.' I fold the food bags and tuck them in among the suitcases.

✈

We're hurtling down I-10 when we spot Don's Specialty Meats, our first stop along the trail. Don's used to have a single location off Highway 49 in Carenco. Recently, they built a huge operation in Scott, just off the interstate Frontage Road. The building looks more like a casino with its enormous neon red sign and sprawling parking lot. We pull between two monster trucks.

Mom takes the Ziploc bag out of her carry-on.

How *do* you sprinkle someone's ashes in a store without alarming the proprietors or the customers? The question hasn't occurred to us until just now. We step inside Don's and feel the rush of air-conditioned air against our skin. The place is packed. There's a long line of people at the counter ordering boudin to go; another dozen shoppers plunder the deep freezers and banks of refrigerators along the wall. I see no way to do this without someone noticing. And suddenly, all I can think of are the sanitation laws we're surely breaking. I'm about to chicken out when Mom comes up behind me gripping a plastic spoon.

'I got this from the girl at the counter.' She grins.

Jennifer posts herself near the front counter and keeps watch while Mom and I wander to the back corner. Mom opens the Ziploc, lifts the lid off the wooden box, and scoops out a quarter-teaspoon of what looks like tiny bits of gravel and grit. She bends low and sprinkles the cremains of my father under the last refrigerator, back far enough that no one will notice. They look pale and gray, almost like silt, against the dirty white floor tiles.

I've never seen Dad's ashes before. I think back on all the years I heard Mom scold Dad for being overweight; how he loved to walk barefoot through the garden we planted behind my house because the feel of his feet in the soil reminded him of his Louisiana childhood – and my mind can't compute. I can't reconcile those memories with the spoonful of dust.

Mom dips the white spoon into the bag again, then looks at me. 'I think we should say something.'

Her suggestion catches me flat-footed. Until now, the tone of our trip has been easy and lighthearted. We've cracked off-color jokes and reminisced about the time Dad glided right off the treadmill and broke his arm. We shake our heads in wonder at the time he took twelve Aleve tablets in one sitting. It's gallows humor, we know, but it's our way of coping. *Why are we getting serious now?* I wonder. Besides, Jennifer's the better public speaker. Three years my junior, she has always possessed a seriousness, an intensity that makes most people assume she's older. She delivered the eulogy at Dad's memorial that had everyone in tears.

'Well, Dad,' I say, fumbling for words, 'I guess this is it.'

But it isn't it.

As I stand there listening to the refrigerators hum, I think about how, before he got sick, people often mistook him for Muhammad Ali. It was easy to do. He had the presence and personality to match. If he were here now, he'd be sauntering down the aisles, his arms loaded with frozen packages of smoked boudin and andouille sausage, never bothering to disabuse staring onlookers of their belief he might be the real prizefighter. Now, standing under the fluorescent lights in the bustling store, I thank Dad aloud for letting me tag along on all those road trips. I tell him about my book. I tell him Mom's going to be okay and that Jennifer and I are talking again.

When I finish, Mom grabs my hand and squeezes.

We give Jennifer the signal – two thumbs up – and the three of us walk back to the car.

Two more stops and we've established a rhythm. The Best Stop Supermarket. Billy's Boudin & Cracklins. My mother keeps the plastic spoon. We have our goodbyes down to five minutes. We pass through Saint Martinville and scatter cremains in the parking lot of Joyce's Supermarket. Rabideaux's in Iowa doesn't sell boudin so it's not officially on the trail, but we swing by anyway because Dad swore they made the best andouille in South Louisiana. It's a tiny shop with a counter and a single display case. In a place this small we'd get busted for sure, so we mix ashes into the soil of a potted palm near the door.

The Walmart Supercenter in Jennings is our last stop before we call it quits for the night. The place is larger than three football fields and it takes us a while to find the Outdoor/Sportsman section, which is where the insulated food bags are sold. As far as Dad was concerned, you couldn't have too many, so we pick out one we think he would have liked and place it on the bottom shelf. And since we're less concerned with sanitation, we scoop out a heaping spoonful of cremains and sprinkle them liberally underneath. The cleaning crew will mop this aisle by this time tomorrow. At least we've paid our respects.

The next morning we drive to Elton, Dad's hometown. When Dad was a kid, he planted an oak sapling in his front yard. The house he grew up in has long since been razed, but the sapling is now a massive oak tree – four stories tall with roots so thick they've buckled the sidewalk.

Here is a scene: Two sisters stand at the base of an enormous oak—a tree their dad planted sixty-five years earlier. They are surrounded by twenty-five people – aunts and uncles and cousins; their great-aunt Dell, who just turned ninety-three, and a few of their father's childhood friends. Their cousin, Antoinette, steps forward and sings the first verse of 'At the Cross' – their dad's favorite hymn. Her voice is crisp and clear, a siren's voice that rises into the oak tree's highest branches. And when the rest of the crowd joins in the singing, the sound carries down the street and out to the road. The group sings two more hymns, both *a capella*, the way black folks in the South used to sing when the girls' dad was a boy. The moment has an old-timey feel.

When the singing stops, the sisters hold hands. They watch their Uncle Sonny dig a hole between the tree roots. Their mother places the little wooden box inside, and then their Uncle Charles fills the hole with concrete and places a small marble headstone over the spot.

It's done. Their dad is home.

It's a long drive back to New Orleans. Jennifer and I are speaking again, a gift of my father's illness – but no-one has much to say. We pass all the boudin joints we visited along the way but this time, we don't stop.

I don't realize how different, how sacred, a trip this has been from what I expected till I get to the airport and see them again: my food bags.

They are empty.

KEIJA PARSSINEN is the author of *The Ruins of Us*, which was longlisted for the Chautauqua Prize and won a Michener-Copernicus Award, and *The Unraveling of Mercy Louis*, which was named a 2015 Must-Read by *Ploughshares, Bustle, Bookish, Pop Sugar, Style Bistro,* and more. Her work has appeared in Lonely Planet's *Better Than Fiction*, as well as in *Five Chapters*, the *New Delta Review, Salon, Marie Claire* and elsewhere. An Assistant Professor of English at the University of Tulsa, she lives in Oklahoma with her husband and son.

My Family's France
KEIJA PARSSINEN

When my family began to fall apart, we turned to France. My parents, deep in money trouble and increasingly desperate, came up with a hare-brained scheme: rent out the Texas McMansion we couldn't afford and move our family to Brenthonne, a tiny Savoyard farming village in the foothills of the Alps. The thinking was, simply and insanely, that by moving to where we had once been happy, we would become happy again. Never mind that my parents had no jobs secured, little money saved, and no plan for schooling. Place would be our salvation; we would move into the upstairs rooms of our friends' farmhouse, and there we would recover ourselves through fresh air, good wine, and long walks in velvet green fields.

Brenthonne was to my family what the Hebrides were to the Ramsay family in Virginia Woolf's *To the Lighthouse*: a haven of peace and beauty, a vacation spot where we could leave the struggles of a difficult world behind for a few weeks every summer. Every July, we left behind the heat and dust of our home in Saudi Arabia for the cool mountain air and pastoral loveliness of rural France. At first, we stayed in a rented farmhouse, a rambling three-story place with a mossy water trough out front where my sister, brother, and I would bathe in the cold water. We children marauded around the property in nothing but our underwear, climbing plum trees to pluck the sweet fruit and let the juice run down our chins, and turning nut-brown beneath the sun. In the morning we threw open the green shutters and sang to the cows that moved lazily in the fields below. When we tired of the country, we drove a short way to Thonon-les-Bains, rented a pedal boat and glided far out onto Lac Leman, where we swam until our bodies couldn't stand the icy alpine water any longer. Floating on the lake wrapped in a warm towel prickly from air-drying on the farmhouse line, I felt happy in the way a child does: like it was my birthright, eternal and unremarkable.

Over the years, my parents struck up a close friendship with the farm's proprietors, Henri and Madeleine, and soon we were invited to stay in the family home just up the road from the old farmhouse. We had made the leap from tenants to close friends, and as formalities fell away, we reaped the benefits of cross-cultural friendship. Henri took us hunting for *champignons* in the wet field flanking the nearby creek, where we learned to distinguish edible mushrooms from poisonous ones in the shadow of a mysterious abandoned farmhouse; we were privileged with evening visits from the neighbors, who wanted to enjoy a glass of Gewürztraminer and banter with *les Américains*; and Madeleine let us harvest the bounty of their huge summer garden, bringing in bulging *tomates* and lettuce heads smelling of earth. Later, she would serve the tomatoes sliced and drizzled in a Dijon salad dressing that I have tried to replicate for years without success. Mornings, we gorged on *tartines* spread with Madeleine's homemade jam and bowls of *chocolat chaud*.

We ate long, lazy meals under the striped awning of the patio, the Alps rising to the west, lights flickering on in distant chalets as evening fell gently across the valley. The only disturbance came when my father and Henri discussed Algeria, where Henri had lost his finger in the war. My father believed Arabs were people; Henri did not. Perhaps we forgave him this bias because his wound meant he had seen things we had not. One year, we came at Christmas, hiking into the mountains to find the perfect pine tree. For lunch, we built a fire and roasted potatoes in foil, and Henri tried to scare us with stories of the fearsome *sangliers*, wild boars with tusks perfect for goring naughty children. On Christmas Eve, I dressed in black velvet and accompanied the adults to Midnight Mass, feeling very grown up, and very tired. When we returned to the house, I tasted my first champagne, but the golden bubbles disappointed me, bitter when they should have been sweet. Our visits were distinguished less by season and more by an overriding sense of joy and well-being.

I can almost forgive my parents for thinking that France would cure us, would reinstate joy in their marriage, which had grown increasingly fragile after our transition from Saudi Arabia to Texas. Tired of living in shabby company housing on the oil compound in Arabia, they built a grand home of white Austin stone filled with pink Saltillo tile. But my father struggled to find work. Savings dwindled and tension mounted. We no longer had the funds for lavish vacations to France.

When my parents told us we were moving to France toward the end of my freshman year of high school, I was thrilled. Sure, it meant I wouldn't be able to play competitive basketball any more, but I'd have the farmhouse, the garden, Henri and Madeleine, maybe even a French boyfriend who rode a moped to school. I told everyone I wouldn't be back for sophomore year and felt a swell of pride when I told them where we were going, *France*, the word so elegant and full of promise.

But we never made it to Brenthonne. At the last minute, my mother nixed the plan after her therapist convinced her it was madness, just another example of my father's faulty decision-making. In the fall, I re-enrolled at Lake Travis High School, slightly embarrassed to be back. A couple of years later, my parents divorced, and I went to college. My memories of Brenthonne grew gauzy. When I did finally make it back, I went alone on spring vacation during my junior year abroad in Scotland. While the farm was just as beautiful – the roses obscenely large and fragrant, the birch trees by the creek shimmering silver – it had a haunted quality about it now, my family moved permanently from the present to the past tense. At dinner, Henri pressed me to explain *why* my parents had divorced. *C'est fou!* He admonished them from afar. At night, I lay alone in the upstairs bedroom I had previously shared with my sister, listening to a passing train sound its whistle. The magic, I realized, wasn't just the place.

MARIE-HELENE BERTINO is the author of the novel *2 A.M. at The Cat's Pajamas* and the collection *Safe as Houses*. She is at work on several projects, including essays about the year she spent working and traveling around America in the wake of 9/11. She teaches at New York University and in the low-residency MFA program at IAIA (Institute of American Indian Arts) in Santa Fe, New Mexico. For more information, please visit: www. mariehelenebertino.com.

American Daughter

MARIE-HELENE BERTINO

We had been driving around America for a year because we were tired of 9 to 5, though we had no right to be tired. Four and three years out of college respectively, Dana quit a marketing job to do the trip, and I quit theatre. The whole thing was my idea. The reason I gave her was an ambiguous choking feeling I had in Philadelphia. I have always read too many stories whose main characters say fuck this, and leave. I was ready to say fuck this, though I had no right. But I did, and then Dana did, and then her grandfather said the eternal fuck this and left her a Buick Regal in his will. We would leave on September 13, 2001. We made a list of who we knew where and Dana bought bags and bags of dried fruit. Two days before our scheduled departure, a group of religious zealots flew two planes into the World Trade Center.

Dana called me in the middle of the night to ask if we should still go. Now more than ever, I said, it was now or never.

Kristi was Dana's childhood friend whose family had moved to Tetonia, Idaho, when they were 12. All Kristi retained from Philadelphia was the return address on Dana's regular letters. When Dana went to college, Kristi married a dry farmer named Kirt. Now she had a four-year-old daughter named Alyssa and a newborn named Wyatt.

Tetonia (population 247) was settled in the stubble of the Grand Tetons on the eastern border of Idaho. On the other side of the mountains, celebrities vacation in Jackson Hole, Wyoming. However, Tetonians aren't star-watchers. Their finicky mountain passes stay closed for most of the year, so their valley remains untouched except for the trailers that move with the weather, and the occasional flourish of small native rodents called pikas, darting under the thrush. The valley had been sucked airless the day we drove up. Alyssa was the only human moving, streaming through her yard to meet our car. Kristi swayed on birth fat in the doorway. She and Dana exchanged a hug that Dana appeared to think would be longer. Kristi gave me a hard rap on the shoulder and introduced us to Alyssa.

Alyssa had a pudgy face and a mop of orange hair. She wore a shirt with a rainbow ribbon she could tie by herself. She was tying and untying it when she asked me if I liked my eyebrows. My eyebrows are bushy, and if I let them have their way, they'd connect. People used to mention them to my mother constantly when I was growing up. I love them, though, and I told her this.

We went inside and watched television. From the car, Dana brought in her photo album that detailed the first six months of our trip. We had worked as housekeepers in Montpelier, Vermont, for foliage season, then had spent five weeks driving out to the West Coast. In San Francisco, we found an apartment and jobs – me as a barista and Dana as a babysitter for a famous musician's children. Dana is an only child, and good with kids. I'm the baby of the family. I've had to fight for food and attention, so what's mine is mine.

Dana meticulously maintained the scrapbook and expected people to look through it and be wowed. Kristi seemed uninterested, and brought Wyatt to her chest apologetically. Dana held up the book, turning the pages as Kristi nursed.

Later, we heard the loud aluminum sneeze of the screen door as Kristi's husband, Kirt, slammed in. 'Too fuckin' hot out there, Mom.' He cracked a beer. 'Lo, Dana.' He took a long swallow and looked Dana up and down. Then he said hello to me.

He told us the other dry farmers called him 'short pants' because he rode the baler every day wearing them. Every day, the ground rebelled by throwing up jags of stones and dirt as he roared by. He propped his leg onto the counter and showed us his scars. Over the years, aided by the sun, these stones and dirt had caked themselves into a second skin. Kirt's original skin color could be seen only on the palms of his hands and thighs.

After dinner, we gave Alyssa the kite we bought her in New Orleans. It was a purple butterfly that, supine amidst the ashtrays and magazine on the coffee table, seemed exotic. It looked up as if to say, where the hell am I? Alyssa wanted to fly it right away. Kristi consulted the small window above the couch.

'No wind, Alyssa.'

Later, Kirt's father arrived and we sat on the prairie scorching marshmallows over a fire. Alyssa called him Pappy and sat on his lap as he worked a marshmallow over the flames. The stars were as bright as people tell you about when you're not listening. We pulled blankets around us.

'Everybody in this valley at some point worked for my grandfather,' Pappy said. 'He and his brothers made moonshine. They'd hide it along the posts of the old road. Someone would come into the store wanting moonshine, and they'd tell 'em what post they could find it behind. That way, no one could track it to them.' He hacked up a dusty giggle and shook his head.

'Yep,' Kirt said.

'One day, a couple agents from the FBI came looking for my grandfather and found one of his brothers. He wouldn't tell them where he was. They said they'd pay him a lot of money. "Give it to me now," he said, "cause if I tell you where he is and you find him, you ain't coming back." ' Pappy and Kirt hacked up more laughter.

Father and son were long and lean and buckled in the middle by a similar brass set of initials. In fact, Pappy and Kirt differed only in that Pappy wore oversized glasses. When he told stories, they reflected the entire prairie: its horizon, the rough bushes that outlined the yard, our bonfire. It was as if each of his eyes was burning from the middle.

I allowed myself to think sloppy thoughts about America. I thought I could do worse than live a life of moonshine and hay bales. I likened Pappy to Woody Guthrie and sang old songs in my head.

Later, Alyssa slept in his lap as he told stories about a hell ride he had through Niggertown in Chicago. They had to lock their doors. Those people are nothing but animals, he said, and handed his marshmallow tenderly to his granddaughter.

Alyssa's life unspooled in front of me. I saw her outgrow the cuteness of being six to the ruddy toughness of the teen years. She'd be on a softball team, holding up a wooden bat to a camera's flash. She wouldn't leave the prairie but would slam out of the screen door over and over to whatever truck awaited, as all of her relatives' opinions solidified into walls inside her thinking, as much a part of her as the brick-red hair. I felt sorry for her in advance and wanted to take her with us when we left. Then just as quickly, I didn't care about her or her future. I yearned to leave and forget these people, who had tricked me into thinking we were in it together. It would be up to her to think beyond the mountains.

The next day Kirt announced it was time for us to meet his dry farmer friends. They'd been chomping at the bit to take a look at 'his city girls.'

'I told 'em you were fat,' he said. 'But they didn't believe me. They want to see for themselves.' He sipped from a can, legs propped over the side of the couch. It was noon and, he said, too hot to work.

The dry farmers arrived as the prairie darkened on our third night. Each man drove up in a blaze of gravel, already consuming a six pack. They leaned against their pick-ups, kicking at their tires until they were invited in by Kristi.

They sat on the counters, folding chairs, and the floor of the kitchen. One of them, a thick-fingered farmer named Meaty, listed every reason he thought we should live in Tetonia. The prairie was quiet, for one. No one would bother us, except maybe the environmentalists, who were trying to lower the hunting quota to one moose per person. But they were fighting that. He drank mud from a jug with a faded label. By midnight, Dana and I were the only ones sober. Alyssa's door squeaked open and she stood in the doorway rubbing sleep out of her eyes. We had woken her up.

Smiling, she dragged her car seat between Meaty and a young

farmer they called Face. She came up to their elbows and a couple times Meaty barely missed her head with his swinging jug.

'What's in there?' she said.

'Don't know, little lady, but they told me it's not what the label says.'

I went into the other room where Kristi sat in a recliner, nursing Wyatt. Her eyes were red from exhaustion. 'Having fun?' she said.

Kristi and Kirt's house was a tetris of three connected trailers. We slept in a fourth that stood detached in the backyard where laundry sagged on ropes. There were no other houses on the prairie. When I walked to our trailer at dawn, the sun was an orange flap, clinging to the horizon. The prairie was dark except for a stubborn rainbow pinwheel, in conversation with the sun.

In the trailer, I used our shared cell phone to dial a number in Philadelphia, though I knew he wouldn't pick up. The way I knew the waitress in Austin would launch the pot of coffee across the counter into the man sitting next to me, and that he would, flinging himself from his chair, upset my newspaper and corn muffin. The way I knew when we entered a bar in New Orleans, tired and broke and the whole city booked, we'd leave with a place to stay. The way I knew the man at the Grand Canyon would turn to his son and not his wife when he let out a low whistle and said, 'Would you believe a river did all *that*?' Somewhere I had acquired a kind of road psychic ability. I had theories as to why that I worked on as we traveled. It had to do with shearing the distractions of one's life until all that remained was the act of following a line on a map.

In my message I said I was scared, that I felt pressed to hang out with a bunch of seedy farmers, that there was no lock on the trailer's flimsy door. These things were true, though I thought these men were most likely harmless. I was still young enough to exaggerate fear to cop a cheap call back from a boy I liked.

It was early 2002, and some kind of scrim had been yanked away from the country, revealing how vulnerable we had been. Yet as the East Coast receded in our mirrors, so did the immediacy of the impact. For some, the devastation was a faraway idea, yielding nothing more disruptive than pinning a ribbon to a sweater or buying a patriotic bumper sticker. The footage played in the background indifferently – in the homes of acquaintances, in town squares, on banks of televisions hanging over empty bars. But most of us understood that there were probably other ways in which we were still vulnerable. We were polite, confused, and prepared to flinch.

I was a city girl who had never heard a coyote. At night, their calls filled that Idaho prairie. They sounded like women screaming.

Where we were before Idaho was Eugene, Oregon, where we stayed with a couple named Don and Julio. Julio spent the week working in San Francisco. Every Friday he took the same plane home, with the same pilot. Their house was built by a student of Frank Lloyd Wright with breezeways and a fireplace in the center of the open floor plan like an exposed heart. It was a house with important windows, on a hill beneath the flight path of Eugene's only airport.

Every Friday at 6.35pm, a shadow crossed the house as Julio's plane flew over. This was Don's signal. He'd save his work, close his laptop, and start dinner.

Julio's HIV had not yet progressed to full-blown AIDS, but it was already cruelly tagging his everyday activities. He paused during conversations to catch his breath.

The fact of that plane, its shadow bleating over the house, triggering the thrill of expectancy: Back when I had no home or romantic partner, it was the most beautiful way I'd ever heard to know your love was near. Now, years later, I have both, and I feel the same.

On our last morning in Idaho we awoke to find Alyssa standing over us, holding her butterfly kite. We had promised her we'd fly it before we left, but there was still no air.

Dana thought of a plan to trick Alyssa into thinking it was flying. Alyssa would hold the butterfly's string, as Dana held it aloft by its belly. They counted to three and then took off, Alyssa first, hollering and making wild circles on the dead lawn. Alyssa's job was to keep enough slack in the string while behind her, Dana yelled updates on how high the kite was. 'It's really going, Lys! It's really high, now!'

When they took a break after a few rounds, Alyssa told Dana that she couldn't actually see the kite flying. 'Really?' Dana said. 'Well, it certainly is. Maybe you'll see it this time.'

Again they lined up on the grass, Alyssa in front. In a clear voice, the little girl counted to three, then yelled go! They exploded across the yard. Alyssa tried several times to turn around while she ran, but couldn't as long as she did her job holding the string.

'Is it flying, Dana?' she yelled. She was singing, hopeful. 'Is it flying?'

LYDIA MILLET is the author of 13 works of fiction, most recently *Mermaids in Paradise,* a satire about a couple honeymooning in the Caribbean who discover strange creatures in a coral reef. Her previous books include the novel *Magnificence,* which was a finalist for the National Book Critics' Circle and Los Angeles Times book awards; *My Happy Life,* which won the PEN-USA fiction award; and a story collection called *Love in Infant Monkeys,* which was a finalist for the Pulitzer Prize. She lives in the Arizona desert and works at the nonprofit Center for Biological Diversity; her next novel, *Sweet Lamb of Heaven,* will be published in 2016.

Rocky Point

LYDIA MILLET

My husband and I had a honeymoon handed to us. We didn't like the wedding industry, and we didn't like the honeymoon industry much either, so our general plan had been to put off a trip until the 105° summer heat descended on southern Arizona, where we live.

Our wedding was his second, and a fairly casual event – a ceremony and party outside our house in the desert, surrounded by towering saguaro cacti and blooming prickly pears. The planning had focused mostly on food and drink; we didn't spend much time on traditional wedding details. I don't enjoy shopping, for instance, and I almost never wear dresses, so a friend of the family who *did* like shopping and dresses just picked out one and mailed it to me. I accepted this favor gratefully and tried on the outfit only once, briefly, before the day of the ceremony. And the marriage vows didn't get much attention either. Both K and I tend to have strong opinions about words, yet our vows were a standard template used by the officiating minister – one of no specific faith that K had found through a quick google. She'd handed the page to us in a crowded, faintly unpleasant coffee shop in a mall and told us to look over it quickly. And look quickly we did, anxious to get away from the latte-drinking hordes.

Friends told me after the ceremony that when I was asked to repeat the line "I will honor you with my body," I looked quite surprised. I seemed to be hearing it for the first time, they said. Apparently I grimaced and pronounced the words as though they were in air quotes.

But at the reception a generous guest surprised us, gifting us two nights in her condo in a small tourist town named Puerto Peñasco on the Sea of Cortez ('Rocky Point' is what the Tucson frat boys call it when they drive down there to party). It was just four hours' road trip from where we lived, so we thanked her and decided we'd nip down and back in K's beater truck – feel the ocean breeze on our faces, hear the waves crash on the shore.

We got to the seaside in the afternoon, dumped our overnight bags in the apartment, and drove to the town's beachside strip, where we promptly found an open-air patio and ordered a couple of margaritas. It was a hotel bar beside the hotel's swimming pool; its floor was colorful tile and the tables were wrought iron. We sat at a two-top along a wall, peering over the stucco edge at the rocks far below, splattered white by seagulls and awash with sea foam and floating plastic litter. For a minute, with our margaritas on the table between us and the gulls drifting nearby in hopes of table scraps, we had that curious feeling of suspended time you get in the resting stops in travel – the confusion of leisure, the limbo of an empty day. What should we do with it?

We never had to make a choice. We'd taken only a sip of our drinks when there was a muffled *boom* and the place was rocked by an explosion. The floor seemed to shudder beneath our feet; a huge mirror shattered behind the bar. We heard screams and jumped up, staring at each other wide-eyed. This was early 2003, and the attacks of September 11 were still fresh in our minds. When it came to explosions, everyone's nerves were raw. We abandoned our table and ran for the restaurant next door to the hotel, from which smoke was billowing. The restaurant building was on fire – people, injured, were already tottering dazedly in the streets like zombies, their faces shocked and immobile. On the second floor, we saw two elderly ladies trapped on a balcony.

K climbed up to help them get down safely. They were American tourists like us, it turned out, as we shouted back and forth over the faint background noise of more yelling and sirens. Small black flakes floated in the air – ash, I guessed—and there was a smell of burning. The older of the two wouldn't agree to be lifted down onto safe ground unless K first took her purse and handed it over to me. (This he did; the purse seemed more important to her in her panic than her own safety.) Then he lifted her off the balcony with me at the bottom to receive her, purse dangling off my forearm. The second woman climbed down with less help, then wandered away the moment our backs were turned. We were focused on Rose – the one who had zealously protected her purse – because we saw, now that our adrenalin rushes were subsiding, that she was terribly hurt: the pale, frail skin of her arms, already as thin as parchment, was deeply burned. She needed medical help right away.

In a moment the sirens were keening close at hand, winding down, and our hopes soared when an ambulance pulled up on the street beside us. But they were quickly dashed when the rear doors were flung open and two uniformed EMTs jumped out: children. Well, teenagers, we saw on closer inspection, but they looked even younger because their faces were blank and confused. Behind the ambulance, we could see more victims roaming the streets, burned and shell-shocked.

The ambulance contained no equipment save for a single stretcher and blanket. There wasn't even a first aid kit that we could see – not even a Band-Aid.

Rose spoke no Spanish and the child paramedics spoke no English; she seemed disoriented, even scared, and the teenagers did too. Although our own versions of Spanish were crude, we figured they might be better than nothing. So I asked one of the teens where the ambulance would take Rose, and after we watched it pull away, we ran to our truck, looked up the address on K's phone, and drove.

It turned out to be a clinic run by the military, maybe four rooms in total: later we found out there'd been so many people wounded in the accident – a boiler explosion – that the survivors had to be spread out among all the town's medical facilities. We waited as they worked on Rose's burns, and when she had been treated and lay recovering in her bed, bandaged up, we stood beside the bedside. We did our best to translate what the doctor and nurses said to her, and what her responses were to them. Rose was 93, she told us. She was still shaky, but managed to communicate with us her urgent worry about her traveling companion, Jerry.

'He's just a *young* man, you see,' she said. 'His name is Jerry. Please, go look for him! I have to know if he's alive. You see, he'd gone to the back of the restaurant. He got up from the table and went to the bathroom…' And with that she gave a small sob and closed her eyes as the sedatives kicked in.

We knew from the medical staff's descriptions of the explosion that this meant Jerry had been nearer the boiler than Rose had – Jerry had been at higher risk. But by now it was late and we could hardly even speak, we were so tired. The doctor told us our search would be more fruitful by daylight, so we went back to the condo and collapsed.

The next morning we got up early and strategized about how to find Jerry. We weren't confident we could make ourselves understood in Spanish over the phone, or understand anyone else's Spanish either. We'd have to hit the pavement. So we brewed some coffee to go and started making the rounds in our truck, driving to every medical outpost in town, one after another.

Our worst stop came in the early afternoon: the town's central hospital. Outside it, milling on the sidewalk, were crowds – families waiting to hear the news and families who had just heard it, standing huddled in pairs or small groups and crying. We walked through these clusters of mourners with our faces down, not wanting to disturb them, trying to be invisible as ghosts. If we'd been home, we would have caught fragments of speech, would have had words to hang onto, words to give the dead and injured, and the people mourning them, detail and personhood. Maybe we would have spoken to someone. Here, where the language wasn't our own, it was like wading through a sea of grief – we couldn't see where our feet were.

But Jerry wasn't there, and he didn't seem to be anywhere. Again and again, no Jerry. Only after many hours of long and frustrating searching – our childlike Spanish kept our progress through the levels of bureaucracy to a snail's pace, and some places we visited twice – we finally found our man.

He wasn't too badly hurt, though he, like Rose, lay weak on his back in a hospital bed. We understood the second we saw him why our description of 'young' Jerry hadn't resonated with staff at any of the hospitals or clinics: 'young' Jerry was in his late seventies. Clearly, by Rose's standards, he was still a spring chicken. When we told him she was alive, he burst into tears.

After a few minutes he asked us to do something for him while he was bedridden. Could we make a trip to retrieve his documents and money from his car? He'd left them in the compartment under the armrest, he said, because Rose had been paying for their lunch that day. Their passports were in the armrest, he said, with their cash and insurance cards. The vehicle was in the parking lot beside the restaurant; he described its location and gestured for the plastic tray that contained his belongings so we could pick out his key ring.

The lot was cordoned off now, and police were teeming over it, dark forms in the dusk. Once we explained why we were there, they lifted the yellow tape for us. We walked along the rows of cars toward the building wall against which Jerry had left his Jeep parked. And there the Jeep was, or what remained of it. No keys would be needed, clearly. The car was gutted, with nothing left of its body but a few blackened metal bones. We stood beside the husk, looking in between those metal bones. One piece of vinyl had survived completely intact, so pristine that it looked as though it had never been engulfed in flame at all: the armrest compartment on the center console. It was still perfectly whole. We pried open the lid of the compartment, and inside, also in perfect condition, found Jerry's and Rose's documents – and hundreds of dollars in mint-looking cash.

A couple of minutes later, trying to leave the parking lot again, we were forced to hand over Jerry's bundle of bills to the policemen. We counted it carefully first, suspecting corruption (as it turned out, we were able to reclaim the money for Jerry at the police station the next day after filing about a ream of paperwork). The documents, though, we were allowed to take to the two clinics, Jerry's and then Rose's, where we gave them back to their rightful owners. We also had to file a report on what we'd witnessed; for that, too, we spent hours waiting in lines at the police station. And when we weren't making our way through dense hedges of Spanish-language formalities, we carried messages back and forth between Rose and Jerry. Administrators at Rose's facility were making plans to airlift her back over the international border, and Jerry needed to be moved to her clinic beforehand so they could ride back in the helicopter together.

By the time we saw them reunited – Jerry at Rose's bedside, both smiling and crying as they held hands – it was the last day of our trip. After they were airlifted out, we, too, would cross the border and go home, back to everyday routine and our jobs in Tucson.

We ended up at a different bar on our last evening, after saying goodbye to them. (We'd never see them again, as it turned out: we parted company without asking for phone numbers or addresses, and both of their names were common.) This second bar was right next to the condo complex, instead of downtown, and frequented mostly by Anglos. It had a more generic feel – a bar that could have been anywhere, or at least anywhere-USA. Spatially it was in Mexico, but its culture was pure American empire. We drank beers instead of margaritas and walked back to the condo, still exhausted, after only two. The feeling of empty time was gone; leisure had passed us by.

We never did take a classic honeymoon vacation, strolling aimlessly and happily on white sands. Years later, divorced but still close, we came to feel that was alright. The time with Rose and Jerry and a small-town Mexican bureaucracy had been about shock, the sadness of others and the practical work of picking up the pieces – no idylls at all. Then again, neither of us is really cut out for free time; most hours will find us bent unhealthily over our laptops.

These days, with a little girl who's 11 and a little boy who's 7, we travel mostly for work – me to promote my novels, K to promote the conservation of endangered species. We do that travel separately, but we've still managed to take the children to Hawaii together, and to Europe, and for road trips and river trips across the West.

For us real travel is travel that isn't just a commodity or a rest from real life. It's more often a change of texture, a shift into rawness and vulnerability. When you venture into unknown places, especially places where you don't speak the language, you give up much of the social power you've come to rely on as an adult. Travel has a way of turning us into children again, whether we're 93 or only 35, and how vulnerable that makes us is mostly a matter of chance, money, and the kindness of strangers.

But as long as we come out in one piece, it's not so bad to be vulnerable. It's not so bad to be surprised, even by hardship.

LLOYD JONES is a writer based in Wellington, New Zealand. Among his published works are *Biografi: An Albanian Quest, The Book of Fame, Mister Pip* (which received the Commonwealth Writers' Prize and was shortlisted for the Man Booker Prize), *Hand Me Down World*, and *The Man in the Shed*. His most recent book is *A History of Silence*.

In Smolensk

LLOYD JONES

Our paths would never have crossed, but for an official in the Kaunas city office telling me a few days earlier, 'Well, course, you will have to go to Smolensk.'

A desk divided us, and the official and I leaned back in our chairs. For a pleasant half hour he shared the problem surrounding the bones of Napoleon's Grande Armée turning up in the ploughs of farmers each spring.

The difficulties, he said, were of a diplomatic nature. The French don't want the bones repatriated, and the local farmers don't know what to do with them.

The 'bones impasse' had come up in conversation after I'd told him of my plan to retrace the route taken by Napoleon on his disastrous invasion of Russia in 1814.

So many of the invaders caught by a barbarous early winter never made it back across the Neiman River. The retreating army froze to death or died spectacularly – catching light as they tried to warm themselves, or were eaten by bears, or run down by pursuing Cossacks, or drowned in the snow and blizzards, slowly capsizing into a sleep from which there was no return.

Some of the survivors never made it back to their country of origin (for this was one of the first 'great coalitions of the willing') and stayed on in Russia, absorbed, or adopted, into local communities.

The city official told me the murals in one of the local churches had been painted by one such straggler.

I can't recall the church or its whereabouts, or a single detail of the paintings I took in later that day, but I do retain a vivid memory of the woman whose knees were swaddled in bandages as she crawled and dragged herself across the flagstones in the direction of the altar.

I thought at first she was crippled, and I watched appalled by the spectacle of this poor woman's attempt to drag herself up the aisle to get closer to, presumably, God or his emissary.

I went and bought an ice cream (vanilla) from a huge woman in a white apron scooping it out of a wooden vat on wheels next to a chocolate-coloured phone box.

I don't recall much of the road to Vilnius bifurcating the historic oak tree where, the official said, Napoleon had taken a nap.

I do remember my eagerness to see it, and my edge-of-the-seat concern that the driver might have already passed it.

I am not even sure of where I caught the train to Smolensk. I suspect it was Vilnius. Probably it was. Of the train trip, nothing passing in the window has stuck as well as the magnificent pastel-coloured station with its cathedral atmosphere that I strode out of that spring morning in 1995.

A road climbed to the old walled town of Smolensk. A section of its stone wall was still intact, and nearby I spied a Ferris wheel. There was no line. I have an idea I was the first customer. And I think it was my idea for the operator to stop the wheel at the top of its arc.

Of the view I don't recall much, apart from the unnerving height at which my bucket seat came to a rest, and my sudden awareness of the disheartening amount of rust and corrosion in the framework around me.

I probably made notes; that's what I usually do. But where are those notes now? I have no idea…

I am in Smolensk that day for no other reason than to search out my own event while in pursuit of another.

My train is scheduled to leave Smolensk for Moscow that evening, so there is the rest of the afternoon to kill. I am, I suppose, just another mysterious and clueless visitor pretending they are not lost. *That* shop and *that* corner lead me to another, and another, and then I am crossing a busy road to a park. Here I may relax, because the obligation of anyone in a park is to forget where they are; a wander in a park is the nearest thing to dreamily treading water in the sea.

The day has turned unexpectedly warm, and wintry faces grimace in the mad wind that is suddenly sweeping the park. Across the road the doors of the Lenin Institute are banging loudly.

The woman approaching me on the path has been caught out, apparently like everyone else, by the soaring warmth. The man at her side also wears a coat, although his is dark and suavely hangs off the points of his sloping shoulders.

He is tall, and thin. He seems agitated. More so now, as I think back to this moment. The way he stops, and starts. He stops when she doesn't want to. He moves off again before she is ready to, or is convinced – her face is one you see at checkpoints; it wants to be persuaded of something which he is withholding. That is how it seems to me now. But that is after many replays. At the time their progress simply appeared to be marked by some minor disagreement.

They are still making their slow way along the path when they stop again, this time for the man to shake a cigarette loose from a packet. His coat falls off his shoulders. He reaches for the woman. Alarmed, she takes half a step back. He still manages to catch her and place each hand on her shoulder, then his knees bend and he proceeds to slide down her front, melting away from her, to sit, and to roll on to his side, dead.

The woman calls out in distress. She kneels down and gently shakes his shoulder. She strokes the man's cheek, talking to him, hoping no doubt that he will suddenly spring awake until she looks up for help, and her eyes alight on me and she begins speaking hurriedly and urgently in Russian which I don't understand, have at best only a few words for asking directions and in the politest possible way saying, 'No, thank you' and 'Yes, please.'

She has one hand beneath the man's shoulder, so that part of him is slightly raised while his head droops back.

I say something in English (probably 'Can I help?'), and then, for a moment that feels unbearably long, certainly long enough for the absurdity of the situation to take its full measure, we stare at each other – the woman with a look of incomprehension.

Another arrives, a knowledgeable and useful person, and he crouches down to check the fallen man. He and the woman quickly converse, and reach agreement. The woman gets to her feet and scrambles off, presumably to find help.

Now, years later, I have just remembered she is carrying a large handbag. And this ridiculous accessory swings uselessly from her arm as she hurries away. She wants to run but has long forgotten how. And we watch her topple into the lanes of traffic and make a beeline for the crashing doors of the Lenin Institute.

The other fellow seems quite unbothered by the dead man. As though it is a regular occurrence. Especially on Sunday afternoons, and at this time of the year.

He lights himself a cigarette, then he crouches down to get his hand under the dead man's shoulder, and together we hoist the poor fellow on to the park bench. We are able to arrange him so that the bench supports him as far as his waist; however, we leave his legs drooping down to the ground, and his shaggy head turned away from the public.

We squeeze in to the little remaining space, and we sit, and we wait, the Russian man with his elbows on his knees, blowing smoke at the ground, and myself, colossally inadequate to the requirements of the moment, totally extraneous to the scene, but implicated by the chance of my being there, as history was made.

Who were they? Man and wife? Lovers? Is the woman still alive?

I imagine I have featured many times in her account of the day 'Ivan' died, so unexpectedly, so heartbreakingly, and the first person on the scene was someone from the other side of the world and without a drop of Russian.

I imagine she has furnished me with details that I can't recall of myself – what I wore, my expressions, my responses, and the strangeness of an encounter which the invaded will recall with clarity for generations after.

SOPHIE CUNNINGHAM has been on the publishing scene in Australia for 30 years. She is a former publisher and editor, as well as the author of two novels, *Geography* and *Bird*, and two books of non-fiction, *Melbourne* and *Warning: The Story of Cyclone Tracy*. Her next book will be about walking places. She has travelled widely and her writing about those travels has been published in a range of anthologies, magazines, and newspapers. Her hometown is Melbourne, Australia, but she currently lives in San Francisco, California.

Into the Canyon

SOPHIE CUNNINGHAM

When I was nineteen, a backpacker, and in Paris, many years ago, I looked out a train window and saw the Eiffel Tower. I'd forgotten about the tower's existence so it was as if I had not only personally discovered it, but was the first to understand its stark, industrial beauty. This is one of the particular pleasures of travelling while young. Everything is new; everything is waiting to be discovered. You don't know how many millions have done *that* elephant ride, *that* trek, or that wherever you are staying used to be *so* much better before it was discovered (ten years, twenty years, fifty years ago). You can find your way into experience that feels like your own.

When I saw the Grand Canyon for the first time, back in the early '90s, I felt a similar sense of overwhelming surprise and pleasure, despite the fact that in this case I'd sought it out. I'll never forget that moment of getting out of the car in a relatively prosaic car park and walking towards the North Rim. Despite the canyon's enormity – it is close to 2000 square miles – it comes upon you suddenly as you walk towards its edge and look down into it: this extraordinary ravine that plunges deep into the earth. It was late afternoon and the canyon walls were a series of striated purples. The rocks and the light – it was hard to distinguish one from the other – shifted from grey to lilac, from dark purple to black. I was awestruck. The visit was so brief that when I left the next day it was as if I'd dreamt the landscape, one so beautiful it's hard to believe it actually existed.

But you can't pursue the purity of the unexpected moment, and ignorance isn't an answer. It certainly pays to know what you're doing when you visit the Grand Canyon. Despite the fact that it's one of the most popular national parks in the world, with around five million visitors a year, only 1 percent of these visitors ever make it below the rim – one of the best ways to appreciate the grandeur of the place – and of those who do, around 250 need to be rescued each year. Worse still, a not inconsiderable number of them die. Over the 96 years of the park's existence, an average of twelve people have died a year.

It's easy to see how this happens. If you're not an experienced walker, it's hard to imagine how demanding the descent to the Colorado River far below, and the return from it, will be. You can't imagine how much water you might need when the sun beats on you from above, or what it's like to bake in temperatures as high as 120° Fahrenheit. This is why signs everywhere warn you not to be casual when you estimate your endurance, and discourage you from hiking from rim to river and back again in a single day.

When I arrived at the entrance to the South Rim of Grand Canyon National Park late last year, I had no desire to walk to the Colorado River and back in a single day, but nor was I aware of the dangers of doing so. All the first sign at the gate warned us of was the fact that there would be no refund if weather conditions meant there wasn't a good view. My partner and I looked at each other. Do people really do that? Demand refunds if the canyon doesn't display its extraordinary dimensions, its subtle light shows? Apparently so. We pulled into the car park further down the road and I tried to repeat the moment when I'd first spied the canyon some twenty years before. Alas, it's hard to recycle profundity.

That night the decision was made to walk some of the Bright Angel Trail, the path that descends from the rim to the river. I knew about it because my 21-year-old godson had told me it was a good walk, though 'kinda challenging'. I certainly hadn't read the report of Spanish explorers in 1540 who, after several hours and having covered only a third of the distance to the river, had returned to the rim, reporting that 'what seemed easy from above was not so'. Now I can report that they were correct and that in this, as all things, perspective is everything. The descent (and ascent) along the trail is so sheer that you can't see what's in store for you when you look at it from above. Two days later, *after* we'd walked down Bright Angel Trail to Plateau Point and back, about 11 miles roundtrip, we cycled far enough along the rim to get a better view – and it was then that we understood what it was we'd undertaken.

However, the morning when we headed off on our impromptu hike, our band of four adults and two kids under thirteen was as deluded as most of the Grand Canyon's other visitors. It was a cool day, so we didn't struggle with high temperatures. The first part of the walk, down to Indian Gardens, was easy enough and the zigzag of the paths, the sheer walls of the canyon, and the persistent plodding of the mule trains were hypnotic. The gardens, when we got to them, were an oasis, sitting at what we first thought was the bottom of the canyon, though in fact they were a good quarter of a mile above it as the crow plummets. Cottonwood trees lined the creek, and leaves glittered gold, brown, and pale yellow in the autumn light. The grass was green and the harshness of the canyon's sheer walls faded away. Havasupai Indians lived and farmed these gardens until 1928, when the National Park Service drove them out, and I tried to imagine what it was like to live down here in such a private, remote, and dramatic place. The contrast between the gardens and the one-and-a-half-mile trail to Plateau Point added to the drama. The flatlands around the trail were populated with thousands of purple cacti, and within ten minutes of walking through them, we felt as if we'd been walking an hour, not because it was strenuous but because it was so otherworldly.

But the point of this story is not the walk, it's that walking on and down into a landscape bonds you to a place, even if that walk includes a five-mile hike back up the canyon during which you ascend close to half a mile straight up: an incline that at first leaves you cursing, but soon reduces you to speechlessness. Over the eight hours it took to walk what was only eleven miles, we became sensitive to the moods and light of the canyon, which shifted from shaded to gentle morning sunlight, to harsh midday sun, then back towards those purplish hues I remembered from my first trip.

We fell in love with the canyon even more the following day when we cycled the rim and spied a condor, some mule deer, and a stand of conifer carved by the wind into a dreamscape of bonsai.

By the time we left, four nights after we arrived, we'd been at the canyon long enough to get down into it, travel around it, and see it in every kind of light. We were sated. We certainly had no expectations of our final morning. As we packed the car, half-asleep in the almost dark of dawn, my partner gestured to the canyon: 'Look at that'.

So I looked. What I saw was a great ocean of dense white cloud that pulsed, and shimmied from side to side, as well up towards, then down from, the canyon rim. The entire gorge was filled with thick clouds and mist. It throbbed as the rising sun played across it. Day broke in a series of pale greys and blues, then pink with golden flashes. The tips of the peaks scattered through the canyon floated like tiny islands. Later I was told that what we had seen was called a cloud inversion. It was rare.

We stood at the rim for some time, just outside the Bright Angel Lodge. People slowly realised what was happening and stood silently, with the exception of the woman who muttered that the clouds were ruining the view. We wondered if she was going to ask for her money back. Native Americans working on the heritage building sites along the rim all laid down their tools and joined the crowds. It was as if we were all of us, a group of strangers, worshipping nature.

There is a word to describe this sense of giving over to some greater force: numinous. Some use the word to mean religious ecstasy, but for me it was a reminder of why we seek nature out, what we are losing as the wilderness is driven into increasingly remote pockets of the earth. I felt honoured. It was a reminder of the privilege that travel can afford. A reminder that travel will never stop surprising us, even when we're standing in the midst of one of the most densely touristed places on the planet.

STEVEN AMSTERDAM is the author of *Things We Didn't See Coming* (*The Age* Book of the Year winner, *The Guardian* First Book Award longlist) and *What the Family Needed* (Encore Award shortlist; International IMPAC Award longlist), and is currently working on his third novel. His writing has also appeared in *The Age*, *Conde Nast Traveller*, *Five Chapters*, *The Huffington Post*, *Meanjin*, *The Monthly*, *Monument*, *Overland*, *Salon*, *Sleepers Almanac*, and *Torpedo*. Born in New York City, he lives in Melbourne, where he also works as a palliative care nurse.

Getting Lost

STEVEN AMSTERDAM

My family never went a-rambling. I'm not complaining, but I was always in awe of those parents who put the kids into the car on a Saturday morning and when asked, *Where are we going?*, told them, *We'll see.* The sheer joy of the wind in our hair or where the day might take us was never the draw.

We travelled with purpose, to places that had already been researched by an advance guard, usually the esteemed Automobile Club of America. As soon as we were buckled in, these questions were answerable: *When will we get there?*, *What will we see?*, and *Where will we eat?* In this way we expanded our range slowly outward from the Upper West Side of Manhattan, establishing safe, knowable boundaries – to the maternal grandparents in Brooklyn's Sheepshead Bay, to the Franklin Institute in Philadelphia, to the relatives in DC, to historic Boston and Colonial Williamsburg, and so on.

We celebrated the purchase of a maroon '75 Valiant by driving Route 95, extending our reach to Florida (and the paternal grandparents). Eventually, there was air travel, both cross-country and overseas. My father was the consummate guide for each of these adventures, plotting our trail weeks in advance, anticipating every step with an up-to-date Michelin or Fodor's guide, a stack of relevant articles at his side, and one magically assembled AAA Triptik, which personalized our vacation one loose-leaf page at a time. AAA knew everything. When the driving was done for the afternoon, my father would drop mother, sister, and me at the pre-booked Days Inn (quiet location, ideally with a view of the pool, and a AAA discount) so we could have a swim while he would go suss out the nearby restaurants, three stars or higher.

This is how travel happened: You unfolded maps across the kitchen table, followed suggested itineraries, and incorporated advice from the cousin who'd been there three years ago. When all the phone calls were made and the schedule was firm, you packed (two days in advance), and if you were flying, you were at the airport three hours early (even domestic). When there were screw-ups – a wrong turn, a lost reservation (or this one time in Villa Vizcaya in Miami, no film in the camera for the whole day) – there were words, followed by silences, but mostly we buzzed along in bliss, confident that we had all we needed (crayons!) and knew exactly where we were going.

One Friday, almost two decades later, after I had moved to California, dutifully learned to drive, and bought a '74 Dart, a friend suggested we break it in with a trip to the desert.

'To where?'

'Wherever. Does it matter? Bring a toothbrush.'

'A toothbrush? How long are we going for?'

'Does it matter?'

'How can you live like that?'

'How can you not?'

A few hours later we were alone in the hills of the Anza-Borrego Desert, which I hadn't known existed until a few minutes before we drove through the entrance to the park. Then and there (at least according to my memory), I vowed to predetermine as little as possible. Travelling without a destination, map, or even a plan would provide its own kind of orientation, maybe even improve my sleep.

From that point on, whenever I saw the chance, I slipped out of town. I would fill a bottle of water and drive, telling myself the freeway would decide. If I could see a town or a park that had an enticing name or looked good from the road, I made the turnoff. These outings wobbled at first. More often than not, they brought me to forests that were less pastoral than they were weedy and towns with charms too subtle for my discernment. The wisdom gained was usually that it was getting dark and I was hungry. But I did learn patience with the road. If there was no place to get to, what was so bad about a wrong turn?

A few years later, I was back in New York looking for a job, no clearer ambition than *something in publishing*. After one interview, the universe obliged with an offer. I told the boss I could start in a month, then booked a ticket to Beijing, using United miles I'd been hoarding for years. Four days later, I landed in China with a backpack and no guidebook. This was a test. The airport bus dropped me at a concrete hostel, situated on a ten-lane boulevard, a few miles from the city center, where jet lag helped me appreciate the morning rush of trucks, lawn mowers, bicycles, and Mercedes.

My China itinerary was intentionally empty, except for the

Forbidden City, which I discovered the next morning was closed for the week. I decided to view this not as a setback but as a challenge. Or better yet, a choice: A, I could flagellate myself for not having done my research and hunker down for the wait, or B, I could float easily onwards, maintaining a half-smiling bubble of Zen whateverness.

I chose B. The Forbidden City wasn't going away. Some place quieter beckoned. How about Mongolia? That sounded far.

Without even looking, the ticket agent told me there was nothing to Mongolia for two weeks. The speed with which she said this was suspicious, as if I'd failed to proffer the password to get to Ulan Bator. Should I stand my ground or move on? Again, I chose option B.

A poster of limestone mountains in the south provided enough spark. I bought a ticket for Guilin, departing the next morning. A prepared traveler, I rose early the next day and caught the bus to the airport with ample time to make my plane. Somehow the express bus seemed to lose its mission midway to the airport, however, and began getting on and off the highway in a route that seemed local, almost circular. I tried not to sweat, willing myself to focus on my fellow riders and their various planes, and to believe that if I missed mine, something good would turn up. In the end, my plane was just as delayed as the bus. China, I decided, was a fine place to be plan-less.

Even from above, the mountains near Guilin are ridiculous. Artfully scattered around twists of the Li River, they shoot straight up as if they had bloomed from the fields. They have well-cragged peaks topped with gnarled cypress trees that aren't afraid of heights. Footpaths, made by and for centuries of tourists, circle sheer forests and lead all the way up to mountaintops that are lost to cloud cover in the morning. There in the mist, a tiny dot of a wooden shrine may be visible, ready for prayer or a photo op with the pastoral plateau below. A first-timer could be forgiven for thinking the landscape was inspired by ancient paintings and not the other way around.

At the airport, the streams of people looking for transportation into Guilin made my choice easy. I found a nearly empty bus headed in the other direction, and took it to a town at the southern end of the mountains. Rooms were cheap and came with shared toilets and calendar-worthy views. Every other building seemed to have a stack of bicycles leaning up against the doorway, all yearning to be rented.

I thought I'd discovered Shangri-La. Flipping through a Lonely Planet on the hostel bookshelf told me a decade of backpackers had beaten me to it. Immediately, the comfort of the place was suspect, which is to say that although I appreciated the muesli, yogurt, and honey that came with the low-key breakfast buffet on the wooden porch at the back of the hostel, I wanted more.

Yes, I had knocked together a holiday on short notice – radical, given my influences, but no huge feat for a first-world tourist with a functioning credit card. There had to be a greater risk/reward out there. I envisioned a true walkabout, consisting of equal parts epic beauty and epic danger. My fantasy had one more ingredient – assured survival, ideally by my own wits. To be clear, there are degrees of lost – being mapless in the Louvre and mapless in the Amazon Delta are different things. I was willing to accept slightly less danger for tidier closure. A true explorer would embrace the possibly suicidal nature of the mission: Truly getting lost may mean staying lost. For me, anything that didn't end up involving the American Embassy would suffice. And no injuries or illnesses, please.

The next morning I set out to find it (what?), this time for real. I paid for my room a week in advance so I wouldn't be missed if I didn't make it back that night. (Surely Amelia Earhart never threw such caution to such wind.) To further hide my tracks, I walked to the far side of town before renting a bicycle and heading north. I took random lefts and rights as fast I could, always veering away from the main road to Guilin, and into the foothills of the thickest cluster of mountains. The further I pedalled, the more I left the majestic for the rustic. Persimmons and tomatoes were laid out on sheets in the sun, meaty smoke poured from the chimney of an old brick house. Women and men rode past me on bicycles that had seen far less maintenance than mine, with side baskets carrying grass, eggplants, and swaddled pigs. No one bothered to even acknowledge the *gwai lo* in their midst. All the better.

In high valleys, a few steeply planted farms provided perfect disorientation. I turned onto an overgrown dirt trail, seeking true oblivion. At first, it complied, serpentining and steepening downward, leaving me to pump the useless brakes and swerve around dips in the road to keep from wiping out. When it finally levelled, civilization returned, with the overgrowth pulling back from the road to reveal that I was coasting right into a village on a bend of the Li River, easily identified by the large tourist boats drifting by. Foiled, but not stopped.

A single low wooden boat, painted with a distinctly non-standard pink Nike swoosh, bobbed at the shore. People were boarding it from the water's edge, carrying their vegetables, already limp from the sun, and chickens, trussed into passivity. I parked my bike, then negotiated a seat on a splintering bench in the back, next to an apparently unaccompanied chicken. Once the boat was moving, I used my pitiful sign language to ask if one of the humans could write down the name of the town. A middle-aged woman, wearing a baby in front and a toddler on her back, complied. I thanked her as best I could, folded the writing I couldn't read, and zippered it into my backpack. (Yes, it was one breadcrumb, but I wasn't enlightened enough to consider abandoning someone else's bicycle.)

The boat drifted from one village to another. Another bend in the river, another market closing up for the day. I disembarked at the fifth stop. Neither Dad nor AAA nor even Lonely Planet had prospected this town before. One of the stalls there was selling a pancake + vegetable + dark sauce item that looked appetizing. It was taken apart, reheated in a wok, reassembled with extra sauce and grandly presented to me, piping hot and practically gift-wrapped in rapidly melting toilet paper. That would be my lunch, and maybe dinner and breakfast too. Who knew?

I ambled straight up into the hills, mixing my rights with my lefts, mindfully stopping every now and then to *just sit*. After a few hours, my meditative spirit was interrupted by the question of where I was going to sleep. I considered: The nights were mild, I had a change of underwear and socks in my pack – all was good. And besides: What did it matter? Negotiating a truce between camping out and tramping out, I meandered toward a settlement in the distance. There were hills in the way and, after a while, what seemed close did not get any closer, spurring more intrusive worry. A moment of thirst devolved to early symptoms of dehydration and a lonely, parched death. I attempted to replace this thought process with the memory of the red plaid thermos we used to take on car trips, usually filled with Minute Maid lemonade – if we were lucky, the pink one.

A moment later, a child, a barefoot boy of about five in homemade green overalls, stepped out from some bushes, carrying two glistening plastic bottles of water, recently refilled. He saw me look at them and immediately held one out in offering. I accepted and, after thanking him in the wrong dialect, went even more clueless, and attempted to give him some change. This didn't register a response. Instead, he crouched to examine the stitching of my hiking boots while I happily drank the water. When he figured out that I wasn't giving up my boots, he stood up and continued on in the direction I'd come from. After a minute, he had disappeared back into the woods.

Eventually, as night came on, moonless and still, I arrived at the town I'd been aiming for. It was the one where the boat had let me off. Except for a trio of blasé cats, no one was around. I accepted the circle of this part of my trek as a kind of randomness – maybe all roads are loops – and walked through an untended field of thistle to sit down by the water. There was an old tarp on the ground, ideal for stretching out. I could sleep right there until the sun came up. I could do this.

'Mister Steven! Mister Steven!' A man punted a rowboat onto the nearby sand. He waved me over, smiling but urgent. I half-hoped that, like my young water bearer, I'd conjured this boatman to bring me to the next stage of my journey. When I saw the bicycle I'd rented that morning laid flat in the back of the boat, I knew that this wasn't quite the case.

Even more humiliating than having to pay for the bicycle and boat return after dark, was reckoning with the fact that stupidly trampling around, inconveniencing the locals, then throwing extra dollars down for their trouble, only reconfirmed that I had transcended nothing. I was another tourist, just less prepared. The only difference between this and the travel of my youth was that I'd probably gone right past all the five-star views in the area.

And I had not disappeared into the landscape at all. Sure, the sun had shone all afternoon, the views had been lovely, and, in the end, someone was there to take me back to a bed. But was that my whole adventure? The most dramatic part of the day was when the kid gave me some bottled water for free. Was this going to be the big story from my itinerary-free, Upper West Sider Gone Wild trip to China?

At the hostel I was welcomed back with a crazy shake of the head from the owner. *Foreigners.*

The next week, as scheduled, I flew back to New York to start as assistant map editor at Fodor's Travel Guides. Punchline, I know. Our sole mission: keep people from getting lost. The desk job suited me. Now and then a few comped trips turned up, plus, occasionally, more exotic gigs such as fact-checking hotel listings on the coast between Georgia and South Carolina. I thrived there, for a while.

In the years since, despite finding many other ways to stray from obvious paths, my travel habits have reverted to their mean: I usually know where I'm going and what's going to happen next. It may be genetic predisposition or a simple love of the tangible outcome (or that I'm controlling), but the prospect of a mystery outing is not nearly as compelling as reliable geolocation beforehand. Without it, hours would be wasted; we'd miss the key destinations; and we'd eat bad food.

Technology has evolved in lock step with my needs. Well-meaning cell phones, mapping apps, and an entire troposphere streaming ungrammatical reviews by strangers all conspire to keep me from making any improvisational turns. I let them. Picture me in the middle of a forest, holding my phone up to the sky at different angles until I get enough bars to figure out exactly where I am.

I recently asked my partner, 'Do we ever get lost?'

'Never,' he said. 'You're too controlling.'

What I like to think he meant is that I plan a good trip, and that this may sometimes come at the price of enduring a carefully orchestrated schedule. What is that price?

I would like to formally apologize to him and to my wayward self who yearned to wander. My father made me this way and, despite the fact that I'm three careers past the Fodor's gig and living on the other side of the earth, it turns out that I have not come very far.

When we arrived in Buenos Aires last year, I spread out travel guides and maps across the bed. The highest rated tango and steak, etc, were checked against at least one app or website, and later cross-checked with a genuine local. Even though we couldn't stay awake late enough to see the best of the best tango, my planning kept us from middling steak, and gave us experiences I would consider peak, if not ur. See? Planning pays off.

But then why, when prompted to write about a transformative travel experience, does an uneventful walk more than twenty years ago come so clearly to mind? Was it the inevitability of my rescuer and his rowboat, ready to escort me safely home? Or was it simply the last time I almost got away?

Getting Lost

SHIRLEY STRESHINSKY is the author of four historical novels and four works of non-fiction, as well as numerous travel stories for such publications as the *San Francisco Examiner, Conde Nast Traveler*, and *Travel + Leisure*. Her most recent book, with historian Patricia Klaus, is the biography *An Atomic Love Story: The Extraordinary Women in Robert Oppenheimer's Life*.

Travels with Suna

SHIRLEY STRESHINSKY

The flight from Calcutta was crowded; the sari-clad woman named Suna took a seat up front, while I pushed on down the aisle and found a window seat. My view of India from the air included the Boeing 737's wing and engine. We were on our way to Bhubaneswar, a city of temples, but would be making a stop at some small outpost in between. After about half an hour, we started our descent.

I watched as the ground came up to meet us, and glanced around to see if anyone else was concerned with what seemed to me to be much too rapid a descent. No-one was. I pulled my seatbelt tight and took a deep breath. Then I looked out the window just in time to see the whole back of the engine fall away. *Dear God, we're going to crash.* I wanted to scream but I couldn't breathe. I felt myself go numb, covered my eyes, and waited for the explosion.

We touched down, bounced once or twice, then rolled to a stop. Passengers busied themselves pulling out bags crammed in overhead bins.

'The engine,' I croaked to one of the attendants, 'the engine, part of it fell off.' The young woman pressed her hands together, fingers up, said, '*Namaste*,' and turned away. I had to do something. I could not get back on this plane without alerting someone to the problem; it would be irresponsible. I waved to Suna. She would know what to do, I was certain of it. I had sat next to her on one of the bus trips that our group had taken; she had grown up in India. She exuded calm.

'We must go to the pilot and tell him what you saw,' she said. Action, yes. Without hesitation, with perfect equanimity.

The pilot came out of the cockpit along with the co-pilot. Suna spoke to them; they nodded and suggested we follow them onto the tarmac to inspect the engine.

'You see?' the pilot asked. I didn't see. I looked down the runway, which was surprisingly short, but there was no evidence of the missing piece of engine.

'Not to worry,' the co-pilot assured me, but he didn't say why.

'Are you certain?' I asked.

'I am certain,' he murmured, god-like. Later, Suna told me he mentioned that English women regularly reported engines falling off. She didn't know what to make of it and neither did I, so we continued on to the city of temples.

Back home in California, the reporter in me pushed for answers, so I called Boeing to ask what exactly had happened with that errant engine. They obliged: On older versions of the 737 the back of the engine acts as a thrust reverser; the clamshell design allows one part to slide down during landing. It is part of the braking system, often used when a landing strip is short and requires a fast landing. When I covered my eyes to wait for eternity, I failed to see the clamshell slide back up and lock into place.

I was embarrassed, yes, but mainly what I felt at the time was gratitude to Suna Kanga for being willing to risk standing up with someone who was making a fool of herself.

More than three decades later, I wince when I think about how close I came to missing that meeting with Suna altogether, and so never discovering the gate she would open for me.

The year was 1981, and I was at a loss to know why the Government of India would invite me on a press trip and I did not plan to accept. My family rebelled. Not just my photojournalist husband, who routinely traveled the world on assignments, but our 13-year-old son and daughter as well. *You have to go*, they chimed in. *What could be more exciting?* 'But I'd miss your 11th birthday,' I told my daughter. She said I could bring her presents.

I didn't try to explain to the Government of India that I was not a travel writer, that I wrote articles for magazines about people like a Navy nurse who had been court martialed for protesting the Vietnam War; about the Berkeley schools' radical new integration plan; about the killing of a young white bus driver in the riots after Martin Luther King's assassination. I had just published my first historical novel and was about to begin another. Still, my only foray outside of the US had been to London, to interview two survivors of the Holocaust. I tended to write about what was wrong with the world; it seemed to me that travel writing by its nature was expected to cover much that is right, to pay more attention to pleasure than to problems. I asked myself how I could possibly do that in India, of all places. The answer was: The only way to know is to go.

When I returned, I wrote a story for a travel magazine. It was titled *Interlude in India*, and it began: 'It had not occurred to me that I would go to India, ever. The Taj Mahal floated in my mind like some shimmering mirage, cold white and dream marble… The India of my mental landscape was monochromatic, brown as the river Ganges, sere and dusty and filled with too many people, too many poor. I didn't realize how vague was my notion of what I was about to encounter… I am not a traveler by inclination; I should not have come.'

'The days between New Delhi and Calcutta were spent touring Hindu temples and second-century Jain caves, traveling to ancient forts and holy ghats on the Ganges. Our guides delivered long, sonorous lectures – stories about ancient struggles between the elephant and the crocodile, good and evil, about Mogul emperors and Sikh gurus. In their lyric, embroidered English, the well-versed guides would chant out interminable tales, explaining all the subtle variations in all the myriad religions, until finally I tuned out the words and listened only to the cadence of their voices. And that is when I began to hear India.'

'I would wake before dawn in my hotel room and lie quietly, waiting for the light. Then, through an air vent came the softest imaginable chanting, drifting up through the air-conditioning system, lulling and beautiful and strange: the morning prayers. In the distance I could see a mosque outlined against the gathering pink of the sunrise. After a while the smell of smoke would drift up and into the room, smoke from a thousand braziers on the street, lit to cook the morning meals.'

'In India all of life can be viewed on the street – cooking and bathing, hair cutting and sewing and the patting of cow dung into small round cakes to be dried in the sun and used for fuel. In the streets, movement is perpetual. My monochromatic India, all brown and dusty green, was actually alive with movement and color – outrageous, amazing splashes of cerise and jade green and saffron yellow, glittering with silver and gold.'

'…At the Harmandir Sikh temple people crowded about, curious, as we washed our feet in a trough before covering our heads with saffron-colored scarves so we could enter the temple, where we were taken on a tour that included a visit to the common kitchen where food for a thousand is prepared each day. I don't know what I expected, certainly not what I saw. Two shadowy stone rooms, dungeon-like, had only a few shafts of light penetrating through narrow windows. Open fires blazed in trenches in the floor. The heat was choking, yet women and children squatted, hour after hour, patting out flat bread on the stone floors. I stood in the suffocating heat and watched a tiny girl, no more than five, methodically slap the bread rounds with a splash of water.'

'When I came back into the full sun of the plaza, something lurched inside me. I was walking next to a Belgian journalist named Andre, and I was surprised to hear myself tell him, "I feel like crying, but I'm afraid if I start I won't be able to stop." He looked at me for a long moment, then he said, "Either you leave India and are so repulsed that you never want to return, or you will have to come back." After his first trip, he told me, he spent two years reading everything he could find about India. He comes back every chance he gets, he explained, "to try to understand".'

'In Calcutta, the women carrying babies high on their breasts would walk alongside me, chanting a peculiar incantation which might have been memorized for Western women: "Oh mommie," they droned, "Oh baksheesh, oh baby, no papa, oh Mommie." But I did not give them baksheesh, and I would not cry for them. If you weep your way through India, if you cannot see beyond the squalor, you will miss the grace and the beauty and the promise.'

'...From a distance it looks like all the photographs you have ever seen: floating in space, heat waves diffusing its focus. It is not until you pass through the Jilo Khana, the red sandstone gateway, that you really see it: The central tomb of the Begum Mumtaz-i-Mahal, white marble, soaring and brilliant in the midday sun. You run your fingertips over the traceries and arabesques formed by semi-precious stones inlaid in marble. You shade your eyes and peer up at one of the towers, glaring white against a blue sky, a remnant of a past only dimly understood, as well as an astonishing measure of possibilities for this crowded subcontinent.'

It was easier to leave India than to return home. Now that I had seen the slums of Mumbai and the beauty of the Taj Mahal, I understood my massive failure of imagination. I had written: 'I am not a traveler by inclination; I should not have come.' India taught me that I had no choice, that I had to find a way to experience the larger world.

On that 1981 press trip, I learned that Suna was the journalist representing Singapore, where she lived with her husband, Rusi, a pilot for Singapore Airlines, and their two teenagers. I watched Suna navigate comfortably, both within the international group of writers and in the chaos that was India at large. In Suna's world, everyone got the benefit of the doubt; no one was beyond redemption. There was something completely guileless about her. She could also be formidable, as I was to discover. And she was prolific; her stories appeared in magazines and newspapers in Singapore, Hong Kong, and India.

As it happens, her daughter was considering a college near my home in Northern California. When the family came to check out schools that summer, I invited them to dinner. In the following years, both Kanga kids would choose West Coast colleges, and both would be in and out of our house. Over time, my husband, Ted, would perform the wedding ceremonies for both (using his Internet credentials) and our children would become friends. I ended up recording the story of the 'crash' of the Boeing 737 for a travel program on National Public Radio; Suna included it on a tape of stories she put together for her grandchildren, and it became their bedtime story.

Eventually our families would blend to include extended family and good friends, but at first it was just Suna and me traveling on our own. She was easy in the world in a way that I was not, and she made me feel comfortable; in effect, she became my gatekeeper, a conduit into a wider world.

Our first foray together was to Hong Kong, where we signed on to one of the small tours into mainland China, to Guangzhou. It was Suna's choice because it included a visit to Shamian Island, once a foreign enclave.

When we arrived, our guide told us that Shamian Island had been removed from the tour. Suna objected quickly without raising her voice. The guide said there was nothing he could do about it. Her face took on a look that I would come to recognize:

total determination. Quietly, purposefully, she found one reason after another to bring up the question of Shamian Island. The guide took me aside to ask why my friend was being so insistent.

'She was born there,' I told him. 'Her father was a businessman, and he was President of the Indian Association. During the Japanese Occupation, he was falsely accused of spying for the British. He was arrested and tortured, and he died soon after. On Shamian Island.'

The Chinese guide grew quiet. 'I see,' he said, 'it is a matter of the heart. I myself will take you there.' And he did. Late that afternoon, I followed Suna as she walked around the gray European-style mansions where the foreign business community had been confined in the years before WWII. Suna had childhood memories of the house, of a bridge over the river where she used to play. The guide and I trailed after her, until she found the once elegant house where she lived with her family and younger sister. It now housed eight families. We invited our guide to tea at a nearby high-rise hotel recently built to attract tourists. He was delighted; Chinese were welcome there only if they were with registered guests… or two foreign women, it would seem.

After that, we found reasons to explore other destinations in various parts of the world, sometimes with effects that would play well in an action movie. We were chased out of Puerto Rico by an impending hurricane; the first available flight landed us in New York City at midnight, in a downpour and without luggage. In Goa, the only available driver had spent the afternoon drinking the local brand of white lightning. In Salt Lake City we had to take shelter in a small opening tucked under the Mormon

Tabernacle when a tornado ripped through.

In Bangkok I was researching a novel that involved drug running, and I hoped to get a look into one of the city's prisons so I could write convincingly. Suna suggested we ask the hotel's concierge. Never blinking, he called over a cab driver who studied us for a long minute, then suddenly smiled and said, 'You ladies want to go to the prison store for shopping.' He managed to maneuver us into an area where prisoners could meet visitors, all of us guarded by soldiers with rifles.

Yet it is other, smaller moments that linger in my memory, like a sultry day in a cab in Mumbai, stalled in traffic, when a beggar boy suddenly thrust his hand through my open window. I happened to be carrying an orange, and plopped it into his palm. He took it and started to turn away when Suna called him back to ask, 'What do you say to Auntie?' A boyish smile appeared, and he looked at me and said, 'Thank you, Auntie.'

Wherever we went, Suna's approach was simply to slow down and settle in, to move through exotic places and absorb the culture of a people without making judgements on how they lived. On all our journeys, she saw what was right without denying all that was wrong.

After Rusi retired, he and Suna became a writer-photographer team, and set out on a series of wilderness adventures. Suna added blue jeans and flannel shirts to her wardrobe and they signed on for safaris, river rafting, mountain climbing; they explored the Amazon, the Nile, and the Danube; climbed on the train to Lhasa in Tibet, trekked to Butan's Tiger's Nest temple. They gave me a copy of the lavish coffee table book they produced together titled *Journey through Colombo: A Pictorial*

Guide to the Gateway of Heavenly Sri Lanka.

During this period, Ted and I met them in Spain, and the four of us explored the White Villages of the south. One day we took a wrong turn and came upon a small, off-the-track village, one which seemed perfect to return to, maybe spend a month or two together, long enough to settle in.

We never did. Ted died in 2003; some months after, I went to India to be coddled and comforted by what seemed the whole Kanga clan, sisters and cousins and squadrons of relatives and friends.

For the past several years I have stayed closer to home, working with a historian friend on a biography titled *An Atomic Love Story: The Extraordinary Women in Robert Oppenheimer's Life*. Suna and Rusi kept up by phone and email, and there were quick visits when they came to the States to see their children. We never let too much time lapse between conversations.

A few weeks after *An Atomic Love Story* was published, Suna and Rusi called to say they would be coming for a short visit. Happily, they were arriving the day before we were to give a reading at a bookstore, with a party afterwards at a friend's house. All my kids happened to turn up, as well as many friends the Kangas already knew. The afternoon was sunny and warm, there was standing room only at the bookstore, the party was in a house worthy of those Suna used to cover for a column she wrote called 'Beautiful Homes'. I have photos of us, taken after most of the guests had left, sitting in a wide circle, my daughter tucked on the arm of the big easy chair Rusi was in. My two sons shared a large bench, Suna and two of my friends were on one sofa. I do not remember the conversation, only the laughter and sense of ease.

The evening before they were to leave, the three of us were

sitting at my kitchen table with cups of tea. Usually there would be a conversation about a next trip, but it didn't come up. I remember Suna asking if I'd heard from her daughter, Nazneen. I said I hadn't, but suddenly I could see how weary Suna seemed, and since they had a long travel day ahead of them, I suggested they turn in.

The next morning I saw them to the car, hugged them both goodbye, kissed Suna a second time. I watched until the car turned the corner and was gone, and then I cried.

Fifteen months later, on the 10th of February 2015, Suna's son, Cyrus, was in town and came to dinner, as he usually did. By then, I knew that Suna had been diagnosed with leukemia three years earlier, and that she had made the decision to reject chemotherapy or any of the other therapies that could prolong her life. She wanted to live fully for the time left to her, she did not want to be treated like an invalid, and so had insisted that only her immediate family know. We were in the kitchen when the call came from Rusi in Singapore. Suna was failing, they were taking her to the hospital. She died five days later, as she had lived: resolute, positive.

The Kangas are Parsis, a religious denomination that came to India from Iran; their prophet is Zoroaster. Suna's final assignment had been a grant from the National Heritage Board of Singapore to write a book about the Parsis of Singapore, their history, customs, culture, and cuisine. She and I had discussed the research it would take, the excitement of dealing with a historic subject; we spoke of the pleasures of writing non-fiction, the satisfaction of being able to add to a body of knowledge. She worked on the book steadily, and was able to finish half. Parsi friends will complete it in her honor.

My travels with Suna are over; we won't be meeting in Rome or Paris, in Hawaii, Hong Kong, or Kuala Lumpur. There will be no more misadventures, no fallen airplane engines in India or random tornadoes in Utah, stories that our children now tell their children. Suna and I covered a wide swath of the world together and in the process we caught our families in a kind of charmed net that pulled us all together, and holds us, with Suna locked in our memories, secure.

And yet, and yet… I cannot quite believe that one day soon she won't call to tell me that the trip is on, that I should not forget my bathing costume. She would remind me, I am certain, that the gate remains open, just the way she left it.

DAVID SHAFER grew up in New York City in the 1970s and '80s, when there was still graffiti on the subway cars. He graduated from Harvard and Columbia. He cast about in his twenties, professionally aimless and emotionally all over the place. He found some footing in his thirties. Once he traveled widely. Now not so much. He lives in Portland, Oregon, with his wife and two children. His first novel, *Whiskey Tango Foxtrot*, was published in 2014.

'The Leaping Prow'

DAVID SHAFER

I will not say that my traveling days are over. That's a quitter thought. But I am unlikely to wander as far in the second half of my life as I did in the first. There's no shame or surprise in that, I suppose; it is a truth shared by many. And yet I find myself turning it into a grievance. I roll home from the opulent grocery store with my one-year-old son in the stroller, his big sister riding the running board like a gangster with a tommy gun. The grocery store provided irrefutable evidence that I live in a bourgeois bubble. Pine nuts are still up around $29/lb, so I bought sunflower seeds instead. I did buy organic pitted prunes for $8/lb. And that was the sale price – it would make my grandma die all over again.

Once I was a wanderer; I traveled widely. Now I have children and a minivan and a mortgage. I have a kingdom of things that need to be cleaned or put back on shelves or put in storage or filed or given away or repaired or thrown out. There is laundry I can see like a straight line to my grave. There are countertops to be *fifzzted* with spray and wiped with the countertop sponge and then made dirty and *fifzzted* again. Sometimes in the midst of fifzzting I find myself thinking that there is a more exciting place I should be, that I'm missing some more interesting life.

There are many reasons why I shouldn't do this. For one, no-one likes to talk to people who think they're supposed to be elsewhere. Then there is that old boulder: *Who cares?* I don't have enough time and money and freedom to travel to distant and romantic places. Shall I pause here while you find your hankie? Anyway, almost every distraction or obligation I can point to, you could point to also and say, *You chose that one.*

But here is an even more basic problem with my whinging like this. The truth is that I can't even say for certain that I *want* to travel to distant and romantic places right now. What if I desire less adventure in my life these days? What if some engine that was racing in me twenty years ago now chugs at idle? What should I do with *that* information?

When I was nineteen years old, I spent three months in La Mosquitia. Some know the place as The Mosquito Coast, a stay-away name if ever there was one. But La Mosquitia is a true frontier. It comprises most of eastern Honduras and some of Nicaragua. It is home to the Miskito and the Garifuna people. It is hot and vast and sparsely populated, and in some sense unmapped – satellites cannot look beneath the thick jungle canopy that hides its terrain. Somewhere in its interior likely lies Ciudad Blanca, the lost city of the Incas. Once, pirates hid from warships in the nooks of its sinuous coast; today narcotraffickers do something similar with airstrips and speedboats.

I came to La Mosquitia to work at a Moravian mission

hospital in a town called Ahuas, in Gracias a Dios, the easternmost department of Honduras. There are no roads that will bring you to Ahuas; it can be reached only by air and water.

My arrival must have been semi-comic. The doctors of the Clinica Evangelica Morava – there were three – expected a medical resident to debark from the single-engine plane that landed on the dirt strip. But what they got was a freshly credentialed EMT, a teenager who wanted to be a doctor when he grew up.

Some of the confusion was due to poor communication infrastructure between Ahuas and the outside world. This was 1992; there was only the hospital's radiophone and mail that arrived irregularly. But the more likely cause was my patron in this arrangement, a dashing and dynamic civil engineer who kept homes in multiple Latin American cities. (His passport was thick with extra pages; he drove an open-top jeep; he knew people *everywhere*, and everyone he met greeted him heartily. I was in awe.) He was an old friend of my father, and had arranged the hospital internship for me as a family favor. I suspect that he may have left the matter of my qualifications somewhat vague.

I had enough sense to be embarrassed by the situation. After a few days during which I could see the hospital staff wondering what to do with me, I presented myself to the chief and offered to go home. Perhaps this impressed him, because after that they did find work for me. I cleaned rooms, I provided childcare for staff and patients, and I assisted the physical therapist, lifting and handling young men who were partially paralyzed as a result of decompression sickness, rubbing oil into their inert limbs. The only commercial industry in La Mosquitia then was diving for lobsters. Most divers received no training in scuba, and many were injured when they dove to depth many times a day. The hospital operated one of the two hyperbaric chambers in Honduras. That is to say, *I* operated one of the two hyperbaric chambers in Honduras. Spare a thought for the paralyzed Miskito *indígena* who regains consciousness inside of a pressurized cylinder, and who sees outside the Plexiglas a white guy on a gap year, wearing a Knicks cap. To mitigate the glibness of that last sentence I should say also that if the hospital received these men – boys, mostly – soon enough after their injuries, their chances of recovery were very good; I was helping to do something good.

I listened closely, I took instruction, and soon the doctors let me do more. I helped to deliver babies. I was allowed in the operating room, and then I was allowed to assist: to read numbers off the indicated gauge for the obstetric surgeon as he delivered stillborn twins to save the mother's life. One night I heard a strange and beautiful sound that went on for hours, and only learned in the morning that it was ritual keening for deceased kin. I traveled into the interior with a visiting dental team; we went up the Rio Patuca in wooden longboats powered by noisy outboards, to visit the villages strung sparsely along the banks of the wide brown river. The dentists examined the mouths of hundreds of children every day; I carried cases of equipment from the boats to the shore. At night we slept on the floors of one-room schoolhouses and I heard the grunts and roars of howler monkeys and, once, the growl of a jaguar. I contracted malaria, and hosted a voracious intestinal parasite. On Sundays, I went to the clapboard church and tried to sing hymns in Miskito, which, luckily, is written phonetically.

Do these count as memories? Even to me, the one who made them, they have the polished quality of an alibi. Through repetition, these anecdotes have become my Official Record of the events; they've lost the fidelity they once had. Because I don't think the howler monkeys or the unseen jaguar were the important parts. Nor should I pretend that I was the Doogie Howser of tropical medicine. Though I think I was helpful around the hospital, it is unlikely that I was net helpful: The doctors who decided to let me stay were essentially taking on a liability, a keen but unskilled young man who needed to be fed, housed, and kept from death or injury, and who would take more from the place than he would give.

They let me stay because I was up for anything: I was happy to sleep on a floor or carry heavy cases or provide childcare or do whatever else was asked of me. I woke and went to sleep looking only forward. (It's also likely they let me stay because the dashing civil engineer paid for my room and board.)

I was nineteen and fearless, or blithely unaware of my limitations anyway, and I could have landed in no better place than in Ahuas. Now there is this pining, nostalgia-inclined part of me that wants to mourn the never-coming-backness of that time and place. But then I'm missing the more important point: I was changed by those months in that tiny town on the bend of a slow river on the baking coast of a strange and wild land, maybe in a way that will forever elude my understanding, but also in a way that stays with me always. Ahuas taught me how to be adventurous; Ahuas gave me a hunger for places strange to me. In the years that followed, I fed that hunger with Beirut and Aleppo; the Andes and the Atacama Desert; Catalonia and Amazonia; Rio de Janeiro and Buenos Aires and Ushuaia, Sri Lanka and Myanmar, Dublin and Berlin and Copenhagen and Ephesus; Graceland and Death Valley and that redwood tree you can drive your car through. (Please forgive the list; to some it will seem boastful and luck-laden, to others it will seem paltry and pedestrian. It is just my list, the one I jumble and mumble to myself when I want the comfort it brings.)

For now, my daily life is humdrum. But this period of staying home is no miscarriage of fate; I know I chose it, and I will choose it again tomorrow. My wife and I will get some work done here. My children like the back yard and their friends down the street. I like the back yard and my friends down the street, and apparently the eight-dollar prunes.

But in blessed moments when the sunlight comes in at a certain angle, when my mind and mood allow it, I can find the thrill in the hum and the surprise in the drum, and the bulk aisle is in its way like a souk, and a city I've known for twenty years shows me a strange new face. These moments always surprise me, and for an hour or an afternoon, I am connected to the bravery that turns any trip into a journey. As when I saw my son's first upright locomotion between the coffee table and the piano bench, or my daughter round a corner on her cheap scooter, poised and concentrating, her rear leg swept high behind her.

The poet James Merrill was interested in this too when he wrote his poem 'The Thousand and Second Night'. Not in that thing about children and scooters – but in travel and making sense of it. The poem is about Merrill's trip to Istanbul and how it changed him. Anyway, I think that's what it's about; it is a fortress of a poem. Whole pages of it confound me. But sparkling like a gem in the middle is this quatrain:

The past recedes and twinkles, falls asleep.
Fear is unworthy, say the stars by rote;
What destinations have been yours till now
Unworthy, says the leaping prow.

I've never been to Istanbul. But I will go one day. The Blue
Mosque, the Hagia Sophia, these await me, *Insha'Allah*. My
traveling days are not over, I promise myself. So in this patch of
staying put, the stroller will serve as a leaping prow and I will
find distant lands in what is close to home. And if at times I dote
too much on fading memories of travels past, there is no harm in
that. I must only remember that those memories are not travel;
they are material. Travel is what's in front of me.

ALIYA WHITELEY lives in West Sussex, UK, with her husband, daughter, and dog. She writes in many genres. In 2015 her dark fantasy novella *The Beauty* was shortlisted for the Shirley Jackson award and the Saboteur Awards, and was also included on the Honours List of the James Tiptree Jr. Award. Her short stories have appeared in publications including *The Guardian, McSweeney's Internet Tendency, Strange Horizons, Interzone*, and Lonely Planet's first *Better than Fiction* anthology. She can be found on Twitter as @AliyaWhiteley.

The Places Where We Wait

ALIYA WHITELEY

Ray wasn't a soldier when I met him. That happened afterwards, when I was already in love, and all the misgivings I felt about becoming a military wife no longer stood tall in the face of love. Nothing belittles long-held opinions quite like it.

But not long after the wedding those misgivings rose up, helped along by the declaration of war against Iraq for the second time. Ray was given a three-week leave of absence before he was due to report to RAF Brize Norton, to fly to Basra on a C130. He would be away, this first time, for six months. He broke the news to me quickly, and then said, 'But three weeks off, quick, get in the car, let's go. Somewhere. Anywhere.'

We took a ferry from Dover to Calais and bought camping supplies from a *hypermarché*, one of those palaces of modern convenience that contain both foie gras and thermos flasks. We threw a tent, a sleeping bag for two, a stove, crockery and cutlery, tins and bottles, into the largest size of shopping trolley, and formulated a plan. First we would head downwards, in search of spring sunshine, which must surely be lurking on the Riviera. Then we'd go back up through Italy, and over the Brenner Pass into Austria. Germany, Holland, Belgium, back into France... How far could we get in three weeks? How much could we cram into this little car?

That first day we travelled and talked, driving down quiet roads lined with tall, straight poplars. We were filled to bursting with plans for the rest of our lives, due to start as soon as the six months were up. We did not speak about what the next six months might hold, except for a moment when he asked me, over a crunchy baguette at a service station, 'What will you do while I'm away?'

I told him I would do nothing. Nothing would happen. I would wait, and everything would remain exactly the same. I pictured those months as dark water that must be softly, slowly waded through, leaving no ripples, in order to reach the glittering beach of our future on the other side.

That first night we found a cheap hotel at Laon. In the morning light there was the surprise of the cathedral, rising up through the mist, and a *pain au chocolat* from a tiny bakery on the road. It brought a reality to the journey. We were someplace new, and there was so much further to go – and higher, too, climbing the long backbone of the country.

The car struggled up hills that turned into mountains, and the roads twisted around themselves, leaving all straight lines behind. The occasional patches of white grew more common and knitted together into blankets, and still we climbed. At the end of the afternoon, past Grenoble, we spotted a blue sign for camping at La Grave, which led us to a sheltered spot in the shadow of a most impressive mountain. There was a washing block, just a hut really, and a small stream hiccupping along nearby. And one tent: the old-fashioned kind that formed a point and looked just big enough for one person, if they tucked their legs up when they slept.

We pitched our tent, learning as we went, and it looked sturdy enough by the time we finished. It smelled of new plastic and looked curvaceous, like a series of dips and rises in contrast to the mountain above us. The sun had already fallen behind it, turning it black and brooding, and so high; it was difficult to look all the way up to the jagged teeth at the top. I stared, and shivered. The air was turning colder.

'Food,' said Ray.

He got the stove working, and the ring produced a hissing but dependable blue flame. From the selection of tins I chose cassoulet, and poured it into our cheap saucepan. Beakers of red wine followed, as the smell of the beans and sausage chunks in their sugary tomato sauce intensified. It warmed and bubbled in the pan.

By the time it was ready to eat, the owner of the pointed tent had returned from what must have been a long and serious hike, judging by his backpack and sturdy shoes, and had set off to the small washblock with a towel thrown over his shoulder. He returned as we ate and raised a hand in greeting. Then he towel-dried his hair with his back to us, looking up at the mountain too.

I've never been a fan of beans, but that evening they were delicious, and so was the black instant coffee with squares of dark pistachio chocolate that followed, broken from the packet in turns until the entire bar was gone. The man continued to stand there, not more than twenty feet away. It grew colder still. I could picture the freezing air rushing down from the tip of that great black mountain, over the icy stream, to us. We got out a pack of cards and played, sitting on our travel rug, until it seemed ridiculous to not speak. Ray called to the man, and he turned, and came over to us as if that had always been the unspoken plan.

He was older than us, although not much more than forty. Any age looks old to the young. His walking boots had long red laces that had been knotted in elaborate loops, and his beard was trimmed, close to his face, so neat in comparison to his tousled hair, still damp. I liked him straightaway, although maybe that was the effect of the wine.

'What are you playing?' he said. His accent was Scandinavian, maybe.

'Rummy,' Ray said. 'Do you want to play?'

'No, no, but I'll watch, if that's okay.' He folded his towel on the grass and sat beside me. I poured him a beaker of wine, which he took and nursed without drinking much, as we talked and played our cards, one after the other, without much thought.

'You're not skiers,' he said. 'You're on a walking holiday?'

'No,' I said. 'A trip around Europe. We just decided to go, and here we are. You?'

'Just here. I come here every year, in the quiet time. I used to come with my wife. Every year. Now it's just me.' He started to talk about La Grave, and I realised we hadn't simply fallen upon a quiet place to pause in our travels. For some people, this was the end of the journey.

The mountain had a name: La Meije. It had been thought unscalable, and was the last major peak in the Alps to be climbed. Off-piste skiers and ice climbers came to it, looking for danger. Many of them found it, and deaths were not rare. The man told us these facts without emotion, or interest. It was as if he had said these words many times before, if only in his head.

Had his wife died here, while skiing or climbing? It was too difficult a question to ask. Perhaps nothing so terrible. It could be she had simply tired of him, and his existing obsession with the mountain. It was impossible to know which had happened first: his love for her, or his love for La Meije. Or maybe it wasn't love when he looked up at those sharp points, so high above. It was the fear you feel for something that lives and cannot be willed out of existence. It was the shark, in the deep, that needs to be watched, watched, watched. If you turned your back, it might bite.

'You are a lovely couple,' he said. 'I hope you have a good holiday.'

Ray thanked him, and I shifted position on the rug. The cold was eating at my fingers and toes, and yet I couldn't stand the thought of crawling inside the tent and lying there, alone, under the mountain. Perhaps Ray read my mind, because he got up, stretched, and said it was getting late, and he needed a quick wash before turning in.

'Of course,' said the man. 'Of course, you are travelling onwards tomorrow. You have a long way to go?'

'Yes,' I said. 'I think so.'

I watched Ray fetch his washbag from inside the tent, and walk down to the block, in the last moments of light. I wanted to call out to him, to make him turn around. How ridiculous I was; how needy.

The man smiled at me. 'You seem a little sad,' he said. 'It's difficult, when you're a couple. You have to be...' He searched for the word. 'Vulnerable. But it's a good thing, really.'

It didn't feel like a good thing, not at that moment. He must have seen my feelings in my face.

'No, no, don't mind me, don't think about me,' he said. 'I must stay here; it's the only place where I know how to – because this was her favourite place. Then she was gone, and I stopped...' He moved one hand over another, forming a wheel, a continuous circle of motion. 'But you have your lives ahead.'

Sometimes the strictures of society part, and a gap is left in which two people, strangers, can see each other. I saw him then, and he saw me. We shared, in that look, the knowledge that every journey must end.

Ray returned, the gap sealed up, and the man wished us both a good night. 'If I see you in the morning, before you go, I'll make you some good coffee,' he promised. We crawled into our tent and unrolled the sleeping bag. It was a double, the material flimsy, better suited to the Riveria than to the Alps. It would have been stupid to undress; instead we ended up putting more clothes on, and huddled together. The cold was intense and the presence of the mountain was strong, worse somehow for being on the other side of the tent's curved sides. I shivered and pressed myself against my husband, in the absolute dark. I let all my fears take hold of my imagination, and rob me of all my good intentions. I could not be brave. I could not go back home, and tell him goodbye.

It's funny how everything is different in the light of morning. I awoke, and Ray was already up and about and had made coffee. I uncurled my aching limbs and stretched, reaching up my hands to the sun. It had reappeared, in a gap between the mountains, and everything had shrunk in comparison to its shining face.

Ray nodded towards the tent, and shrugged. Maybe the man was already out walking, or maybe he was in there, thinking his own thoughts, not wanting to be disturbed. We packed up our gear, vowing to get a warmer sleeping bag at the next opportunity, and drove away.

A month later, Ray was far away, fighting a war that I could not imagine, and he did not want to describe in our short telephone calls. That was the best thing for both of us. 'I'm here,' I would tell him. 'I'm waiting.' Then we'd talk, not of the future, but of our holiday: the ice cream houses of the Riviera; the bikers roaring around our car over the Brenner Pass; the watercolour canals of that last-minute stop in Bruges. And of the man at La Grave.

'It's weird,' said Ray. 'I feel like he might still be standing there.'

The television was an enemy, keen to spill its bad news every day. I took to avoiding it, and instead poured myself into books, fighting down waves of nervous sickness. But the sickness got worse, until I had to face the fact that something was wrong. I was changing inside; I could feel it.

It did not occur to me, until the doctor said the actual words in a kind, quiet tone of voice, that I was pregnant.

I don't remember the walk home from the surgery. I remember taking a bath, and while lying in the water I pictured La Meije, that giant mountain, towering over me. 'You have your lives ahead,' the man had said. He could not walk away from the blackness, but I could.

I sat in the bath, in the house where I had wanted to do nothing but wait. But we don't always get to choose whether we wait, or we move. We try to stay so still, and yet our bodies are always travelling, travelling.

DON GEORGE has edited eight previous Lonely Planet literary anthologies, including *An Innocent Abroad*, *Better Than Fiction*, *A Moveable Feast*, *The Kindness of Strangers*, *By the Seat of My Pants*, and *Tales from Nowhere*. Don is the author of *The Way of Wanderlust: The Best Travel Writing of Don George* and of the best-selling *Lonely Planet Guide to Travel Writing*. He is Editor at Large and Columnist for *National Geographic Traveler*, Editor of the Words & Wanderlust section of BBC Travel, and Editor of Geographic Expeditions' blog, Wanderlust: Literary Journeys for the Discerning Traveler. Don has been Global Travel Editor for Lonely Planet, Travel Editor at the *San Francisco Examiner & Chronicle*, and Founding Travel Editor of Salon.com. He has received dozens of awards for his writing and editing, including the Society of American Travel Writers' Lowell Thomas Award. He appears frequently on NPR, CNN, and other TV and radio outlets, is a highly sought-after speaker at conferences and on campuses around the world, and hosts a national series of onstage conversations with prominent writers. Don is also co-founder and host of the Weekday Wanderlust reading series in San Francisco, and co-founder and chairman of the annual Book Passage Travel Writers and Photographers Conference.

Also from Lonely Planet

TONY WHEELER'S DARK LANDS Lonely Planet's founder, Tony Wheeler, goes deeper into the world's darkest corners to explore a rogue's gallery of troubled nations. Join him to find out if there's a happy ever after in these tales.

LIGHTS, CAMERA... TRAVEL! Editor Andrew McCarthy asks some of the most widely travelled people in the film industry to share their own personal, inspiring and funny stories from their time on the road.

A FORK IN THE ROAD Award-winning editor James Oseland invites you to a 34-course banquet of original stories from food-obsessed writers and chefs in this James Beard Awards-nominated collection.

BETTER THAN FICTION A collection of original travel stories told by some of the world'sbest novelists, including Isabel Allende, Peter Matthiessen, Alexander McCall Smith and DBC Pierre.

AN INNOCENT ABROAD Some of the world's best-loved writers, including Dave Eggers, Cheryl Strayed, Tim Cahill, Richard Ford and Sloane Crosley share the travel experiences that made them the people they are today.